I WAS A TEENAGE LIBERAL

I WAS A TEENAGE LIBERAL

SECOND EDITION

MICHAEL MULDOWNEY

To

The Great Teacher,

C.S. Lewis

Contents

I WAS A TEENAGE LIBERAL

Apology

Dear Liberal Friend,

I present this slim volume with apprehension that it will be misunderstood in some quarters. I have many friends who are regular voters of the Democrat party, and some call themselves Liberals. You are soon to discover that some of the things I may say about Liberals in my little book are, well, honestly, somewhat less than entirely flattering. Most of my friends are very decent, kind folks who are pretty much as Conservative as I am. Some of you vote Democrat because you have done so for many years and can't conceive of doing otherwise. Some of you consider yourself Liberals because you are very generous people who are concerned for those who have less than you have. I respect that. Your intentions are good. What we intend to achieve, however, is often not what is actually achieved. In trying to do good, we may in fact be doing very great evil. In a complicated world, it is easy to be deceived. I ask you to read my little pamphlet in full, and ponder it for a bit. Maybe I have a point or two worth considering.

In using the term Liberal, be advised that I use the term to refer to the real hard-core Liberals, Barney Frank, Nancy Pelosi, San Francisco Liberals, New York City Liberals, Congressmen who have dined with Fidel Castro, Hugo Chavez, or Daniel Ortega. Many of the people who call themselves Liberal are actually Moderates and Non-Politicals. You can use my handy chart of the Political Spectrum to find where you really stand! You can thank me later. If my scribblings leave you cold, please understand that I must say what I think, and not sanitize my thoughts to please others. God gave me a brain so that I could use it; these are the thoughts that the brain has condensed. If I have offended you, I ask you to forgive me my trespasses as I strive to forgive those who trespass against me.

Foreword

Like any book touching on the subject of politics, this one is likely to be embraced by one side and hated by the other. Liberals and Conservatives would both like to see a world where all people are free, happy, healthy, and prosperous. My purpose in writing this little booklet is to encourage people to analyze their perspectives and their actions, and to pursue the policies that will most effectively achieve their vision of the world. There are a great many good people who advocate very bad public policies in the belief that they are doing the right and good thing. Their intentions are good but the results of their actions are bad and destructive. They do not mean to do evil, but, through ignorance or misinformation, they do great harm to our country and to the world. This is not to deny that there are some very bad people in America, people who would fit in very well with Bolsheviks, Stalinists, and Maoists. No, that's outrageous, you can't say that, we don't have extremists of that kind in America! I wish. We should consider that there are many people in our country who have not hesitated to associate with the mass murderer Castro or the Communist Sandinistas. There are people who would not shrink from whatever actions they find necessary to implement the Socialist Utopia. Pray that they never get the chance to prove me right.

Throughout this work, I use the term Liberal, but in order to pin them down a bit, we need a more comprehensive term. In the late 1800s, they called themselves Socialists; when that didn't sell, they changed the term to Progressive; when that acquired an odor, they shifted to Liberal, which at that time meant what we now refer to as Conservative; and now that the term Liberal has acquired the status of an insult, they are shifting back to Progressive. They haven't used that one for a few decades, so they figure that they can fool folks for a while with that one. To eliminate confusion, we will coin the comprehensive term Liberal Marxist Progressive Socialist Democrat, or LMPSD, pronounced "limp-seed". That should encompass all their disguises.

This book is written for people who wish only good for all mankind. This book is written to people who are good but are tempted by the falsehood that *the end justifies the means*. I hope that I can address those folks and convince them that the end *never* justifies the means. The road to Hell, paved with good intentions, is the easy way, the path of least resistance, the slippery slope to destruction. My hope in writing this book is that I can persuade you to eschew that popular thoroughfare. Some will surely say that my little booklet is short on facts and statistics.   That is very true.   I have avoided arguments over facts and figures and interpretations and passing issues of the day. My aim is to write a book that can be read a hundred or a thousand years from today and still have the same relevance to the human condition. It's a think piece.

As I type these words, Freedom and Individual Liberty are under attack in the United States as never before. The last time we saw a President who fought such a war on Capitalism, we experienced a Depression from which we might never have recovered without the greater evil of world war. This time around, we will see if the advent of a more sophisticated and educated citizenry, talk radio, the internet, along with other forms of communication independent of government and Liberal control, will enable Freedom to flex its muscles and throw off the yoke of Socialism that is descending upon it. As Mark Twain said, "History doesn't repeat itself, but it does rhyme". I dare to hope that this humble pamphlet will have some infinitesimal effect in the outcome of this struggle. In the process, I hope to ignite a buzz, perhaps a sensation, maybe even an uproar, or if I'm really lucky, a brouhaha.

Read on, friend.

I Was a Teenage Liberal

Yes, it's true. I'm not proud of it. If you were born the son of Irish immigrants in Boston City Hospital in 1954, then you would have been one too. It's sort of baked in the cake. In our home, in the early 1960s, we had a portrait of JFK, from the Globe, up on the wall, right next to a picture of the Pope and a Crucifix. These were the glory days for the Kennedys, the Irish fulfillment of the American dream, and no greater man could be imagined than Jack Kennedy. The Kennedys had defeated the hated Yankees (the descendants of the Puritans, not the even more hated baseball team), taken over the Commonwealth of Massachusetts, and had finally fulfilled Joe Kennedy's obsession to place a son in the White House. JFK's election, in many minds, marked the elevation of the American Irish to full equality and respectability, just as Barrack Obama's election would signify a similar milestone to black Americans. Jack Kennedy, his beautiful wife, and their adorable children were the focus of all eyes, admired by the world. People of Irish descent everywhere could not help but be proud of Jack and Bobby. Heady times indeed.

My Dad was born in the west of Ireland. He was orphaned at age five and grew up in a poverty that is unknown in America. My Mom was also born in Ireland, to a more prosperous farm family. As a boy, Dad worked the fields of England as the B-17s flew over to fight Hitler. Dad has little use for Republicans. Quite apart from being the opponents of the Kennedys, the Republicans had always tried to keep the Irish down and had opposed Irish immigration to America. They put up signs saying "No Irish need apply". We saw Republicans as the people who got to America first, grabbed all the good stuff, and then didn't want to share. Dad worked hard at a union job, he and Mom bought a nice house in a Republican suburb with good schools and good quality of life, and they raised seven healthy children lovingly, if not quietly.

Except for my Uncle Mike, a union carpenter in New York City but an independent-minded fellow, nobody ever entertained the idea that there might be any sane alternative to the Democrats. At one point, it even dawned on me that Uncle Mike might be hinting that Republicans were not all evil. Maybe I misunderstood.

I loved to read, and still do. A book from the Scholastic Book Club told the story of a family escaping from behind the Iron Curtain by riding under a train. The book had a profound effect on me. It was my first look at the horrors of Communism. Now I could understand what JFK was talking about when he spoke of the battle against totalitarianism and why it was so necessary, about the importance of Liberty and why we must defend it to the death.

> *Let every nation know . . . that we shall pay any price, bear any burden, meet any hardship, support any friend, oppose any foe, to assure the survival and the success of liberty.*
>
> —John Fitzgerald Kennedy

Such words would be sufficient to get one promptly expelled from today's Democrat Party, but at that time, anti-Communism was an important linchpin of American Liberal Democrat orthodoxy. Our American system was an earthly heaven compared to the hell and slavery of Communism. I felt that my attitude toward Communism was identical to cold warriors like JFK and his successor, Lyndon Johnson. I took great comfort and security in knowing that my fellow

Massachusetts Democrats felt the same way. After all, JFK was our earthly king, adored and worshipped. His powerful words were quoted as the highest wisdom. Had there ever been such a brilliant and beautiful President of the United States? Not by a longshot.

As a child of the 60s, I of course learned to look forward to The Revolution, when Capitalism and Un-Niceness would be overthrown and all people would live together in Peace and Love   There would be no greed or fear and there would be plenty of everything for everyone without anybody actually working too hard, if at all. Then we could all pursue lives of happy self-actualization and achieve our most poetic existence. The details were sketchy, but there were songs about it and everything. Our high school song was "Imagine". I was right on board with that. Who could oppose the universal peace and tranquility that seemed to be right around the corner? As a child, I saw the world with childish eyes. I had little experience of the world; my powers of critical thinking were, let's say, less than fully developed. While I was bright enough to be a good high school student without working too hard, I didn't want to appear to be uncool by paying excessive attention to school. I rebelled as much as I dared, got into a few scrapes, nothing serious, and didn't do anything bad enough to get on my permanent record, whatever that was. I never shot a man just to watch him die or anything like that.

In college, we learned more about Marxism, but I had some difficulty in being fashionably totalitarian at the University of Massachusetts at Amherst, an institution sadly famous not for scholarship, but for ideological lunacy. Secretly, I nursed a love for Freedom, but of course not for its financial manifestation, Capitalism. After all, Capitalism was the process by which the rich capitalists stole the wealth of the poor people; but I did feel that, while people had a right to enjoy a healthy percentage of what they earned—after all, they earned it—those who did not work for their money had no such right. Therefore, I backed a 100% death tax, so that everyone could start out in life with the same financial capital. The leftovers of the rich should be distributed amongst the poor. That way, people could compete fairly in life's game, without lucky offspring of the rich being handed the world on a silver platter. Everybody would start out in life as equals, and the financial carcass of the rich would provide nourishment to those starting out in life. Everybody would have an equal chance to succeed in life; racism would be eliminated by leveling the playing field and allowing free people to rise to their highest potential. This policy would eliminate inherited privilege and equalize opportunity. The Evil Rich would be finally defeated!

As the 70s passed, it became more and more apparent that the policies of the Great Society were in the process of failing miserably, as people came to understand the term "unintended consequences". Spending a semester in Washington, DC, I did my Liberal duty as an intern in the old Legal Services Corporation, which fought for the interests of poor people. I found that the recipients of taxpayer dollars were less than grateful for the largesse so generously heaped upon them. On the contrary, they seemed to feel that they had a right to the taxpayers' money, as if the taxpayers were the workers and the welfare beneficiaries were the employers. I didn't get the warm, fuzzy feelings of gratitude that I was expecting. In fact, they seemed to view little old Liberal me as an oppressor just because I was white. Not very nice!

Back in Amherst. One day in spring of my senior year. A person atop the ten-story university library. A crowd chanting "jump, jump". He did.

The most important class that I took in college was an Honors seminar in Political Science titled "History vs. Logic". The course discussed whether Human Logic could negate and overcome the forces of History to create a better world. For one session, Professor Russell asked me to report on an essay of Karl Marx. When I was finished, he said, "Good synopsis. Now criticize the essay." I was speechless. How could one question Marx, who had so surely predicted the inevitable coming of World Socialism? Was the Professor suggesting that Marx was less than infallible? Was it possible that Human Logic could fail to end all human misery, fail to construct a perfect world? That's not what people at UMass thought. By the end of term, I began to understand what critical thinking is. Thanks, Prof.

Even though I was a bit resistant to some of the radical insanity at UMass, it would be wrong to foster the impression that I had become a Republican or anything of that nature. After all, there was nothing good about Republicans. President Ford and the GOP were still trying to save our Vietnamese allies from Communist invaders from the North, just as JFK had done, and I could not believe that we would soon betray the people who had put their trust in us, to the everlasting shame of the those who perpetrated this obscenity; but really the Republicans were just a bunch of rich people and I was a student without much income, so I had nothing in common with them. Despite some curiosity, I never took a class in Economics; why bother, since Capitalism was headed for the ash heap of History? I eagerly voted for George McGovern and for Jimmy Carter. Everybody I knew did the same.

After completing a Master's Degree in 1977, I met real life. It was a tough time to do so. Unemployment and inflation were high and rising. At that point, I saw no possible outcome to History except the decline of my beloved America. We seemed to be losing on all fronts. Carter was weak beyond description in dealing with every problem, foreign and domestic. His primary policy was surrender. There could be no doubt that America was in decline and that it was just a matter of time before the stalwart Russians intimidated the spineless Americans into defeat and submission. No one I knew had any idea how America could get out of the death spiral we found ourselves in. I could not contemplate the possibility of having children, for it would be mere cruelty to bring children into a Socialist world where they would be slaves of the state.

In 1980, this Reagan guy fought his way to the top of the Republican ticket. Where did they dig up this old fossil? I remembered him from television, where he rode the Boraxo wagon to introduce the weekly Western. Everyone said he was a far-out lunatic who would cause nuclear war. No one I knew took him seriously. I punted in 1980 and did not vote. I could not vote for the hapless Carter, but everybody I knew said that Reagan was too dangerous to be President. Why bother voting? I could see no way that the planet could arrive at a happy outcome. The free world was going down the tubes. It was a dark time. All my Liberal friends agreed that the United States had no future and would soon reap the fruits of its evil ways. Reagan's words sounded good in an old-fashioned, square kind of way, but even if Reagan had some good ideas, what could one man do against the ineluctable tides of History that were forcing the United States of America onto the rocks of economic disaster and military decline?

Well, we all know the answer. Ronald Reagan did more than I could ever have imagined. Ronald

Reagan disintegrated the Soviet Union, leaving it on the ash heap of history. He changed the world. Somehow, against all logic, the disorderly, self-oriented capitalists, under Ronald Reagan, utterly defeated the monolithic totalitarians. It is said that the difference between fiction and non-fiction is that fiction has to make sense. You can't write this stuff. Beyond the economic and military revitalization of America, Ronald Reagan renewed the American spirit to a level as high as at any other time in our history. People came to believe that Freedom and Liberty might actually be able to exist in this wicked world. And if it could happen in America, it could happen everywhere. All people could be as wealthy and as free as Americans. All that was necessary was for America to stick to American principles. The United States would be a light unto the nations, an example that all people could emulate. Hope was reborn. It was a revelation to see how one man, the greatest President since Abraham Lincoln, could turn the world around. I have been a committed Conservative ever since the Reagan Revolution.

As I look back to my youth, I find that my vision of what constitutes an ideal world has changed very little: people living without the interference of government, whether it be a hostile military force, a totalitarian oppressor, or a busybody bureaucracy. Who could disagree with that? I now understand that there are many people who are opposed to that dream—totally.

Young Minds at Risk

Youth rebels unto itself, though none else near

—Shakespeare

I know you, young and dumb,
I know where you're coming from

—Pete Townsend

Young people are at great risk of Liberalism, which has a natural attraction for the weak-minded. Liberalism appeals to the emotional animal nature within the sometimes-rational human being. Immature people have not yet developed their powers of critical thinking, and are subject to the excitements of their hormones and inexperienced minds. The human animal has a natural inclination to rebel against authority, and it is well that this is so. Without a strong, vital, and even rebellious temperament in young people, most of the great accomplishments and endeavors of the human race would never have occurred. Without the rebellious spirit of youth, new ideas, inventions, explorations, discoveries, would be much more rare; old ways, entrenched interests, and "inside the box" thinking would endure far beyond their period of maximum utility. Without the spirit of rebellion, human progress would be far less than it is; the world would be a primitive and savage place.

Unfortunately, the average young person does not understand how far humanity has advanced, or, how fragile our technological civilization, the most advanced in the history of the world, truly is. We accept our everyday life as a given, as the default mode of human existence. We accept modern America's freedoms and conveniences without thinking, without gratitude. Young people lack the historical and worldwide perspective to realize how far man has progressed in some countries, and how little he has progressed in other vast areas of the planet. They are simply not in a position to understand the uniqueness of America at this time; they just do not comprehend that never in human history have so many people lived such a prosperous and healthy existence. After all, how would they know such things? They would have to have intellectual curiosity; they might even have to read and study. Unfortunately, most young people are not curious or educated enough to understand how very unique the

United States is. They assume that technological progress has put the whole planet on a one-way track to the world of The Jetsons. Most youths have no concept of true poverty, as it exists in many area of Earth. If or when they come to realize the extent of their blessings, they realize that they owe a great debt to God and country.

The major stumbling block to the acquisition of historical and economic wisdom by America's youth is the Liberal educational complex. Curricula in recent years have gone from Civics and American History to Global Warming and How to Put a Condom on a Banana. The Liberals know that young people without knowledge and without critical thinking skills are easy prey for their Socialist nostrums. From textbook choice to classroom instruction, school districts that do not actively confront and combat the Liberal indoctrination efforts find that their children are subjected to a constant Deconstructionist assault. Some contend that Liberal teachers know that Critical Thinking is a potentially fatal threat to their entire agenda; but I am not sure that the Liberal mind goes that deep. Many LMPSD teachers do not possess the Critical Thinking or analytical skills necessary to understand what Critical Thinking is; the teachers are often the victims of Liberal education as well as its enforcers.

Let us be fair to the LMPSDs. In a certain sense, the Liberals are idealists, pursuing their beautiful, impossible dream despite the unpleasant intrusion of reality. One must pity them: they are in a hopeless position, for they are incapable of being happy in this world, which can never conform to their idealized Utopia. They lack some critical element that is necessary for human happiness. Many if not most people are Liberals when they are young. Like Robert Kennedy, they ask, why can't the world be perfect?

> *There are those who look at things the way they are, and ask why. I dream of things that never were and ask why not?*

And that reflects something that is good and admirable in their nature, a desire for the good of all people. Unfortunately, there are very good answers to RFK's question, which experience of the world will teach to the young mind as it matures. Why can't food be free? Ask a farmer. Why can't everyone be rich? An economist will enlighten you on that topic. Madison says, "If men were angels, no government would be necessary." All men, and women too, are corruptible and corrupt, and the world will be corrupt as long as it is populated by human beings. "To expect men to be angels is to expect that which never was and never will be." As we grow in experience, we learn, in small ways and in large, that the policies of Socialism do not achieve the ends that we had expected, no matter how many times and in how many ways they are implemented. As we mature, we gradually develop a view of the world and of human nature based on reality and not on our fantasies. Or vice versa: developing an accurate view of reality, seeing the truth behind the veil, is the definition of maturity.

> *When I was a child, I spake as a child, I understood as a child, I thought as a child: but when I became a man, I put away childish things*
>
> —Saint Paul

We gain in understanding of the world and its wicked ways as we gain more experience of life. Every day is a learning and growing experience for an open mind.

But not for Liberals. The true Liberal is inherently unable to adapt to the new information about the world. He clings to his fixed ideology as a drowning man clings to a life preserver. He is unresponsive to reason and reality whenever they do not conform to his ideology. The Great Society destroyed the black family? Hogwash! High taxes depress the economy? Never! Ronald Reagan defeated the Soviet Union? How silly! Buying houses with no down payments caused the housing market to collapse? Crazy talk! The true LMPSD never learns, and thus remains a Liberal, rather than an intellectually open human being who grows in knowledge and understanding. Liberals are correctly described as cases of arrested development. To learn and to adapt to the realities of the world is to grow past Liberalism and to mature into a normal human being.

I suppose I would be remiss if I failed to quote a very famous line that strongly makes my point:

> *If a man is not a socialist in his youth, he has no heart. If he is not a conservative by the time he is 30, he has no head.*
> —Clemenceau (1841-1929)

As I looked up this quote, slightly revised by Clemenceau, I found that the original author was Francois Guizot (1787-1874). We so often think that the issues of our time are so new and unique to the modern world. Is it not remarkable how little human nature changes over the centuries, even as technology and society evolve beyond our wildest dreams?

The Political Spectrum

When one finds oneself in a political discussion with a Liberal, we will observe that they enter a state of high dudgeon when the results and the implications of their policies are pointed out to them. For example, if one says that giving free money and apartments to single mothers encourages more women to become single mothers, they are outraged at the suggestion that people respond to economic incentives. Why, the very thought that a person could be so venal! Only a Conservative could have such a low opinion of human beings!

The Liberal congratulates himself on helping someone by giving them money—not his money – perish the thought!—Other People's Money. The thought that this money is being removed from the pocket of a hard-working taxpayer, or from the pockets of the current taxpayer's children or grandchildren, does not enter his consciousness.

The problem here is that Leftism is not rational. One of the prime characteristics of the LMPSDs is that his powers of Critical Thinking are poor; if they were not, he would not be a Liberal. A Liberal learns his dogma, and nothing can ever change his mind on any subject.

When one breaks down the assumptions that underlie Leftist thought, we find that there is something missing; there is no foundation there, except within the nostrums of Marxist ideology. The more closely we examine the intellectual and moral foundations of Leftism, the more obvious it becomes that there are no intellectual or moral foundations beyond Karl Marx. There is no ore in that mine, except for Marxist fool's gold. In the Communist countries, one could cite Marxism as the intellectual, moral, historical, even spiritual authority. In the Western democracies, Liberals hesitate to cite Marx no matter how deeply they believe in his philosophy; to be an unabashed Communist is to marginalize oneself politically, even in Liberal Europe. When one drills down on the Liberal philosophy, when one proves the shallowness of its foundation, when one shows the inevitable results of their policies, the Liberal will say, well, you can't tell me what I support and what I think! You can't read my mind! That's your opinion! You have no proof!

Those were the old days, my friend. It is with great pleasure and pride that I here announce, for the first time ever on Planet Earth, that I have objectified the political spectrum. In so doing, I have cut off the escape routes of the Liberals, reduced their wiggle room to zero, and decimated their camouflage. The tool that will expose Right and Left in their innermost beliefs and philosophies is called *Muldowney's Spectrum of Politico-Economic Ideology*. Of course, it is only Liberals who try to convince others that they are not Liberals; they often try to portray themselves as Conservatives, especially at election season; *hypocrisy is the homage that vice pays to virtue*. Conservatives are proud to be identified as Conservatives. With this new tool, we can analyze and identify the political and economic philosophy of any individual with just a few easy questions.   The Spectrum allows me to pin down the political profile of anyone like a bug on a specimen tray. It's so good it's copyrighted!

The conventional wisdom holds that we have people of the Left and we have people of the Right and we have people somewhere between the two and we call these folks Moderates.   These middle-of-theroaders might vote for either the Conservative (Republican) party or the Socialist (Democrat) party in any given election. By definition, they have voted for each at one time or another. In many people's minds, there seems to be an implicit assumption that there is great virtue in being in the middle. These middlemen are free from the ideologies of Left and Right and have achieved a sort of Golden Mean where they are above the partisan battlefield and have risen to a transcendent status. If they are between two extremes, then they must be in the correct place, since they split the difference between the polar opposites. Quite Solomon-like! Half a loaf is a fair compromise. The moderates are like Switzerland, beyond partisanship. It might even make sense if there was not one party that trends ever Leftward.

We must grant our friends the LMPSDs one thing: they are very clear in their goals. They know what they want. They desire to deconstruct the existing order of things. They desire to expropriate Other People's Money, which they regard as expropriated from the people who have no money. They desire to eliminate Capitalism, Freedom, and Individualism (even though they vehemently deny it if the question is put so bluntly), and to usher in the

Socialist / Communist Utopia. There is no hesitation, no doubt, no grey area. No cogitation is necessary for them to reach the conclusion that they will take Other People's Money (or Other Corporation's Money, which is the same thing) to further the Socialist agenda, by whatever means necessary. They know what they hate and what they endeavor to destroy. They know who the enemies of World Socialism are. There is zero probability of their voting for a Republican. As Stalin said, no enemies on the Left. The LMPSDs will always vote for the Leftmost candidate.

Similarly, Conservatives understand that Liberals desire to destroy the Normal and the Just. They know that the LMPSDs are the enemies of Freedom and that they desire to eliminate Constitutional government, Individual Liberty, and America as we know it. Conservatives know that even a so-called "moderate" Democrat will vote for whatever Socialist program is advanced by Democrat leadership in Congress, and will therefore advance the Socialist agenda. For example, Obama care is the ultimate example of an overwhelming and anti-Constitutional expansion of government power; any politician who voted for the imposition of an unproven, unpopular, radical experiment that completely transforms one-seventh of the American economy is a Socialist and a radical, in any sense of those words. Therefore, there is, and should be, zero probability that any true Conservative will vote for a Liberal-Marxist-Progressive-Socialist-Democrat of any description.

The Moderate enjoys no such clarity. He might vote for Obama or he might vote for Ronald Reagan. Certainly there are millions of people who voted for both. How one person can vote for a Conservative Reagan and a Socialist Obama, who disagree on every conceivable political issue, is mind-boggling. Yet, there are millions and millions who did so. To one who is politically conscious, whether of the Right or Left, this lack of certainty is incomprehensible. Many in the non-ideological center are quite simply non-political; they have no interest in politics and do not study or understand the issues very deeply. They do not understand politics and would not understand this book. Some Moderates are of a very non-confrontational temperament and are uncomfortable taking a position that might be offensive to someone. Others are confused by the arguments that either side advances and make a calculation that splitting the difference must be the rational course. Some make decisions based on personal attractiveness of the candidates and are unaware of issues. As muddled as these folks are, they are the swing voters who ultimately decide elections. No wonder Churchill said that democracy is the worst possible form of government—except for every other form of government.

Commentators have suggested that the Left and Right each constitute 30 to 42 percent of the population. These numbers seem to be remarkably consistent in the United States. Democrats usually have had higher party registration than the GOP, but many independents, and some Democrats, are in fact Conservatives. The hard core of LMPSDs is considerable smaller, with some surveys showing as low as 10 to 20 percent. Certainly some who call themselves Moderates are actually partisan, or at least more sympathetic to one side or the other, but they are sufficiently wary of controversy to deny affiliation with either party; or, they say they are Independent just because it is, of course, good to be independent. (After all, who would want to be dependent? Oops! Let's not go there.) Being independent carries an aura of deep consideration and cogitation.

We sometimes hear a person say, "I vote for the best person for the job." If you say that, we must conclude that if Jesus ran on the Nazi party ticket, you would vote for him. The quality, however defined, of the candidate means nothing in comparison to the policies he proposes to implement. It would be more accurate to say that these Moderate folks are straws in the wind, and they will blow with the prevailing breezes. They can be fooled by a Carter and an Obama, but they correct the mistake as soon as reality bites and their folly slowly, inevitably dawns on them. When the Builders, that is, the Republicans, are in power, they repair the damage caused by the Decons as best they can; but the GOP is every bit as subject to corruption as is the other side of the aisle, and the voters will not countenance corruption and abuse of office. In fact, the Conservative party may be more likely to be financially corrupted because they are friends of free enterprise and do not treat businessmen as evil thieves, as the Decons are prone to do. Of course, a weak economy on Election Day can be harmful to either party, but the Decons are much more likely to damage the economy through the implementation of their Socialist schemes. When you think about it, it never makes sense to put Socialists in charge of a free market economy; they just don't understand economics. They think the Republicans are just making the whole thing up as a way to keep the money. They really do. Let's be frank: many LMPSDs are not deep thinkers; their politics are based on emotion and not on sound judgment.

Our Moderates will often say, "I decide based on the issues". That statement makes perfect sense, but it implies that Makers and Takers do not decide based on the issues. To the Maker, the issue is always, "the government that governs best is the government that governs least"; to the Taker, the issue is always, "give me Other People's Money". Let us see if we can break down these questions into more discrete paradigms.

Having determined that we have three broad classes of people, the Conservatives, the Deconstructionists, and the Middlemen (also known as the Squishy Center, the Confused, the Easily Led, or the Weathervanes), let us ask, what do these classes of people believe in? After considering the matter at great length, I have constructed what I like to call *Muldowney's Spectrum of Politico-Economic Ideology*.

COLLECTIVIST

LEFT — RIGHT

LEFT		RIGHT
opposes	individual rights	supports
opposes	private property	supports
opposes	rule of law	supports
supports	government takings	opposes
supports	government power and control	opposes
supports	government social intervention	opposes
supports	government economic intervention	opposes
supports	taxation and regulation	opposes
supports	centralized decision-making	opposes
supports	expanded government	opposes
supports	redistribution of income	opposes
supports	government solutions to problems	opposes
materialistic	view of man and society	spiritualistic

LEFT	RIGHT
views men as servants of government	views government as servant of man
views man as ethnic/racial/gender/class unit	views man as individual
views government as source of wealth	views individual as source of individual wealth
views "I" as the "grammatical fiction"	views "I" as center of universe
views man as social animal	views man as spiritual being
societal responsibility	individual responsibility
ends justify means	ends do not justify means
views human life as commodity	views human life as inviolable

INDIVIDUALIST

Muldowney's Spectrum of Politico-Economic Ideology

COLLECTIVISM

| COMMUNISM | SYNDICALISM | NATIONAL SOCIALISM | FASCISM | SOCIALISM | LIBERALISM | THE NON-IDEOLOGICAL CENTER | CONSERVATISM | CAPITALISM | LIBERTARIANISM | ANARCHISM |

INDIVIDUALISM

The most important and overarching aspect of the Spectrum is Collectivism or Statism versus Individualism or Liberty (although we can substitute Takers versus Makers, Deconstructionists versus Builders, Deceivers versus Achievers, and many other paradigms).   All of politics and economics is encompassed by this overarching concept; the other layers of the Spectrum merely flesh out the details of the whole.   Human beings, being human, have a consistent pattern of being inconsistent; we will find Marxists who oppose abortion, we will find Conservatives who support high taxes; but overall, one can track one's political positions and get a pretty good idea of where one stands on the Spectrum. I imagine we could readily devise a point system that would define folks pretty well; but we'll save that for a later edition of this highly successful and best-selling book. Starting from the Left, we find the extreme position occupied by Communism.   All individuality is extinguished; there is no right to do or think anything that is antithetical to the interests of the Collective. The very concept of "I" is a betrayal of the Collective. An ant colony functions very well as the ideal of the Collective, each individual subordinating their will, their desires, their individuality, their freedom. In the all-encompassing collective, there is no such thing as spirituality; the world is entirely materialistic. Law as we know it does not exist, as the only law is the will of the Collective. There is no private property, which would create inequality. Government intrudes in every area of life, since totalitarianism requires total fidelity to the will of the Collective, however expressed. Government decides who works, based on their ability, and who receives, based on their needs, as dictated by the all-powerful government.

On the other extreme, we have Anarchism. I need to clarify that this term does not refer to the radical Communists and Syndicalists of the late 1800s and early 1900s or to today's violent protestors. These were and are Communists through and through; they call themselves "anarchists" only to signify their total indifference to the rule of law. In philosophy, they are the opposite of Anarchists; they fight for the totalitarian state. Anarchism refers to a total lack of government, no laws, no taxes, unlimited individual rights; it also implies a spiritual society, which values people as individuals and as bearers of immortal Souls. Each individual acts as he believes proper. In short, totally impractical and impossible, given human nature. I do not know of anyone who is an Anarchist in this sense. Why do I even mention Anarchism?

Only to establish it as the antithesis of Communism: total ascendancy of the Individual as opposed to total ascendancy of the Collective. The closest philosophy to this theoretical Anarchism is Libertarianism. The category "Capitalism" applies to a philosophy such as Ayn Rand's Objectivism, which stresses individual achievement and responsibility.

When a LMPSD looks at this chart, he will immediately, invariably, squeal loudly that National Socialism (a name they would prefer to forget and substitute the condensed and non-descriptive term "Nazi") is of the Right and not the Left. We hardly need to look beyond the very name of the party to overrule this objection. As we analyze the policies of National Socialism, we find that it is only mildly distinct from plain Socialism. While private industry was not nationalized, it did take its orders from government, just as in Fascist Italy, or as was attempted in the unconstitutional National Recovery Administration in the American New Deal. All the other National Socialist elements of state power, including the practice of eugenics and genocide against ethnic populations, reveal their heavy use of state power and the complete lack of respect for individual rights. The person who says that the National Socialists are of the

Right is only telling us that they themselves are farther left than the National Socialists, in other words, that they are Communists or Syndicalists.

The Liberals will also be thrown into a fit when they see that the Spectrum shows that they are opposed to individual rights. Nothing could be further from the truth, they shriek. In truth, they are very eager to encourage free speech that attacks Conservatives; the right to attack the Right must never be infringed. When it comes to speech that does not favor their agenda, their response is the opposite. They hatch schemes to destroy talk radio and the fantastically successful Fox News Channel. They regulate speech on college campi with speech codes where the emphasis is not on actual conduct but on how a member of a favored group might "feel" about something that is said. Always, the rights of the individual are subordinated to the wants of the state and of their favored groups. When the Supreme Court ruled that corporations had free speech rights, the LMPSDs howled with anger; apparently there is some lack of clarity in saying that "Congress shall make no law...abridging the freedom of speech". Inexplicably, they did not complain that the same rights were extended to their allies, the unions.

As for gun rights, don't even go there. The Liberal firmly believes that the individual has no right of self-defense, but must depend on the government for protection from criminals. As for government taking of private property, well that's just fine, the more the better, whether it's for a government whim, as in the *Kelo* eminent domain case, or for spreading the wealth, as in the case of high taxes on the rich.

To the voter who says, "I decide on the issues", I ask, what in the Spectrum really changes from election to election? Are you for free enterprise in one election year and opposed to it in another? Are you a Communist in one election year and a Capitalist four years later? Do you wish to empower the government in one election and protect individual rights in another? As you look at yourself in relation to the Spectrum, consider where you stand and whether the transient issues of the day should really change your choices. Are you so blinded by the trees of campaign commercials that you cannot see the forest of our ongoing civilization? Are you maintaining the perspective that an intelligent human being should have as you lend your voice, through your vote, in deciding the future course of history? Have no doubt, the free voter in America determinant of the history of the human race. We are the sovereigns of the United States. When you cast your vote, do you consider the big picture, gentle reader?

The Spectrum shows the two polar opposites. Which is more important, the individual or the state? The state is composed of millions of individuals, not just one. The state is perpetual; it goes on, potentially, until the planet is consumed by the sun, while the individual life, at best a hundred years, is a brief flicker, a spark. On earth, we are all temporary phenomenona. Compared to the interests and needs and wants of the millions of citizens of the state, how important is one person, who is one in 6,000,000,000 (that is, six billion)?

Let's look at a hypothetical situation where the state could realize great benefits by violating the rights of one person other citizen in a nation of one million had one currency unit. By confiscating and redistributing the wealth of this one person, every citizen of the state could double their net worth. Would it be moral to confiscate the wealthy man's fortune? For the true Liberal, the answer is simple. There is hardly a question there. The true Socialist instantly expropriates that citizen's property and divides the spoils in the name of fairness and equality. After all, why should one have so much when others have so little? They would hardly pause to consider that they have created a system where their own assets could now be taken from them at will. Their system of values sees no problem in violating the one to benefit the many. After all, it's only fair that all should be equal. To the Liberal, there is no other consideration.

For a person who follows natural or Judeo-Christian law, the question is entirely different. Can we do good by doing wrong? Do the ends justify the means, or are the means more important than the ends? Can good fruit come from a poisoned tree? The answer is no. The ends do not justify the means. The material benefits are transitory but the damage to the Soul is long-lasting. The hard-core Communist denies not only the soul, but the individual itself. We can prove the existence of the body and of the state, but we cannot prove that "I" exists. "I" is, in Arthur Koestler's memorable words, the "rhetorical fiction". To Descartes' "I think, therefore I am", the true Communist says "you have no proof"; since the self, like the Soul, has no physical manifestation, there is no question of the rights of the individual; he has none. Subordinating or even restraining the power of the state is heresy. The state is the objective reality and must trump any subjective sense of individualism. Any suffering, deprivation, or even death that serves the interests of the state is not only justified, but greatly to be desired. I find that many people have great difficulty in comprehending this critical element of the Leftist consciousness. Only when we understand this unhuman mindset can we understand the murders of tens of millions of human beings carried out in the name of Communism. Only by understanding their disconnection from all notions of human morality can we understand Stalin, Mao, and Pol Pot. While they were not institutionalized, they were absolute madmen, driven to actions no decent human being could contemplate by the inexorable logic of their godless religion, Marxism.

When I was a young Liberal, I subscribed to the conventional wisdom and assumed that there must be truth and wisdom in the center of the Spectrum. I no longer believe that. The question is not Right and Left; it is Right and Wrong. On every issue, on every paradigm, on every question, the Left represents error and policies destructive of the Good, both in a moral and an economic sense. The policies of the Left are destructive to human Liberty and to economic prosperity. Every country that has embraced them has brought only misery and poverty to its citizens. The Soviet Union is gone; China is still totalitarian but economically capitalist; Cuba and North Korea continue to bleed. Liberalism in America has brought only class envy and hatred, along with economic distress.

But surely there is a huge difference between being a Socialist / Liberal and being a Communist? One could view the Socialist / Liberal as a moderate Communist who does not profess the more extreme positions of the Collectivist agenda. The more important point, however, is that the Liberal is on the wrong side of the Spectrum, the anti-individual, anti-freedom, intrusive government side: the dark side. He shares the Marxist assumptions of the Communist; his morality is based on Marxist materialism, not Jeffersonian Liberty. Whatever condition a society finds itself in, the Socialist / Liberal will push ever Leftward. The Liberal Marxist Progressive Socialist Democrat coalition travels together down the Leftward road.

What do we wish for the world? The only person I can speak for is myself. I would like to see a world where people can live in peace and prosperity, free to raise their children and to live as they choose, untroubled by tyrants and bullies. I think most people would agree with that statement. That was my hope when I was a child and it remains my hope to this day. Even Liberals and Communists would say that they agree with that statement, as Marxist ideology predicts that the state will "wither away" as all the problems of the world are solved by Communism and government becomes unnecessary. Jefferson and Marx agree that, "If men were angels, there would be no need of government". The difference is that Marx requires a totalitarian government that regulates every aspect of human life—including one's own thoughts—to exercise unlimited control over all people, until some point in the far future when their character and behavior are modified sufficiently to eliminate all vestiges of human nature. If that change in behavior is never achieved, which of course it never can be, then necessarily the totalitarian state, allowing zero individual rights, will continue perpetually.

I humbly hope, gentle reader, that the Spectrum might help people to clarify what they believe, who they want to be, and what they want to stand for. Know yourself. As one of the sovereigns of the United States, you have important decisions to make, decisions that will affect the freedom and prosperity of this and future generations. If you are a dedicated Statist, understand what you are; if that is where and what you want to be, then so be it. If you find that your heart and mind do not accept the doctrines of the Left, then we welcome you to the Right side.

Liberals versus God

Let's talk morality. That is a difficult topic, since the Left will aver that there is no objective standard of goodness. The atheists must decline to recognize any concept of goodness, since without God there is only Chaos, a vacuum of moral values, unless the Liberals make them up, which they do, but only at the sacrifice of logic. Let us put the atheists to one side for now and restrict our argument to those of a more religious bent. Specifically, let's deal with a rule set accepted by Jews, Christians, and even implicitly endorsed by Mohammed. I refer to the Ten Commandments, which are the most clearly stated compilation of law in the Bible and, perhaps, in all of pre-modern writings. These are laws given by God to the Jews and later accepted by Christians, along with the entire Old Testament. The Koran endorses the teachings of the Hebrew Scriptures in full, although people who have not read the Koran might be surprised to learn this fact. Many Liberals tell me that they are Christians; let's see what they mean by that.

I. *I am the LORD your God. You shall worship the Lord your God and Him only shall you serve*

Many Liberals don't even pretend to believe in God, and many more actively deny his existence. There are, nevertheless, many Liberals who claim belief in a deity; in fact, the churches are full of them. As we listen to their explanations, we find that the god they believe in bears small relation to the God of the Old or even of the New Testament. I find that many "religious" liberals wish to somehow put the Ten Commandments and the stern prescriptions of the Old Testament aside, and to dwell on the forgiveness of the New Testament. What they end up with is not religion but an "I'm okay, you're okay" nothing sandwich, bearing no relation to the God of the Bible. The greatest lunacy of the liberals comes from those who state that "Jesus was not a god-man, but he was a great moral teacher." Wrong. Jesus was either the Messiah or a lunatic; there is no middle ground. Anyone who says "I am the way and the light, and he who believes in me will have eternal life" is either God, or barking mad. One would need to discard a vast portion of Jesus' words to reduce him to a secular humanist. Of course, clarity of thought is not a prerequisite for being a Liberal; in fact, it is an impediment to Liberalism. One may believe in the authority of the Old Testament and/or New Testament, or in the doctrines of Marxism, but not in both. The two are mutually exclusive. Liberalism is the antithesis of God. A person who follows the Commandments and adheres to the plain language of the Bible cannot simultaneously believe in the LMPSD philosophy, any more than one could believe that they are in light and in darkness at the same time. While some folks will perform prodigious mental gymnastics to suggest that Jesus was a Liberal and a Communist, their efforts are ludicrous. LMPSDism is in fact a negation of God. Liberalism goes far back before the time of Marx, but atheism has always been a necessary part of it. Marx believed that the forces of History drive mankind toward equality of all people. History was his god, and the Liberals follow that philosophy of historical determinism as their religion. For that reason, Liberals often call themselves Progressives, because they believe that their political actions advance human equality and thus are in harmony with the currents of History.

Marx was correct in postulating that there is a direction in the affairs of men; but he was wrong to postulate that the driving force is Equality; the true driving force is Freedom. When Communist regimes fall, we see that Marx' theory of historical inevitability is pure bunk. The Liberals will never accept this truth as long as they are Liberals; when they finally understand this truth, they will no longer be Liberals. They will forsake their false god of Marxist determinism.

History is not the only false god that the LMPSDs worship. They also worship their own variety of human reason and elevate it above God. They reason that they cannot prove the existence of God; therefore, they must not believe in God. To be neutral on something that they can neither prove nor disprove, or to even admit the possibility of the existence of God, is not tolerable. They must have absolute proof of the existence of God or else the absence of proof becomes proof of the non-existence of God. That statement is, of course, totally irrational, but that fact does not deter their blind adherence to atheism. To the Liberal, their concept of Godless Reason is elevated above any possibility of the spirit. The Liberal universe is cold, pointless, purposeless, futile. Man lives and dies—end of story. From dust he comes, to dust he goes; but for the LMPSD, there is nothing more, no spirit or soul in the universe. Rather than follow a God who offers eternal life, the Liberal blindly follows the dictates of their Godless Reason based on their Liberal assumptions. Their philosophy is based on their belief, which they hold with religious fervor, that man is not an eternal spirit "passing through nature to eternity", but a mere animal that must be trained by them to his appropriate social role. He must be taught his place in their ordered society. To the true LMPSD, a man is no more than an ant in an ant colony; the sooner he learns his role and learns to like it, the better for him and for society. And the Liberal is happy to hasten that day.

The Liberal god, Godless Reason, dominates all their worldview. Is the economy not as egalitarian as they wish it to be? Is the cost of health care too great? Are mortgages requiring twenty percent cash down too onerous for groups favored by Liberals? No problem; government bureaucrats will develop regulations to remedy the inequality. When the unanticipated (by Liberals) consequences and disasters inevitably appear, they will write new regulations that create new problems. The vicious cycle never ends as they squeeze the balloon, trying to mold it to the perfection that can never be achieved. Matters get worse instead of better. Will they ever stop their interference and deregulate something? Heresy! Perish the thought! One of the most destructive cases of unintended consequences involved the pesticide DDT. An environmentalist, without anything in the way of scientific evidence, alleged that DDT was killing birds. In knee-jerk fashion, the Liberals banned the pesticide, without any analysis of costs versus benefits. Since then, tens of millions of people, mostly poor and African, have died of malaria. Unnecessary deaths on the altar of Liberalism. Where are the apologies and retractions? Being Liberal means never having to say you're sorry.

The hard-core LMPSD has an unbounded confidence in the ability of Liberals to use Godless Reason to shape society; this practice of social engineering reflects an arrogance and hubris that amounts to a worship of their own abilities. Secular Humanism is well described as The Godless Religion. Man—Liberal Man, that is—becomes his own god, changing and perfecting the economy and society into their ideal of the Socialist Utopia. The economist Adam Smith wrote of the invisible hand that guides economic activity. Whose hand is that? There's a question. What we do know is that it is not the hand of a government bureaucrat. Societies, cultures, economies, industries, businesses, crafts, and professions develop not according to rules imposed by bureaucrats, but by trial and error over many years. They are organisms that evolve as they grow. A new practice or technique is introduced; if it works well, it is adopted and becomes part of the culture until someone comes along with a better idea; if it does not work well, it is discarded and another practice, old or new, replaces it. Without government interference, the society, culture, economy, industry, business, craft, or profession grows and evolves to a greater and greater degree of perfection. Our friend the Liberal approaches a target, whether it is a society, culture, economy, industry, business, craft, or profession, and says, we will change this to make it better according to our values. Just a little tinkering will make all the difference, they tell us. That is when the Liberals begin to destroy their target, until the voters sober up and elect new leaders to pick up the pieces. For this reason, Liberals highest goal is to impose programs that cannot be reversed regardless of the financial and economic destruction they cause. That's a Liberal grand slam, whether it's a Ponzi scheme called Social Security, or programs for our grandchildren to pay for our health care, such as Medicare and Obamacare. As Margaret Thatcher said, "socialism works great until you run out of Other People's Money". Which you always do, eventually.

Liberals would like us to believe that Jesus was a Communist; after all, didn't he say that it is easier for a camel to pass through the eye of a needle than for a rich man to enter the Kingdom of Heaven? Yes, he did say that. What he did *not* say is, take the rich man's money and give it to people who you think should have it. The question of the rich man and the Kingdom of Heaven is between the rich man and God; there is no third party involvement of a redistributionist government mentioned. Jesus does not admonish the Romans to confiscate the rich people's property and give it to the poor. Doesn't the Bible say that Jesus said that a man should give away all his possessions and follow Jesus if he wishes to enter into eternal life? Yes it does; but it does not say that the authorities should expropriate the man's possessions and give them away to favored groups, nor that such governmental action would grant the man an entitlement to eternal life. The duty of charity does not imply a moral directive of government redistribution. Quite the opposite: if government seizes and redistributes people's property, there is neither opportunity nor need for charity. God commands us to perform charitable acts not to create an egalitarian society, but to ennoble human character. Charity is a spiritual exercise. Larceny is not.

Saint Paul states, "who does not work, neither shall he eat". All have a duty to work for the glory of God. God does not send souls to earth to become lazy and pampered pets of the state, nor to be drug addicts or other drains on the resources of society. Work is essential to our character and dignity as human beings. Let us return to the outright atheists. Their morality is easy, since they can make it up as they go. Or, let the United Nations do it. That collection of dictators and oppressors, with a few democracies thrown in, can create an unlimited listing of rights and benefits that are due to all, rights that are regularly denied to the majority of the dictators' subjects. Of course, the UN can just as easily repeal those rights, since they are based on nothing except getting a majority vote. Without a moral grounding in something, their ethics are shifting sands, fads of the day, lighter than air, not to be taken seriously. Why do we believe that humans have rights? Are we born with them? Are they created by UN proclamation? If the UN created them, then the UN can as easily rescind them; in that case, they were never true rights; they were privileges granted by an institution. JFK knew "that the rights of man come not from the generosity of the state, but from the hand of God." Without God, we must manufacture a list of privileges and call them human rights.

There are also Liberals who take an alternate approach and deny that humans have any innate rights. PETA (People for the Ethical Treatment of Animals) is an organization that works to prevent baby seals from being clubbed by humans so that they can be "naturally" mauled and devoured by polar bears and sharks. They have a different philosophy: a mosquito is equal to a boy. They imply that man is just another animal and does not have a Soul. In so doing, they are not raising the animals up to man's level; they are reducing man to the animal level. We must respect PETA in that they are ideologically consistent with their atheism. They don't pretend that humans have any rights that a bug or an amoeba do not have; the government will dictate what rights, if any, will be assigned to the various species. The Liberals certainly do not see Man as Shakespeare did:

What a piece of work is a man! How noble in reason! how infinite in faculty! in form and moving how express and admirable! in action how like an angel! in apprehension how like a god! The beauty of the world! the paragon of animals!

To the true Liberal, man is not the Crown of God's Creation, but a quasi-intelligent beast to be broken and domesticated to his given function, as determined by Liberals.

Christians have many disagreements with a fellow named Mohammed, but on one thing, we must agree. He says several times in the Koran: look at the world, the mountains, the seas, the sky; how can anyone look at these and doubt the existence of God? When we look at nature, we see beauty; but how can we appreciate beauty if we are creatures of chaos? When we see beauty, we are seeing through the eyes of a higher creature, one who could not have evolved from nothingness. When we see beauty, we are seeing through the eyes of the Soul, not through the eyes of our lower, animal nature. Our comprehension of beauty can only originate from a higher consciousness; our simple animal natures are incapable of comprehending beauty or even the idea of beauty.

We noted that some Liberals may believe that they believe in God, but they certainly serve other agenda. Even many who claim religiosity will scoff at the idea of Creationism or even intelligent Design. While even the most wild-eyed Liberal must concede that Evolution is nothing more than a theory, they treat any deviation from the orthodoxy of what we may call Accidental Evolution as true insanity. They seem to think that this world that we inhabit was not the result of any Creation, but somehow exists merely by happenstance. Let me see if I understand their theory: they are saying that at one time the universe was an infinitesimal point that exploded into a chaos of simple atoms of hydrogen, (almost as if someone had said, "let there be light!"). And these simple atoms were drawn into groups that eventually achieved such a size and temperature that nuclear fusion occurred. First helium, and then other heavier elements came into being. In the larger stars, heavier elements were created, including oxygen and iron. These giant stars exploded into supernovae, thus creating all the heaviest elements, and spreading these heavy elements throughout the universe. These heavy elements condensed into planets, where, purely by accident, the exact conditions necessary for the emergence of life occurred: the correct mixture of gasses in the atmosphere; the combination of hydrogen and oxygen that formed molecules of water, without which it would be hard to conceive of the possibility of life; the temperatures and sunlight that were just perfect for the emergence of life; the force of gravity which, purely by accident, was of the perfect strength to hold the atmosphere to the earth; the iron core that creates a magnetic field to protect all earthly life from deadly radiation; the rising of the land so that the earth's surface would not be covered by water; and a million other necessary factors. On an infinitesimally tiny speck of rock flying through an incomprehensibly vast and dangerous cosmos, the dust has taken form, opened its eyes, looked around, and become conscious that it exists. And we are asked to believe that all these intricate events occurred by chance, without any guidance or design from a higher source. St. Thomas called the Creator of the world the Primum Mobile, the First Mover; but our friends the Liberals say, no way, it just happened, without any plan or design. Just lucky, I guess.

One old chestnut runs, if you had a billion monkeys banging randomly on a billion typewriters, one of them would eventually create the works of Shakespeare. And by this logic, life would arise and evolution would and must eventually occur. Just one problem with that theory; it's not true. Mathematicians who have run the numbers have discovered that the probability of that occurrence is so infinitesimally low that it would not occur in a trillion trillion universes, that is, statistically, never. People who believe in evolution are devoted to an irrational belief without foundation in science. It's like they are in some weird godless religion that has an unquestioning belief in things that are mathematically impossible; they really hate it when they themselves are forced to concede that Accidental Evolution is, for all the *Sturm und Drang*, just a theory. The fact is, we have theories and we have ideas, but no human can honestly claim that they *know* the truth of the origin of the universe or of Man.

Recent discoveries suggest that there is even more that science does not know about our universe. It seems that astrophysics has determined that the galaxies could not have formed and could not maintain their existence without the influence of a force that we know nothing—absolutely nothing—about. This force can not be observed; we only know that something must be holding the galaxies together because physics predicts that the stars of the galaxies should fly apart; there is not sufficient gravity to hold them together. We have no proof or even a theory of what this unseen force is; but mathematics tells the astronomers that it must exist. The scientists give this unknown force the misleading name: dark matter. In truth, it is not dark, since we cannot see it; it is actually the opposite of dark, that is, it is invisible; and we don't really know if it is matter in any sense of the word. It would be more accurate to call it an invisible force, rather than dark matter, but that term sounds a bit, well, let's say, non-scientific. Human beings know only a tiny fraction of what there is to be known.

The physicists and the chemists might say, well, the nature of physics and chemistry created the possibility, if not the necessity, that all these things could or would happen. These permutations and combinations of matter were inevitable because of the inherent properties of energy and matter. Fair enough. But who created the matter and the energy of the universe to be such that the dust would live, sit up, and ask questions? Who or what determined what the properties of Nature would be? Just plain old dumb luck, say our Liberal friends. Mathematically, however, nothing could be more improbable, to the point where it is statistically impossible, than for the star dust to evolve into rational human beings without some great guiding force, a force far beyond human comprehension.

Our friends the atheists can be quite silly at times. When we say, we believe in God, they seem to think that we believe in an old man with a white beard and long, flowing robes, sitting on a big throne. While God took human form in Jesus Christ, the Bible never speaks of God the Father as a physical entity. Artists may take liberties to communicate their vision to us, but no Christian really believes that God looks like the painting in the Sistine Chapel. The ways of God are not the ways of man. The ways of the Spirit are not intelligible to human reason. Our limited consciousness is as incapable of comprehending God as an ant is incapable of comprehending humans. The Bible tells us just the basics of the journey of the Soul. The Book does not lie, but it tells us only what we are capable of comprehending. As C.S. Lewis said, what God has planned for us is infinitely different than what we can imagine, and infinitely better. "Now we can only see as through a glass, darkly; but some day, face to face." That day will come. In Heaven, you will know everything; on earth, we are not capable of perfect knowledge.

Our friends the Liberals worship many gods, but not the God of the Bible. The First Commandment forms the foundation of all the Commandments. If one does not accept and follow it, there is little point in going further.

II. You shall not take the name of the Lord your God in vain.

I am sure that there is room for improvement amongst believers as well as nonbelievers in these areas. Nothing further on this.

III. Remember to keep holy the Sabbath day.

Nonbelievers, by their own definition, have nothing to keep holy, so it would not be fair blame them incrementally on this count.

IV. Honor your father and your mother.

If we begin with the pure Communist, we find that they not only do not honor their parents, but they actively seek to undermine the ethic and practice of the institution of the family. The hard-core Communist considers the family to be a bourgeois institution and therefore something to be eliminated. This fact is amply demonstrated by social experiments ranging from the Maoist war on the family to the less severe practice of the Israeli *kibbutz*. The extreme Leftist views the family as a transmitter of the bad old ways rather than the new Socialist attitudes required of the New Man. To treasure one person over another because of the accident of birth is, frankly, irrational. A person is not likely to be better than or more loveable than someone else simply because he is related to us. But Liberals are people too, and the human ties of blood and family are not easily ignored by even the most coldly rational among us. There are few things on this planet stronger than a mother's love. You can be sure that even Stalin, the greatest murderer ever to exist, was loved by his mother, who would surely have defended him to the death. I am confident that Liberals treat their children well and raise them using their best judgment, which is, unfortunately, often not that good. But let's not get into a discussion of child-rearing.

The family is the nurturer of young *Homo sapiens* as they grow from a one-celled creature to a fully mature adult. It gives them not only physical support but also the values that will emerge in their adult selves. To a large extent, our family makes us what we are. It can have powerful effects on our psyches and personalities, for good or ill, although the debate about our innate, genetic nature versus our life experiences as a determinant of personality will never be fully resolved. Humans need an environment of love and acceptance in order to develop into happy, healthy individuals. The only possible entity that can care for and nurture human children is the family.

The big social change in America in the last century has been the collapse of the extended family into the nuclear family. In a farming culture, the older folk would conduct the less strenuous labor, which would include minding the young ones while the stronger family members did work more appropriate to their strength. Instead of Grandma and Grandpa taking care of the kids, we now have very expensive daycare. While the elders are liberated to live their own leisure lives, the labor they formerly provided has been lost. In the extended family, they would perform the labor now performed by expensive daycare providers. Each new rule, regulation, and law increases the cost of child care outside the home. Reeling under the cost of daycare, parents make an economic decision to have fewer children. When the elders eventually become consumers rather than producers of care, in many cases they are shipped to very expensive institutions, the cost of which threatens to bankrupt Medicare, Medicaid, and the United States of America. The family can gladly wash their hands of the elderly and rely on "the government" to take care of their elders. Undoubtedly those who are victims of serious dementia or illness require appropriate care, but as the cost of medical and custodial care spiral upward, society will soon find itself asking: can we afford to refuse the child-raising labor of Grandma and Grandpa, replacing it with costly daycare, while shuttling the old folks off to the nursing home at the first sign of decline? Will Grandma and Grandpa always be able to afford their own separate household? As federal deficits reach critical mass and the costs of unlimited entitlements sinks the economy, the answer will increasingly be "no". Economics may one day nudge the American family back from its' nuclear form toward a more extended family life.

As government grows larger and larger, such as it has done in much of Europe, it has become a dire threat to the family. The government provides for its subjects from infancy to old age; they never need to worry that they will not have food or shelter, and many other benefits. People look to government to eliminate all the problems and inconveniences of life. Unfortunately, the welfare state has begotten the mother of all intended consequences. In less developed cultures, families have many children; children represent a ready labor force and a source of support in old age. As societies increase in wealth, the number of children declines, as offspring become more expensive to raise and educate. When the large scale cradle-to-grave welfare state arrives, children become superfluous; they represent a cost without an economic benefit. The result? Exactly what the laws of economics predict. Adults become the children of the state; Big Brother becomes the provider; and the people lose the will to reproduce themselves. The populations of many economically developed countries are shrinking. Their populations are in drastic decline, creating demographic changes that have never been seen before. Stepping in to fill the vacuum are poorer and less educated immigrants. The Europeans have lost an important element of what makes people healthy and happy. By abandoning the family life of their fathers, and forsaking the traditions of centuries, they are not honoring their father and mother. They are in disobedience to God's first instruction to the first humans: "be fruitful and multiply."

In a larger sense, the entire concept of Liberalism is a challenge to the honoring of mother and father. "Mother and father" refers not only to individual entities, but to one's heritage, which includes not just Mom and Dad but an entire culture and set of values. Sometimes we hold a value without knowing precisely what it is based on—but that does not make it wrong. On occasion, the only answer we can supply to a child's (or a Liberal's) question is "because that's the way it has always been", or "because that's the way it is", or "just because". (Helpful hint to parents: respond "why do you think?". Eventually, the kids will learn to think before they ask. That is an outcome devoutly to be wished. Such tactics will not work on Liberals, however; thinking is not something they easily or willingly do.) Such a response often means that there are reasons that we might not know or even surmise, or perhaps reasons that are too complex for us to easily understand or articulate. Any significant change in any complex system necessarily has unintended consequences, different in type and degree than the average person might surmise. The classic example of unintended consequences was the introduction of welfare payments to unmarried mothers. Sounds like a nice thing to do. Unfortunately, when you pay for something, you get more of it, and unwed mothers and fatherless children proliferated as never before. The black family, which had been rising in income and stability, gave back all its gains. Fatherless males are highly likely to become gang members and drug addicts. Social engineering is a dangerous game. Liberals rush in where angels fear to tread.

Another threat to the family is Homosexual Marriage. What is wrong with that? How would that hurt anybody? Why is that anybody's business besides the homosexuals involved? After all, anything goes, these days. A skeptic might cite tradition, but a deeper answer is that the experience of this practice in Europe shows a breakdown of the family, a reduction in the number of all marriages as the institution of marriage is profaned, and a reduction in the birthrate after such policies have been enacted. Gay marriage is a corrosive force on the fabric of the human family and diminishes the viability of the human race. It offers a sterile union as an alternative to the normal male-and-female marriage, which creates new lives, as homosexual unions can never do. What the gay people truly want is: to be normal; but that is the one thing they can never be. The average person might be opposed to gay marriage without full awareness of the demographic cataclysm that it threatens. While their response may be based on tradition and the honoring of our political and religious heritage, they are acting on sound demographic and sociological principles. The populations of Europe shrink as the family structure dissolves and the government's role expands. For the first time in history, we see negative population growth. Every society has a right and a duty to defend and perpetuate itself.

The ease of divorce also contributes to the breakdown of the family. While there are obviously situations where a break has to be made, is it possible that people are just a bit too quick to get a divorce these days? With some people, it almost seems a question of choice rather than a necessity. While divorce may be a necessary evil for couples without children, the situation is very different when children are involved. Divorce creates a tragedy for kids, a cataclysm that leaves deep scars on children. The

Fourth Commandment decrees that we must maintain, support, and defend the concept of the traditional family. A society that does not treasure and protect its young people will not survive—nor does it deserve to.

V. *You shall not murder.*

The author will readily concede that some of the points made in this chapter might require some elaboration or cogitation for full understanding. Some of those points might even conceivably, possibly, theoretically, be debatable. But sometimes we get a softball, an unequivocal and undeniable sign, something which is so clear and obvious that no honest person can take issue with it. God gives us such a clear marker with this Commandment. It's impossible to hedge. For a Liberal to try to reconcile the practice of abortion with this very straightforward Commandment is beyond reason. This one is a no-brainer. Once an embryo is fertilized and becomes a fetus, it is a life form. No question. Is it human? You know the answer. There is nothing more to be said. Some Liberals say that the fetus is not fully human or that it does not have a Soul. When does the mass of cells acquire a Soul? Nobody can say. Since we are ignorant, we must err on the side of safety, and not kill the human organism whether we believe it has a Soul or not.   Anyone who advocates the practice of abortion, or does anything to enable it, is in gross violation of this Commandment.

Enabling abortion includes voting for a politician who votes to fund or authorize abortions, or voting for a politician who votes to confirm a judge who might be reasonably expected to authorize the practice of abortion.   Am I saying that practically the whole Democrat Party is in gross violation of this Commandment of God? It gives me no pleasure to say that, yes, I am saying precisely that. Who can deny it?

I have heard people say, "I am against abortion, but I vote for the LMPSD anyway because of other issues". *Au contraire, mon frere*. If you voted for a candidate who supports or enables abortion, you voted for abortion; your words are meaningless when they are contradicted by your actions. On a deeper level, what good can come from people who call themselves Christian and yet espouse the practice of abortion?

*From their fruits ye shall know them; do
men gather from thorns grapes? or from*

> *thistles figs? so every good tree doth*
> *yield good fruits, but the bad tree doth*
> *yield evil fruits.*
>
> —Matthew

An extreme position on abortion tells a Christian or a Jew everything he needs to know about a person's – or a political party's - character. No good comes from a poisoned tree.

Some people allege that capital punishment violates the Fifth Commandment, but that allegation is untrue, since the Bible explicitly commands that the murderer shall not be allowed to live. We are instructed to forgive a sinner, even a murderer, if we wish our sins to be forgiven; but the law cannot forgo the designated penalty; otherwise, it is not law.

VI. *You shall not commit adultery.*

This Commandment combines with *IV. Honor your father and your mother*, as well as *IX. You shall not covet your neighbor's wife* to support the institution of the family, as we have discussed.

VII. *You shall not steal.*

There are some people in this world who make too much money, and I'll tell you exactly who they are: everybody who makes more than me. That's funny, but it reveals a very deep truth about our animal nature. We all feel Envy; it is an inescapable part of human nature, one of the seven deadly sins, a temptation that we must fight every day of our lives.

Liberal Marxist Progressive Socialist Democratism is based on envy, and on the lust for OPM—Other People's Money. Socialism is a direct violation of the Seventh and Tenth Commandments. We may not steal our neighbor's property, but if we elect politicians who vote to do what we as individuals are forbidden to do, and to make it all nice and legal-like, we are guilty nonetheless. Even if you try to justify stealing from one person to give their property to another as charity, that is not charity; that is larceny. Charity involves giving our own assets, not other people's. Congress can change the legal code or the tax code, but not the moral code. The government may not morally do what an individual cannot morally do.

So let's be clear. Am I saying that a Christian or a Jew cannot morally be a Socialist? Yes, that is exactly what I am saying.

VIII. *You shall not bear false witness against your neighbor.*

The LMPSDs do not believe that Truth is a fixed commodity. After all, it all depends on how you see it. And everything's relative, after all. Everyone has their own truth. Your truth may not be my truth.

We deny it. Truth is ascertainable by inquiry and examination. In the free market of ideas, the truth will always emerge, even if it takes years and decades.

On an earthier level, all should understand that, in the Liberal philosophy, truth is whatever moves the ball toward the goalposts of the Socialist Utopia. To tell a lie is okay if it frustrates the Conservatives. The only moral act is to act in the interest of World Socialism. Any lie, evasion, or deception is not only morally acceptable, but absolutely necessary, if it advances the Socialist agenda. Telling the truth is a foible of the bourgeoisie.   There are no Ten Commandments in Marxism.

IX. You shall not covet your neighbor's wife

Another Commandment to support the vital human institution of the family.

X. You shall not covet anything that belongs to your neighbor.

We have discussed how the entire LMPSD world view is based on the principle of envy. Without the desire to expropriate the property and income of other people, there would be no reason for Liberals to exist. Envy and hatred of non-Liberal people is not only a prime characteristic of the Liberal; it is the motive force behind the Liberal Marxist Progressive Socialist Democrat psyche. Without the hatred that they have for people and corporations that they see as more privileged than themselves, Liberals would not be Liberals; they would be normal people.   Two Commandments prohibit the redistributionist basis of Liberalism. John Adams saw this clearly many years ago when he wrote:

The moment the idea is admitted into society that property is not as sacred as the laws of God, and that there is not a force of law and public justice to protect it, anarchy and tyranny commence. If "Thou shalt not covet" and "Thou shalt not steal" were not Commandments of Heaven, they must be made inviolable precepts in every society before it can be civilized or made free.

Is there any doubt that we have wandered far from these sound precepts of morality and economics in constructing the welfare state? Is it not striking that the precepts of morality and the laws of economics bring us to the same conclusion by different paths? Socialism is a double threat; it places the Soul in jeopardy of sin even as it decimates a free and healthy economy.

"Religious" Liberals often say, well, the Ten Commandments are Old School, they became obsolete when Jesus came to the world; Jesus brought mercy and forgiveness so that it is no longer necessary to observe the Ten Commandments. Some Liberals even suggest that we should disregard the Old Testament in its entirety and read only the New Testament. That is not what the Bible says. When Jesus is asked what one must do to enter eternal life, He says,

If you wish to enter into life, keep the Commandments." Then he said to Him, "Which ones?" And Jesus said, "You Shall Not Commit Murder; You Shall Not Commit Adultery; You Shall Not Steal; You Shall Not Bear False Witness; Honor Your Father And Mother; and You Shall Love Your Neighbor As Yourself.

—Matthew

In the Sermon on the Mount, Jesus says,

Think not that I am come to destroy the law, or the prophets: I am not come to destroy, but to fulfill. For verily I say unto you, Till heaven and earth pass, one jot or one tittle shall in no wise pass from the law, till all be fulfilled. Whosoever therefore shall break one of these least Commandments, and shall teach men so, he shall be called the least in the kingdom of heaven: but whosoever shall

*do and teach them, the same shall be
called great in the kingdom of heaven.*

—Matthew

That settles the question rather well, I think. The Ten Commandments do not expire while this world exists. They are a continuing obligation of every Christian and every Jew. If we do not observe them, we are in direct confrontation with God's Law. The practices of abortion and Socialism cannot in any way be reconciled to the clear and decisive language of the Ten Commandments.

Twin Destinies

Lift not the painted veil which those who
*   live*
Call Life. Though unreal shapes be
*   pictured there,*
And it but mimic all we would believe
With colours idly spread, behind lurk Hope
And Fear, twin Destinies, who ever weave
Their shadow, o'er the chasm, sightless
*   and drear.*

                    —Shelley

One can often detect in the words of political observers a certain assumption, that we have the Right and we have the Left and we have people in the middle who are moderate or perhaps have achieved some type of golden mean. That paradigm does not stand up to analysis. Given that each and every one of the six billion people on this planet is a unique and important individual, I would nevertheless suggest that there are two basic types of people. One type of person is generally happy and optimistic. They are not *always* happy; when life hands them the usual griefs and tragedies, they mourn, they recover, and endure. Their outlook might be described as hopeful; they are optimistic that things will generally work out, both in their personal life and in the wider world; despite all the dangers and difficulties, we will somehow muddle through. This type of person works hard, builds and makes things, and tends to favor a society based on liberty, individual rights, and capitalism. They feel that they must and will take care of themselves and their families, and will not rely on others to provide the necessities of life. They do not feel that the world owes them a living. Why do they favor capitalism? Not because they are serious students of economics and have concluded, after years of intensive study, that it is a system superior to the alternatives. Their choice is made intuitively and unconsciously; truly, it is not a choice but an adaptation to the world in which they find themselves. Capitalism is economic freedom. It is what people do unless government stops them from doing it. Many people do not even know what the definition of capitalism is, even though they follow its principles every day. When people are free, they are capitalists. When free people have an excess of something, whether it is labor, or apples, or skyscrapers, they will trade or sell that something for things that they need or money to buy those things.

They work for their own and their family's good. They may give generously to church and to the poor, after their family's basic needs are met. People of this type tend to see order in the universe, and for that and other reasons, are likely to believe in God. Seeing their community as an extension of their family, and feeling that their environment is not overtly hostile to them, they tend to have a positive relation to, and an allegiance to, their community, state, and nation. Seeing the bigger picture, they tend not to be egocentric; they feel that they have a place in a universe that is infinite but not chaotic or hostile. Let's call these people The Builders. Referring to Shelley's poem above, we will say their destiny is Hope, in that there are optimistic and confident in their outlook on life.

There is another type of person. We will call them the Deconstructionists. They may work, and even work hard, but they are never happy, whether they are rich or poor. They fear and distrust the world, including individuals and corporations, because they are sure that these individuals and corporations exist only to rob and deceive them. They are envious of anyone who has more than they have, even when they are wealthy. Their envy poisons their entire world view. They do not want some people to be wealthy while there are other people who are poor. The question of whether some people *deserve* to be wealthy and other people *deserve* to be poor is not something they consider; such a question is meaningless to them; they don't know what you mean by that; it is simply not within the scope of their consciousness. Equality is all they can conceive; if all are not equal, then someone is being cheated. These people are against economic freedom or capitalism, because they believe that these are evil forces that have deprived them of things that they deserve but do not have. They cannot conceive of people living successful and prosperous lives on their own; they must have guarantees of government benefits. The cards are stacked against the individual; the universe is against him; corporations conspire to pick his pocket, not to provide him the necessities of life; the individual must seek safety in the collective of the group. These people are driven by Fear, along with its allies, Envy and Hatred. What these folks want is to take Other People's Money (OPM) and give it to people who did not earn it, because the Decons believe that the non-earners *do* deserve it. They call themselves Marxists, Communists, Socialists, Levelers, Progressives, Liberals, and many other names. They seek to remake government, society, health care, industry, society, and all institutions, to rebuild the world into the theoretical Socialist Utopia, where everyone has all they want and nobody works more than they want to. To each according to his needs, from each according to his means.

As we observe representatives of the Twin Destinies, Hope and Fear, in life, on television and radio, as we read their columns, editorials, books, we develop an impression of them over time. When we are young, it is difficult to sort them out, but as our minds mature, we learn to can determine what political type they are within minutes. One can see that the Builders are trying to keep the economy going, to reduce the frictional costs of government, to remove barriers to free trade, to do the things that will grow the economy and thereby increase the overall wealth of the people. They oppose and even fight those countries that threaten America's legitimate interests. They uphold the United States Constitution as it is, written in plain language and as any high school student can understand it. They are the champions of the Normal.

The Deconstructors are opposed to essentially everything the Builders want to do. They want to take money from the people who earned it and give OPM to those who did not earn it. They want to increase the size and cost of government even if it means reducing the productivity of the economy, which it necessarily does. They are immune to the argument that taxes and regulation impair the growth of the economy; they act as if economics is something the Builders made up just to frustrate the Liberals' designs. In order to deconstruct society and the economy, they have invented Marxist and Keynesian "economics". The Decons are happy to befriend America's enemies because they share a common enemy, that is, Normal America, and the enemy of their enemy is their friend. They do not respect the Constitution except when it can be manipulated and twisted to justify their often anti-Constitutional purposes.

Liberals are quick to tell us how much they love America, and I have no doubt that they try hard to believe it as the words come out of their mouths. They have difficulty keeping their supposed love in mind, because they often slip and use the word *patriot* as an insult to describe their ideological opponents. But the America that the Liberals love is not the

America that exists, with all its warts; it is a different, reborn America, cleansed of selfishness, disease, want, Republicans, contact sports, bullies, NASCAR, tobacco, trans-fats, individualism; it is an America that does not exist and never will exist.   The America they love cannot exist without eliminating the people who love law and liberty, and the Liberal dream of America is not America as it is, with all its flaws and all its virtues.

Ronald Reagan said that Liberals love humanity; it's people that they hate.   Of course, our Liberal friends would scoff at this statement.   But in truth, the distinguishing characteristic of the Liberal is: hate. Their vitriol comes through loud and clear on television and in writing, although a few of them are getting better at smiling as they rant.   They hate America, they hate capitalism, they hate the Normal, and they hate the God that made them, the God who is so unfair and does not meet the standards they set. Regardless of where they live, they have a particular hatred for the United States of America, for in no other country is there so much freedom, especially economic freedom.   Whatever they can do to destroy America and its economic system, they will do.   It is their hatred that makes them what they are.   Without that hatred, they would be different people, much calmer, at peace with the world and with their Maker. And then, they would no longer be Liberals.

Shelley speaks of "twin Destinies" of Hope and Fear. All people are torn between Hope and Fear, feeling more of some at one time, more of the other at another time. At different points in our lives, each individual will be dominated by one or the other; we are all bi-polar. Those who are consumed by their Fear, and who experience the world as a hostile environment, are Liberals. And Fear leads inevitably to Hatred; hatred of Big Business, hatred of Capitalism, hatred of the Normal, and most of all, to Hatred of those who appear to live without Fear. Their greatest Fear is that there is no God and therefore it must follow that there is no Hope in the long term. Without the Light of God, there is only Darkness. If death is the end, then there is no Hope. If they are confirmed atheists, then their Fear and Hatred must necessarily be overwhelming. "Fear is the mind-killer." It is also the Soul-killer.

Perhaps it is an American phenomenon that we believe that people make their own destiny through the exercise of Free Will, through the choices we make every day. Hope and Fear are the competing influences on us as we make those choices. Without the grace of God, we would all succumb to Fear, and would be doomed to the condition where we are totally separated from God, a condition called Hell.

> *The mind is its own place, and in it self*
> *Can make a Heav'n of Hell, a Hell of*
> *Heav'n.*
>
> —Milton

And as Marlowe's fallen angel Mephistophilis complains:

> *Hell hath no limits, nor is circumscribed*
> *In one self place; for where we are is hell,*
> *And where hell is there must we ever be:*
> *And, to conclude, when all the world dissolves,*
> *And every creature shall be purified,*
> *All places shall be hell that is not Heaven.*
>
> —Marlowe

God does not damn any Soul to eternal Hell; only the individual can do that, by rejecting God's freely offered Love. People who may now be driven by Fear may come to embrace Hope, through God's grace. Are Lenin, Hitler, Stalin, Mao Tse Tung, Pol Pot, Castro, bin

Laden, and countless other murderers and mass murderers doomed to Hell for eternity? Judge not, less ye be judged. God offers redemption and an opportunity for repentance to even such as these. Some theologians argue that all Souls will eventually be saved. This earthly life may not be our final chance at redemption. Perhaps all People of Fear will become People of Hope, Beings of Darkness will become Beings of Light, even if is not in this world. Those whose Fear is overcome by the light of Hope live a much more peaceful existence. Since God offers an eternity of bliss on a higher plane of existence, what is there to fear? The temporary world we are visiting is a stop on the road to a greater eternity, but God uses this life to refine our faithfulness to Him and His Commandments. The person of Hope places strong emphasis on moral action, because God tells us that it is right, in itself, as well as necessary to earn a place in a greater world. Or does the performance of Right action actually create a better world? Is it possible that the performance of Right action will one day lead to an earthly paradise? We cannot know, but we are not required to know. We are only required to believe and act according to our beliefs.

A certain type of person says, "I would definitely believe in God if He gave me proof of his existence." Duh. If God could be proven, then all would believe, because belief would be a matter of Science and not of Faith. While I believe that there are many signs of the existence of a higher being in our universe, and that new developments in science serve only to confirm and deepen those beliefs, I predict that there will never be indisputable proof of God while we inhabit this planet. That is because God requires us to have Faith. Why does He require Faith? The Creator could easily have created beings that were perfectly obedient to His will; instead, He made unruly and rebellious humans. Apparently, God did not want His highest creatures to be pure automatons. One could argue that animals are such automatons; they act according to the rules of their nature; they are not troubled by Hope or Fear, in the sense that humans experience these conditions. But a being cannot be capable of Love unless it is capable of Hate; without the possibility of Hate, there is no possibility of Love. Without the threat of Fear, there is no need for Hope. Without the possibility of Unbelief, there is no virtue in Faith. Without Darkness, Light has no meaning. God willed to create something more than an animal. He willed into existence a race of creatures that would not carry out his instructions blindly and obediently, but would, eventually, come to love Him of their own Free Wills, as a result of their own free choices. He wants his highest creatures to be motivated not by Fear, but by Love.

What motivates you, gentle reader?

The Ten Commandments of Liberalism

I. I am the Lord your God, you shall have no strange gods before me, unless of course you don't believe in God, not that there is anything wrong with that, after all, you have your rights, we don't want to oppress you with our values; if you want to believe in some old guy with long hair and a beard who floats around on a cloud, then that's your right, no matter how silly we think you are; or you could join us and worship the Government, which gives us our daily bread and all kinds of free stuff, using the funds it takes from the filthy, greedy, capitalist pigs.

II. You shall not take the name of the Lord in vain, unless you want to, because obviously you have a right to free speech and you should not be oppressed by imaginary beings.

III. Keep holy the Sabbath Day and be sure that the union workers get time-and—a-half.

IV. Honor your father and mother, and put them in the nursing home as soon as possible so they will not become an inconvenience to you. All they did was raise you, feed you, clothe you, educate you, and shelter you for twenty years. Time for them to move on.

V. You shall not murder, unless of course you need an abortion, the Supreme Court says it's Constitutional, it's settled law, the law of the land. And how can we be sure that it's a human life, after all, a gerbil or a hamster might have found its way up there, and you don't need to be inconvenienced by having any unnecessary babies around.

VI. You shall not commit adultery, but if you do, it's okay, it's easy to get a divorce if you get caught, we wouldn't want to oppress you with old-fashioned ideas like faithfulness and loyalty. If it feels good, do it. Don't be hung up. Gay, straight, go for it!

VII. You shall not steal, but of course it's okay to let the Government do it for you, after all, it's only fair, and we need to enforce equality, that's a Commandment too, isn't it, well no, but I am sure I read it somewhere, and after all I am not stealing if I elect officials who vote to do it all nice and legal-like, so I am not personally responsible for their larceny.

VIII.   You shall not bear false witness against your neighbor, unless, of course, it advances the Liberal Marxist Progressive Socialist Democrat agenda, because the end justifies the means, so if we need to lie through our teeth to the masses to get them to do the things that we know are for their own good, then it's our duty to do so.

IX.   You shall not covet your neighbor's wife, but hey, stuff happens, so don't be a square.

X.   You shall not covet your neighbor's goods, unless he has more than you, and that's really not fair that he should have so much while others have so little, so we'll elect a Government that will liberate his assets and give them to someone whom we find to be more deserving.

Constitutional Quiz

Let's have some fun. Here's a true-or-false quiz:

1. The Constitution explicitly states that there is a wall of separation between church and state.

2. The Constitution explicitly states that there are three equal and independent branches of the Federal government.

3. The Constitution explicitly states that the Supreme Court is the ultimate arbiter of whether laws are Constitutional or not.

4. The Constitution explicitly states that the Federal government can do whatever it wants as long as it does not violate the Bill of Rights.

5. The Constitution explicitly states that anyone born in the United States is a citizen of the United States.

6. The Constitution explicitly guarantees a right to privacy.

7. The Constitution explicitly states that the Supreme Court has the authority to issue orders that the other branches must obey.

8. The Constitution explicitly states that there is a right to abortion.

9. The Constitution explicitly states that only the Supreme Court, and not the Executive and Legislative branches, is responsible for upholding the Constitution.

10. The Constitution explicitly states that the government must ensure the equality of all citizens.

11. The Constitution explicitly states that the individual state governments are prohibited from establishing religion.

12. The Constitution explicitly states that a defendant who commits a crime shall not be convicted if the government violates his Constitutional rights in the prosecution of the case. Write down your answers.

The correct answers follow immediately.

The answer to all of the above is FALSE.

How did you score on Constitutional knowledge? If you are a Liberal, then not so well. As Ronald Reagan said, the problem with our friends the Liberals is not exactly that they are ignorant; it is that they believe so many things that are just not true. For example, the twelve items listed above. To be specific:

1. The Constitution makes no mention of a wall of separation between church and state. The phrase does not occur in the entire document.

2. The Constitution says nothing about three *equal* branches. Given the fact that the Congress is created in the very first article; given that the Founders had just fought a war against what they considered to be an overactive chief executive, George III; given the exhaustive treatment of the Congress and its powers, compared to the brief paragraphs establishing the other branches, it is hard to deny that Congress was intended to be the predominant element of the new government. The executive had important powers, clearly specified, as well. To assume that the Supreme Court has some role that is in any way equal to the

elected branches is utterly unfounded in the text, as well as foreign to the customs and experience of the time.

3.   The Constitution grants no special role to the Supreme Court in the interpretation of the Constitution.

4. The powers of the Federal government are limited; they are clearly and explicitly enumerated in Article One.   The Founders were careful men; to be on the safe side, they wrote the Tenth Amendment stating that

> *The powers not delegated to the United States by the Constitution, nor prohibited by it to the States, are reserved to the States respectively or to the people.*

By writing this amendment, they removed any validity to someone claiming that there are powers "implied" in the Constitution.   As we know, the plain and easily understandable language of the Constitution does not prevent the Deconstructionists from ignoring the Constitution; it just eliminates any credibility from their   arguments.   The   Deconstructionists   will deconstruct the Constitution just as they deconstruct all the pillars of society; that is what they do.

5. The Fourteenth Amendment states that

> *All persons born or naturalized in the United States, and subject to the jurisdiction thereof, are citizens of the United States and of the State wherein they reside.*

There are two necessary and distinct conditions that must be met for citizenship to be granted. The first part is easily determined; if that settled the question, then the amendment would have no second part; but it does. A child is not under the jurisdiction of the United States if his mother has entered the country without the consent of the United States. She remains under the jurisdiction of her home country, just as the U.S.-born children of foreign ambassadors are not American citizens. Some will say that the mother comes under the jurisdiction of the United States when she crosses the border; but in that case, there is again no need to require the second necessary condition; yet there is a second condition; so that argument fails. The legislative history explicitly shows that the purpose of this amendment was to prevent discrimination against African-American citizens after the War Between the States, not to reward illegal immigrants to our country.

6. The Constitution says nothing of a right to privacy.

7. The Constitution does not grant the Supreme Court any power to issue instructions to another branch of government.

8. The Constitution does not mention abortion. Therefore, the Tenth Amendment clearly indicates that abortion is an issue reserved to the States. That is where abortion was historically regulated until activist judicial tyrants perverted their Constitutional role and usurped the authority of state governments.

9. All officers of the United States Government are sworn to uphold and defend the Constitution. The Constitution does not grant to the courts any special role in upholding the Constitution. The process of how a bill becomes a law is clearly defined. The Constitution has no process by which a law can be invalidated or struck down, other than through the legislative process and the elected representatives of

the people. This is exactly what the Founders intended. They did not fight a bloody war to throw off one tyrannical ruler just to create a new class of unelected and unaccountable despots in black robes. The historical record is clear that the Supreme Court, starting with John Marshall, has violated the Constitution by seizing powers that are not theirs.

We have recently seen a troubling trend in the legislative process. Some legislators will say, well, we aren't sure if the Supreme Court will uphold the constitutionality of this law, but we will pass it anyway and let the court sort out the question of constitutionality. This situation occurred prominently in the passage of campaign finance laws that attempted to suppress First Amendment rights to free speech and the right to petition the government. We cannot castigate the Liberals here, as they were faithfully advancing their constant purpose of increasing the power of government, of unions, and of Liberal media, all in furtherance of the Socialist agenda; one can count on the Liberals to happily disregard the mere Constitution and Bill of Rights when they see a chance to increase the power of the Left. The true scandal was the so-called Moderates, who were derelict in their duty to uphold the Constitution, and so violated their oath of office. Did not the Liberals also violate their oath of office? Of course, but they were acting accord to their nature, supporting a greater cause, to wit, the Socialist Utopia, which always and everywhere trumps such trivia as oaths and constitutions.

10. Equality is not mentioned in the Constitution. The Founders were clearly focused on Liberty and Freedom, even if they did not extend that Freedom to the slaves. The Fourteenth Amendment does guarantee "equal protection of the laws", which is far different from guaranteeing equality.

11. *Congress shall make no law respecting an establishment of religion, or prohibiting the free exercise thereof.* Over the years, rogue courts have extended the same restriction to state and local governments. Is this what the Constitution says? Is this what the Founders intended? At the time of the Founding, over two thirds of the states had their own state-supported and official (established) religions. They did not end this practice when the Constitution was ratified; quite the contrary. The Founders did not want a Federal government to establish a national religion, as the British government had; they wanted

their state religions to be left unmolested by the federal government, and they believed that they had accomplished that goal in the explicit language of the First Amendment. To suggest that the Founders wrote the First Amendment to prohibit religious expression at the state and local level is so utterly preposterous that it is laughable. Yet there are tyrants in black robes, aided by radical LMPSD groups, who consistently turn the Constitution on its head and actively prohibit the free exercise of religion at the state and local level. The Founders would be outraged and saddened to find their defense of religion used to prohibit a voluntary prayer at a high school graduation.

12.   The Constitution does not state that a criminal should enjoy any special consideration if the prosecution violates his rights. Many criminals walk away from justice because of minor police and prosecution errors. There is no Constitutional basis for this practice; it is entirely an invention of the legal system. Justice demands that the guilty be punished; if the police break the law or violate someone's Constitutional rights, then the individual police officer should be appropriately sanctioned.   Instead, the courts release guilty and sometimes vicious felons, who remain dangers to the public safety. The result is

that the public at large is made to suffer for the shortcomings of the government.

Reading this analysis, a Liberal will say: "Hey, who do you think you are? You're not a lawyer or a Constitutional scholar! Who are you to say what the Constitution says? We have cases and precedents and rulings and injunctions from here to Alpha Centauri, proving that judges decide what is right and what the Constitution says. Who are you to say they are wrong? The paperwork makes it all nice and legal-like." This is the same type of invective used by medieval clerics against people who questioned church authority before Gutenberg brought the Bible to the people. My Liberal friend, I hold a much higher title than attorney or judge; I am a Free Citizen of the United States; I can read and understand the plain meaning of a plain document written in my native language; and a million Supreme Courts with a trillion rulings cannot change the meaning of that document.

The Constitution does not begin with "We the lawyers". Nor was it written for attorneys, but for the people. Law is too important to be left to the lawyers. A free people must protect the law and the Constitution with their votes. Presidents who appoint, and Senators who vote for, Deconstructionist judges must not be elected or re-elected if the country wishes to live under the Constitution. The whole body of Constitutional Law, created by generations of attorneys and judges, is nothing; the Constitution is everything. The simple language of the original document overrules all arguments against it.

Lawyers use a device that they call "precedent" to change the plain meanings of the Constitution and laws with which they do not agree. A precedent is formally defined as a little, teeny-tiny, itsy-bitsy over-extension of the law that can be sequentially combined with other little, teeny-tiny, itsy-bitsy over-extensions of the law to create a great big corruption of the letter and spirit of the law. By expanding the law just a bit in one case, mendacious attorneys and corrupt judges can expand it a little more in the next case, until they deform the law into whatever form they desire. Thus, an amendment saying that Congress shall not prohibit the free exercise of religion is twisted into a policy whereby Congress funds a so-called Justice Department that does everything it can to frustrate the free exercise of religion. The creation from nothing of a right to kill an unborn fetus is the greatest example of judicial contempt for the Constitution; it would be hard to top that one.

Andrew Jackson and Abraham Lincoln openly defied, or shall we say ignored, the Supreme Court when it overstepped its bounds. They treated the Court's rulings as opinions and nothing more. For most people, and even for states and localities, there is often no restraint on judicial tyranny. There is no one to judge the judges—well, not in this life. The Founders could not have foreseen how judicial authority would be abused; given the times, they were focused on the tyranny of the executive, such as they had seen in King George. The idea of usurpation of authority by mere judges was unprecedented and unthinkable. They should have observed Jefferson's admonition: "Leave no authority existing not responsible to the people". Even when Congress has exercised its power to narrow the jurisdiction of the Supreme Court, the Court has run roughshod over the restrictions, in blatant violation of the law and of the Constitution they swear to uphold. When Congress removed the question of enemy combatants from the Court's jurisdiction, the Court simply ignored the law and ruled by fiat. Few have raised an alarm about this dangerous power grab.

Liberal Marxist Progressive Socialist Democrat judges will say, the Constitution is a "living document", and we must update it as time passes and society changes.   Wrong.   The process for amending or updating the Constitution is clearly specified in the document itself.   That process involves the elected representatives of the people, that is, the Congress and the state legislatures.   Unelected judges have no legitimate role in amending, revising, updating, or otherwise changing the Constitution.   To say that it is a "living document" is to say that it has no objective meaning; that is to deny that is in any sense a Constitution at all.   Therefore, the judicial tyrants will gladly impose their personal opinions over the black letters of the centuries-old document.

Liberals often defend judicial tyranny by saying that Supreme Court decisions with which they agree are "the law of the land".   That's not what the Constitution says.

> *This Constitution and the Laws of the United States . . . and all Treaties made . . . shall be the supreme Law of the Land.*

It does not say that the opinions of the Supreme Court shall be the Law of the Land. But who is to interpret the Constitution? The Constitution does not say, but it clearly does not grant that privilege to the Supreme Court. The Founders expected that questions that might arise would be decided through the political process, by the elected representatives of the people, which most definitely does not include the unelected and unaccountable Supreme Court.

Often, there are Supreme Court decisions with which we agree. That is a welcome example of unintended consequences created by Liberals. We must enjoy seeing them hoist by their own petard. But that does not justify judicial seizure of powers that are not theirs. Overall, judicial activity beyond proper Constitutional bounds, whether we agree with the outcome or not, is a serious danger to the rule of law.

The duty to support the Constitution is equally shared by many parties.

The Senators and Representatives before mentioned, and the Members of the several State Legislatures, and all executive and judicial Officers, both of

the United States and of the several
States, shall be bound by Oath or
Affirmation, to support this Constitution

What is to prevent the perversion of the Constitution by Liberal judges? The fault is not in the document, but in the judges. There are some worthy suggestions, such as ten-year terms for judges, but ultimately the protection of Constitutional government relies on the appointment of judges who are persons of good character, who will faithfully follow the Constitution. If we have the strength to be honest, we must conclude that the above description does not include Liberals, who consistently seek to impose their own radical values over the values of the people, as expressed by elected representatives.

Unions are Bad

All Americans feel sympathy when we hear of a group of humble workers bravely standing up to a mean, heartless corporation that is forcing them to work for peasant wages. Well, not really forcing them, because the workers could always quit if they were unhappy. And maybe not really peasant wages, because the workers freely agreed to work for these wages and, if they quit, there are other people who would instantly take those jobs at the market wage. By definition, there are a practically unlimited number of workers who would take those jobs at the market wage.

Labor unions, however, do not seek the market wage, that is, the wage at which free companies and free individuals agree to hire and to be hired. They want: more. As much as they can get. They demand compensation that is above the market price. We tend to see union struggles as between management and workers, but there are other parties involved. The union strategy is two-pronged: (1) extract as much from the employer as they can, and (2) deny other otential workers the opportunity to accept the wages that they themselves reject. Without the second prong, the denial of opportunity to others, the first prong will be ineffective. The labor union increases the economic well-being of its own members while denying economic opportunity to those who are not union members. The employer does not necessarily suffer from having a union in control of its workplace, as long as its competitors are also unionized. Higher wages mean a higher price for the employer's product. Economists will tell us that the profit margin will remain more or less the same, both because of competition and because the employer's cost of capital is ultimately the same for all players in the industry. Henry Ford was a strong backer of labor unions in his company, but of course he did not foresee that the unions would one day destroy the American automobile industry.

The only real loser in this whole scenario is the consumer, who pays the higher prices caused by the above-market wages paid by the union employer. Union members may read the title of this chapter and say, "Unions are bad? No way! Without the union, I never would have got x, x, x, and y." Precisely. The unfortunate economic fact is that the sum total of benefits gained through union coercion is exactly equal to the sum total of higher costs imposed on the consumer, although the benefit to the unionist is detectable and measurable while the cost to the individual consumer is not seen or calculated. The cost of these above-market union benefits is born by the consumer in every product and service produced by union labor or by every taxpayer paying for unionized government. Unfortunately, this consumer is the same fellow who was not in the union and was denied the opportunity to work by the union. Not only are his economic prospects diminished by his exclusion from the union workplace, but he must also pay the above-market price that the union employer must charge to produce products.

Here's an idea: why don't we all, everyone, everywhere, form unions and then we can all get above-market wages? I hope I don't need to explain why that statement is inherently ridiculous. That is like saying we are all above average. Economists have compared such an idea to trying to pull oneself up by the hair; it is a logical impossibility; it just doesn't work. We can't all be above average. One could argue that the economic situation would be equalized if either (1) everyone was in a union or (2) if no one was in a union; but as long as some people are in unions and others are not, the union members will remain a privileged class, with wages and benefits that are beyond the reach of others. They will earn above-market wages, as long as government colludes with the unions in allowing picket lines and other strategies to "persuade" non-union workers not to seek employment during a strike.

Imagine that you started a business and hired some employees. Let's say that the workers came to you one day and said, we demand higher wages, and we demand less work, and if you don't meet our demands, we are not going to quit, but we are going to stop working and we will do our best to prevent you from hiring people who do want to work under the wages you offer. You would fire the unwilling workers instantly. And rightly so. The unhappy workers were attempting to exercise ownership rights over your business, which is your property. Even though they had no rights of ownership, they had essentially decided to expropriate your ownership rights. Under the Constitution of the United States, they have no right of any kind to your property and no decision-making role in your private enterprise. Certainly the historical record is clear that the Founding Fathers had no conception that the Constitution they were writing could allow any such assault on private property. To condone such an act of larceny would have been inconceivable to them. Under the Constitution, private property is inviolate without due process of law (that is, in criminal cases).

Is there any lack of clarity about who owns the job: the worker or the employer? That is easily determined. Who can close the plant, and end all the jobs? Who can sell the plant and its jobs? Who can move the plant and the jobs to another state or country? Not the workers.

What is the difference between a union and a gang, between organized labor and organized crime? One is legal and one is not. For the first century of the Republic, there was no discernible difference. For many years, the Supreme Court held that unions were "combinations in restraint of trade" under the Sherman Anti-Trust Acct, which they obviously are. The New Deal brought laws that legalized union activities, but there was no change to the Constitution, so these activities remain unconstitutional. Despite legal wrangling over the years, the courts have weakened the right to private property and unions have gained ground. Unions have destroyed the steel, auto, and many other industries in America with excessive demands. As workers and employers gradually came to comprehend the destructive power of unions, they now understand that companies function and employees prosper very well without unions, and the share of private industry infested by unions has decreased dramatically.

Unions are probably the greatest violators of human rights in the United States. The twenty-three "right to work" states allow workers the option to choose to join the union or not, in companies that are unionized. Outrageously, the other "closed shop" states require employees to join a union or to pay dues to that union. What of the Constitutional guarantees of freedom of association? What of people's right to not be forced to pay for the promotion of political agendas and candidates that they oppose? How can a free American be forced to pay money to an organization against his will when the Constitution prohibits involuntary servitude? Despite protections provided in Federal law, unions routinely use the dues of their members to support Leftist candidates even though a large percentage of their members do not support those candidates. The government has failed to enforce the laws that prohibit this coerced subsidization of the Left. Millions of dollars in union pension assets have mysteriously disappeared, causing financial hardship for the members, but the Liberals will do nothing to stop this theft. When laws are proposed to require a clear public accounting, such as is required of any public company, the unions and their hired politicians rush to the television cameras to denounce this assault on the working man. The union members are kept ignorant of where the money goes. And when a union member tries to challenge the union powers that be—he better be sure that his insurance is paid up.

Some workers benefit more from their union membership than others. The best and most efficient workers don't need a union; their work habits and proficiency at their job make them very desirable employees, and they might make the same or even more income without the union. The middle rank probably gets a small net benefit from union membership. The bottom rank includes unmotivated and inefficient workers who would have been fired years ago except for the interference of the union. These workers benefit enormously from their union membership, which not only keeps them employed but gives them above-market income which they would never receive outside the union. For all three classes of worker, the wages are the same, as negotiated by the union. What is the incentive to excel? For most, there is none, except for the exceptional few who will find themselves promoted *out* of the union. For the vast majority, the union stifles all incentive for excellence and creativity.

In recent years, employees have become more and more resistant to the promises of unionism, and have rejected it more and more. To sidestep the inconvenient problem of workers who don't want to be unionized, unions have come up with a plan to bypass the formality of a free vote for unionization of a work force. The so-called "card check" law would allow one-on-one persuasion by union "consultants" who would doubtless have a very high rate of success. The right of a worker to a free and secret ballot, without intimidation by either side, would be lost.

The first duty of a union is to protect the interests of its members. Sad to say, the unions have abandoned their members to pursue a new priority. Historically, union leaders from George Meany to Cesar Chavez have opposed illegal immigration. That makes perfect sense, as reducing the supply of new, cheap labor entering the market is the best way to raise the general level of wages, benefiting all workers. The new, radical LMPSD union leaders have sold out their members and subordinated their interests to the larger LMPSD agenda. Unions now back amnesty for illegal entrants to America, despite the fact that such an increase in labor supply can only reduce any upward pressure on wages, and is thus directly inimical to the interests of its existing members. For what possible reason would they commit such a betrayal of their membership? The union leaders are LMPSDs first, and union leaders second, and they see their highest duty to be advancing the Socialist agenda; they believe, first, that amnestied immigrants will be ready voters for the Leftward party, and, and second, that they will be easy converts in company unionization efforts. The union bosses may eventually find that these new citizens are a little too Catholic and a bit too upwardly mobile to be reliably Socialist in the long run, but that is not the point. The point is that there is no possible scenario in which a flood of new labor can benefit existing union members, whom these union leaders have sworn to protect; but it may increase the political power and influence of the unions and their leaders.

We have seen the harm that unions do to all non-union members by increasing the cost of goods, and we have seen unions destroy industries in the US. As deleterious as their impact is in the private sector, it pales in comparison to the damage done in the public sector. Some states, unlike the Federal government, allow government employee unions to bargain for wages and benefits, a practice that was staunchly opposed by Franklin Roosevelt, among others. This grant by these states of bargaining privileges—they are not "rights", else there would be no need to grant them nor power to retract them— breeds a unique form of corruption as union members elect Leftist politicians who gladly submit to the unions' demands, subverting the public trust. Such a conflict of interest cannot occur in the private sector. The cost to the states threatens to destroy the budgets and the economies of those states foolish enough to follow that corrupt path.

Union-bought politicians have failed to protect the government from unionism, and government at all levels has made extravagant promises to workers and retirees. The level of unionism in government has exploded even as it has diminished in the private sector. Politicians jettisoned the public interest and agreed to fat contracts for union workers, who kicked back a portion of their ill-gotten gains to their pet politicians, creating a vicious cycle of fleecing the public using public money. Private employers (and also the federal government, to a large degree) have moved from defined benefit plans, where the employer bears the investment risk, to defined contribution plans, where the employee is responsible for their own retirement planning; but many state and local governments continued to sign extravagant contracts granting generous defined and guaranteed benefits to workers and retirees. Instead of considering the long-term fiscal health of government, corrupt politicians gambled that they would be retired, dead, or forgotten when the enormous bills came due.

In 2010, a weak economy hastened, but did not cause, a financial crisis in many state and local governments. The easy promises of corrupt politicians hatched into devastating financial expenditures. The result was the practical bankruptcy of many state and local governments. In Chicago, the police union was given a choice of cutting 10% of all officers' pay or cutting 10% of officers. They dumped the bottom 10% without a second thought. The citizens had 10% less police protection, but the older cops did not suffer the loss of a penny. The younger 10% of officers were left to fend for themselves; that is what they call union brotherhood.

Even as unionization of state and municipal workers is more harmful than private sector unionization, there is an even worse abuse that occurs. That is the unionization of teachers. Schools should have only one priority: the education and well-being of their young charges. Nothing can be permitted to deflect or detract from that purpose. The good of the students must be the sole concern of administrators and teachers. We all know that this is not the case whenever a union is involved in education. Just as no man can serve two masters, no organization can have two priorities. Teachers unions have a consistent record of becoming the priority. Many teachers unions run their own slate of candidates in low turnout school board elections, especially during off-year elections. The union stooge members then grant generous salary increases to the union members. The unions argue that these raises benefit the students and increase the quality of teaching; but the only change is that the existing teachers score big cash, while the quality of instruction remained unchanged. This scenario has occurred thousands of times in our country. It is one thing to destroy the auto companies or the steel industry or the airlines; to sacrifice our children on the altar of unionism is unforgiveable.

A very sad event occurred in the District of Columbia in the elections of 2010. A courageous mayor had installed a new superintendent who fired incompetent teachers and demonstrably improved the education of children. He also cracked down on crime and reduced the murder rate in DC. Obviously, the grateful citizens would overwhelmingly re-elect the mayor who had so greatly improved the quality of life. Unfortunately, no. The voters were more concerned about the welfare of the unionized incompetents who had been canned, and the criminals who had been incarcerated, than they were about the improved life chances of their children and the lives saved by removing the murderers from society. Under union control, the schools had come to be seen as a jobs program for the inept rather than a means to improve children's lives. That is very disheartening.

Whether there ever was a time when unions served the interests of the country, that time has come and gone. It is time for the Congress and the courts to enforce the Constitution, including the right to private property, and sharply rein in the activities of labor unions.   Unions must be made financially accountable to their members and respectful of the rights of all Americans.

A Couple of Points on Economics

Some of the nicest people I know are Liberals. Well, at least they think they are. These nice folks are not very political. They see that some people have nothing, and other people have a lot, and they are uncomfortable with this situation. They therefore feel that someone, such as the government, needs to make things more fair. So far, so good. There was a time where I felt exactly the same way. Nobody wants another person to be poor, and nobody but a Liberal would accuse anyone of advocating that life should be unfair. The question is: how do we make the world more fair? There's the rub.

Someone who wants the world to be more fair, and who has no knowledge of economics, would simply say: it is a simple problem with a simple solution: we re-shuffle the deck so everyone gets the same. Complete redistribution of wealth. Then everyone is equal. What could be simpler?

In the real world, of course, things are not so simple. The wealth that exists was created by the efforts of individuals. Those individuals are not likely to be anxious to part with what they have earned for the benefit of someone who has done nothing to create or earn that wealth. People's wealth represents their ability to live as they wish and to support and protect their family from the vicissitudes of the world. It also represents the fruits of years of their hard work. They can become quite upset when someone else, even the government, takes that money from them and their family. What gives the government the right to take money from some people and give it to others? Is it fair to take wealth from people who worked for it and give it to people who did not work for it? Many people would consider that to be completely unfair.

Let us journey to Fantasyland and imagine a world where we could give everyone the same amount of wealth without upsetting the expropriated parties. Everyone at a given moment has equal wealth. Perfection of economic equality is achieved. How long would that perfect situation endure? Not long. Since we are dealing with humans and not with angels, people will make different choices, and some choices will lead to better outcomes than others. Some people will spend very little on their personal comforts and save their money; others will buy heroin and alcohol. Some will put money in the bank and earn a return that, after taxes and inflation, will result in a negative real return and a loss of purchasing power; some will start a bank and pay low interest to those depositors while using the depositors' money to earn high returns for themselves. Some will purchase income-producing assets and hold them for the long term; others will gamble away their funds and sell their other assets at low prices to raise cash for more gambling and other consumption. Some will use their assets to build houses and other assets and then sell those assets at a profit to others who can not or will not build those assets themselves. In short, even if we at one point have a situation where all people are equal in personal wealth, that equality will soon disappear. We would soon arrive back at precisely the same situation we started from, with inequality of wealth. Some folks are just naturally better than others at making money. That's the way God made them.

Our friends the Liberals have a deep and sincere hatred for many things, and one of their most hatey hatreds is for: evil corporations, which includes all corporations except the Corporation for Public Broadcasting, which Liberals control at taxpayer expense.   Ah, why couldn't all corporations be like that!

No one has ever seen a corporation. They have seen corporate buildings, they have seen corporate executives, they have seen corporate assets, but they have not seen a corporation. And they never will, because a corporation does not exist; it is a legal fiction. A corporation exists only on paper. In economic terms, it is a pass-through mechanism. Corporations sell things and take in money; they hire employees and buy materials to produce their product; they retain some funds for future use and distribute the residue to the owners of the corporation, the shareholders, who pay income taxes on the dividends received.   Corporations do not pay taxes.   If government raises taxes on a corporation, the price of their product will increase; it must, because the shareholders demand a given rate of return on their investment, and they will not invest if they are not compensated for their risk as they believe they should be.   Corporate taxes are inevitably paid by the consumer; there is just no way around that economic law. Liberals can never accept the above facts. They are blinded by hate. They will raise corporate taxes at every opportunity, even though it hurts them and their fellow travelers.

If there were no corporate income tax, all the proceeds would flow to the shareholders, who would pay individual income tax on them, more taxes because the corporate profits would be higher. Total corporate expenses would be reduced by the tax cut, competition would force the price of products to decline, and every consumer would benefit. Corporate profits would jump, relieved of the tax burden. Earnings and dividends would increase, as would the value of corporations, which the market prices according to the company's ability to produce earnings. Among the largest beneficiaries would be retirement plans, including union pension funds, state employee pension funds, corporate employee pension funds, IRAs, and 401(k)s.

What of the revenue lost to the government? That is a fair question. The individual tax code could be adjusted to compensate appropriately. The difference is that lower income people and their retirement plans would not be paying the 35% corporate tax; individuals would pay at their personal tax rate. High income individuals would pay a high or higher rate (than the 35% corporate rate) anyway; low income people pay at a much lower rate.

The net result is a bonanza for lower income people. The corporate income tax forces lower income people, including Liberals and union members, to pay 35% rates on income when, without that tax, they would pay at a much lower rate. Truly, elimination of the corporate income tax is a no-brainer. What are the chances of repeal of that regressive tax under Liberal control? You know the answer.

I offer the above information as an example of how people can be blinded by irrational hatreds and blind ignorance into pursuing policies that are self-destructive to their own best interests. The corporation is incapable of pain or pleasure; but the Liberals insist on punishing it even though they are punishing themselves even more. Such masochistic behavior is not Left or Right; it is just Wrong, by any standard you can imagine.

Liberals will often refer to "Marxist economics" or "Socialist economics" or "Keynesian economics" as if there are various viable alternatives and we can pick and choose among them to select the kind that we like best.   That is nonsense. There is only one type of economics, which we might call Classical Economics; it governs all economies everywhere; it rules the world. Economics is the study of the decisions that rational human beings will make in given situations; in a sense, it can be construed to be a branch of Behavioral Psychology.   Marxism and its sub-ideologies are the negation of economics; they say, "Let's pretend there are no laws of economics."   But "let's pretend" only works for so long.   You can have an economy structured on Socialist / Marxist principles, but it will fail, as all have, because of the irresistible laws of Classical Economics.   That is why the Soviet Union is gone and why China has chosen the (somewhat) Capitalist road.

The laws of economics are as powerful as the laws of Physics. They are laws of Nature every bit as much as Mathematics and Gravity are laws of nature. They can be ignored for the short-term, but eventually they will determine the outcome of any enterprise.

What's in a Name?

In politics, the opposing sides are universally referred to as "Left" and "Right". Many observers have traced this paradigm back to the French Revolution, where the Jacobins and their communist allies sat on the left side of the legislative chamber. Actually, the words go back much further, back to the Roman Republic, at least.

The Latin word for "right", in the sense of direction, is "dexter". Another Latin word for "right", in the sense of "correct, proper, honest, upright, natural, plain, straightforward", is "rectus", from which we get "rectitude". Somehow the two Latin words have evolved into one English synonym. Interesting, but what are we to make of this curious current of language?

The Latin word for "left" is "sinister", meaning "on the left hand, wrong, perverse, unfavorable, adverse". It is difficult to understand how the simple concept of one side or direction can have come to be synonymous with such strong and negative adjectives.

I will leave it to others to speculate on left brain / right brain or other paradigms. Certainly it must be upsetting to the Leftists to be described as wrong, perverse, unfavorable, adverse, or even sinister, no matter how accurate these descriptions might be.

The Left / Right paradigm surfaces again in the French Revolutionary legislature, where the radical Jacobins sat on the left side of the chamber. The Jacobins were as extreme and murderous as any Stalinist or Maoist, even though Karl Marx was not yet a gleam in his grandfather's eye. The lack of a formalized theory of history was no impediment to the murder of thousands in the name of creating a more perfect world.

If you expect me to propound a theory as to the deeper meaning of these words and their significance, and to how these words evolved over the centuries, I must disappoint you. Such discussions must be left to a more imaginative and speculative author. Of course, we must also note that, culturally, prior to the development of modern hygienic conveniences, the left was the hand you used to, well, never mind. Because of this historical fact, in many cultures, everyone is taught to be right-handed.

We note that while Socialism has existed for a very long time, many people assume that it was the creation of Karl Marx. The Jacobins of the French Revolution, homicidal as any Bolshevik, committed their crimes in the name of the people, just as the Bolsheviks claimed to be the vanguard of the proletariat. In the Victorian era, the most radical Leftists came to be called anarchists or nihilists. The significance of Marx is that he created an intellectual framework for the actions of Leftists so that they could acquire a patina of intellectual and moral respectability. Rather than being a useless aberration from productive society and a mindless hater of the normal, the extreme Leftist now had a Theory of History that not only justified his actions as a champion of truth and justice but also promised him eventual and inevitable victory due to the ineluctable tides of history.

Who was this man who made Socialism and Communism acceptable to so many millions of people? He crafted a philosophy that turned Christian and Jewish morality on its head. The philosophy of Marx is the opposite of Judeo-Christianity. Seizing the property of a person who might have more assets than you was not a crime—it was your right. If

the bourgeois, you were not committing mu

were eliminating an enemy of the people. D

rights of a member of the bourgeois was nc

bourgeois was evil. One must recognize the ᴗᴗᴗᴗᴗᴗᴗᴗ,

of Marx' achievement in creating a negation of morality

that has caused countless wars and resulted in the

deaths, by war and by outright murder, of tens of

millions of human beings. Any crime was justified if it

hastened the coming of the Socialist Utopia.

Where Are We Going With This?

Let's see where we are. It has been clearly established that Liberal Marxist Progressive Socialist Democratism is not consistent with the moral code found in the Bible, and specifically that the entire philosophy of the Liberal Marxist Progressive Socialist Democrats is in direct and flagrant violation of the Ten Commandments, which are the most explicit and straightforward statements of God's Law for Christians and Jews.

As to the damage created to the economy and to human freedom by the high taxes, ever-expanding government regulation, and endlessly multiplying debt championed by the LMPSDs, that is all too evident. As I put these words to paper, the European financial meltdown shows us our own future, unless we change our ways, and soon. At the heart of all political strife in our nation is the continual battle to possess Other People's Money. This is ironic, because Americans know nothing of true poverty, which is found in Africa and other undeveloped areas of the planet. Even the poorest American has access to welfare and medical benefits undreamed of in the Less Developed Countries, not to mention the tremendous charity resources provided by the American people, who are the most generous in the world, by far. Every American in need is able to knock on the door of any church, government welfare office, or charitable institution and they will be fed and sheltered. Famine is unheard of in the United States. Certainly there are homeless people who have nothing, but their condition is often a result of mental illness, addiction, and a refusal to help themselves, not lack of government and charitable resources. Government bureaucrats pull a number out of the air and arbitrarily state than everyone below that number is in poverty; but if one standard were used to measure poverty on a global basis, there would be no Americans below the poverty line; America's poor would be considered wealthy in many parts of Africa. Our American Liberals do not want OPM so that people can survive, but so that people who do not work will be just as wealthy as people who do work. Common sense tells us that such a goal is not economically sustainable, even if it were morally desirable.

We have discussed the influences of Hope and Fear, pulling us to and fro, swinging us between joy and depression, battling within every human consciousness, like a good angel and a bad angel sitting on our shoulders. We noted that roughly a third of the population is more or less permanently dominated by the dark side, Fear, and its fellows, Envy and Hatred. I would like to think that every one of those folks would read my little pamphlet and say, "you know, this fellow makes a strong case, he points out some things in the Bible that I never really thought about, maybe he is right; maybe I need to consider things a bit differently from now on; perhaps I should not worry so much about what other people have and what I do not have." You would think me a fool indeed if I told you that I expected that to happen. It's not a realistic hope. Some people may be beyond the reach of anything on Earth. Just as God hardened Pharaoh's heart,

> This my long sufferance, and my day of
> grace,
> They who neglect and scorn shall never
> taste;
> But hard be hardened, blind be blinded
> more,
> That they may stumble on, and deeper
> fall;

—Milton

Some people understand the Bible to say that one-third of humanity is beyond redemption and will experience a most unpleasant eternity. Let us fervently pray that it is not so. History has many examples of confirmed Communists whose hearts were changed. The journalist and spy Whitaker Chambers turned against his Soviet spymasters and turned to the side of Freedom, even as he was convinced that he was leaving the winning side and joining the losing side in the battle of History. There are some who interpret the Bible to say that all will be saved; people of Light and Hope pray that that is so.

We have also observed that roughly a third of the body politic strives to observe the Commandments. Certainly, they are far from perfect in their attempts—but they do attempt, and that is the critical point. This one-third stretches across all economic and class levels. A rich person who does not practice charity disobeys God's Commandments every bit as much as a larcenous Liberal or a common thief. No one can be as ugly to behold as a person who has received richly of life's bounty and yet does not show humility, gratitude, and charity. People of Hope understand that a

> *Grateful mind*
> *By owing owes not, but still pays, at once*
> *Indebted and discharged*
>   —Milton

America's richest man ever, John D. Rockefeller, strictly tithed ten percent of his income to charity, even as relentlessly reduced the cost of lamp oil and brought light to every American home (and, incidentally, saved at least one species of whale by making whale oil obsolete). In so doing, he did well and he did well—and the Liberals will never forgive him.

We return to the roughly one-third in the middle of the political spectrum, whom we have called the Non-political. These folks are in constant danger of slipping into Liberalism. Minds and hearts can be changed. It is my fond hope that some of these folks might read my humble scratchings and see some things in a new light. Enlightenment can come to those who have not hardened their hearts. Perhaps we can move a few folks to use their vote to elect leaders who respect and support the tenets of the Ten Commandments.

I have many kind and good friends who are Non-political; I can prove it to them on the Spectrum. They equate their charitable instincts with a proclivity to Liberalism. Friends, you need to understand what Liberalism is, and then you will understand that you are not a Liberal. The LMPSD philosophy leads ineluctably to a nation devoid of Freedom and Liberty, to a world that is morally, economically, and spiritually poor. If you wish to see a world of prosperity and Freedom, observe God's Commandments, and reject those who offer easy solutions and short-cuts to an earthly Socialist utopia.

So let's be clear. Am I saying that a Christian or a Jew cannot morally be a Liberal Marxist Progressive Socialist Democrat? Yes, that is precisely what I am saying. Yes, even though there are political parties, in Europe, that denote themselves "Christian Socialist". That name is a true oxymoron. When we wander from the clear language of the Bible, we fall into moral error, even when our intentions are good.

As Christians, and as Jews, we are called to defend our faith and our families every day. We are called to live our faith every day, every minute, every second, and not just to take it out and shine it up to show it off in church on Sunday. Some people show up to church on Sunday just to check off the "God" box, as an insurance policy against everlasting damnation, just in case all that old Biblical stuff is true—they want to be sure they have all the bases covered. It's a prudent move. Then, they put all that church stuff in the rear view mirror and do as they will, ignoring God's clear Commandments. Abortion, no problem! Other People's Money, yes please! Our faith must be integral to our character, not a garment that we put on and off for convenience. As individuals, we must have one face, not two. We must have integrity: one-ness. We must not deny who we truly are; we must be men for all seasons, not one person in one situation and a different person in a different situation. Christians are called to witness our faith every day and in every way, not just when it is convenient and comfortable to do so.

The sad fact is that, on Election Day, many nominal Christians, after listening to the teaching of their church and the clear language of the

Commandments on Sunday, put all of that aside to cast their vote for pro-abortion Socialists. The results have not been good. How could we have expected them to be otherwise? No good comes from the poisoned tree.

Many people interpret the Bible to say that the world ends in an apocalypse of destruction. I am not convinced that we can accurately interpret these revelatory visions. Perhaps it is wishful thinking, but I nurse a hope that Man can eventually surmount all the myriad difficulties we face and somehow achieve a peaceful and prosperous paradise on earth. I dare to hope that America, the light of Freedom in this wicked world, can lead the free people of the planet in defeating all threats to liberty. I dare to hope that, with the grace of God, people will put aside the behaviors that can never bring happiness and, by observing God's Commandments, hasten the coming of the Kingdom of Christ to this world. Are we not commanded to pray not that we will go to Heaven, but that God's "Kingdom come" to us, which it will when "Thy will be done, on earth as it is in Heaven"?

The long-term course of history, despite all our human flaws, is in many ways a positive one, in terms of health, prosperity, life span, human rights, and in many other ways.   Human freedom is expanding. Most intelligent people do not look to Marxism and other freedom-crushing ideologies as the future of the planet.   Perhaps our short time on earth is an opportunity to prove that we can follow God's guidance through the trials of life and prove ourselves worthy of a higher existence.   It just may be possible for all people to live in peace and plenty—if we can follow the simple Commandments that God has given us.

Gentle reader, thank you for reading my book.

Required Reading for the Intelligent Observer

Alphabetical by author

Witness – Whitaker Chambers

Albion's Seed – David Hackett Fisher

New Deal or Raw Deal? – Burton Folsom, Jr.

The Myth of the Robber Barons – Burton Folsom, Jr.

Money of the Mind – James Grant

The Creature from Jekyll Island – G. Edward Griffin

Darkness at Noon – Arthur Koestler

Mere Christianity – C.S. Lewis. Start here with Lewis and continue as far as you like

The Chronicles of Narnia – C.S. Lewis. The books, not the movies. Watch the old BBC DVD version for a more faithful, less Hollywood, adaptation

Paradise Lost – John Milton

The Tycoons – Charles A. Morris

FDR's Folly – Jim Powell

The Tragedie of Hamlet, Prince of Denmark – William Shakespeare

The Forgotten Man – Amity Shlaes

The Wealth of Nations – Adam Smith

Basic Economics – Thomas Sowell

America Alone – Mark Steyn

The Road to Serfdom – Friedrick von Hayek

The Way the World Works – Jude Wanniski

THE
VICTORIAN PEASANT

'Bridge with mower and man', Guiting Power or Guiting Temple, Gloucester-shire (H.W. Taunt, *c.* 1895). The 'mower' is the double-handed scythe carried on the man's shoulder.

Oxfordshire County Libraries.

THE
VICTORIAN PEASANT

by RICHARD HEATH
Edited by Keith Dockray

An abridged edition of *The English Peasant*
by Richard Heath, with an introduction
by Keith Dockray

ALAN SUTTON · Gloucester
ST. MARTIN'S PRESS · New York
1989

First published in Great Britain in 1989
Alan Sutton Publishing Limited
Brunswick Road
Gloucester

British Library Cataloguing in Publication Data

Heath, Richard
The Victorian Peasant.—Abridged ed.
1. England. Peasants. Social Conditions, 1800–1890
I. Title   II. Dockray, Keith
305.5′63

ISBN 0-86299-517-5

First published in the United States of America in 1989
St. Martin's Press, Inc.
175 Fifth Avenue
New York, NY 10010

Library of Congress Cataloging Publication Data

Applied for

ISBN 0-312-02852-0

Typesetting and origination by
Alan Sutton Publishing Limited
Printed in Great Britain by
Dotesios Printers Ltd.

Contents

CONTENTS

I am grateful to my colleagues Keith Laybourn and Peter Wood for answering my no doubt often naive questions and commenting on this introduction; hopefully, they have prevented me, as a mere medievalist entering the stormy waters of Victorian rural history, making too many crass errors!

INTRODUCTION

No nineteenth-century political, social and moral commentator
on the English rural scene is more renowned than William
Cobbett (1762–1835): his *Rural Rides*, published in 1830, remains a
source of fundamental importance for the social historian. Jour-
neying on horseback around southern England between 1822 and
1826, and recording (initially in his weekly *Political Register*) much
of what he saw and did during these travels, Cobbett proved
himself not only an adept at description – whether of landscapes,
country estates, farms, villages or the people he met – but also a
redoubtable political journalist who passionately lamented the
sufferings and injustices of the rural poor and profoundly regret-
ted the impact of increasingly profit-orientated landowners on a
hitherto contented and stable countryside.

Richard Heath, by contrast, is a deeply obscure later nineteenth-
century observer and commentator, albeit a man whose travels
and chronicles of rural life may be seen as very much in the
Cobbett tradition. Indeed, he even felt moved to publish, in 1874,
a biographical sketch of William Cobbett himself, graphically
describing his eminent journalistic predecessor as 'a peasant politician' and 'perhaps the most perfect specimen of the typical "John
Bull" this country has ever produced.' Four years earlier, in 1870,
Heath had penned a substantial paper on 'The Cottage Homes of
England' for the periodical *Leisure Hour,* a paper largely inspired
by – and to some extent based upon – a study of the 1867 report of
a parliamentary commission on the 'Employment of Children,
Young Persons and Women in Agriculture.' Moreover, so
aroused was his interest in rural society in general, and the lot of
the agricultural labourer in particular that, between 1870 and 1874,
Heath himself undertook a series of 'pedestrian tours' through

many counties – ranging from Kent to Dorset and Suffolk to Northumberland – whereby he 'came to realise the truth' with his own eyes. A spate of further articles presenting his findings resulted. Furthermore, as he tells us in the preface to a collection of many of his pieces reprinted in 1893 under the title *The English Peasant* (of which this book is an abridged edition), 'the growth of convictions resulting from practical experiences supplemented by a careful looking up of authorities' soon led him, as well, to embark on an historical survey of the agricultural labourer since Anglo-Saxon times: the resulting essay – 'The English Via Dolorosa; or, Glimpses of the History of the Agricultural Labourer' – appeared in 1884. Continuing concern for the well-being of rural workers, this time inspired by the parish council elections of December 1894, resulted, in turn, in 'The Rural Revolution' (originally published in the *Contemporary Review* in 1895 and reprinted here in a much shortened form).

There are many indications in these papers of the nature of Richard Heath's source material as well as of his own firmly held attitudes and beliefs. Clearly, the bulk of the information – and the plethora of stories and anecdotes – derived from the author's own careful observations while travelling around the country and his conversations with the many people he met. As he remarks when writing of a visit to Northumberland in the summer of 1871:

> . . . I sought to find out, as far as I could, what it was made the Northumberland peasantry so superior. I visited Wooler and its neighbourhood, walking along the base of the Cheviots as far as Rothbury, and during my rambles I took every opportunity of conversing with the people, and learning from their mouths the true state of things.

Charm, affability and the common touch he must surely have had: not only were labouring men and women of all kinds prepared to talk to him, it seems, but also often invite him into their homes (however dreadful they might be), ply him with tea and even

allow him to sketch what he found there. As for available written sources, he recognised that they might not always be reliable. When discussing the 1549 Norfolk rebellion in 'The English Via Dolorosa', for instance, he commented:

> The annals of the Poor are nearly always lost or distorted. They have no friendly scribes to chronicle their doings, but what comes down to posterity, even when honest, is full of misconception through want of sympathy . . .

For his own times Heath frequently cites – and, indeed, quotes from – official reports (although almost always as a supplement to his own observations and discoveries). Two figure most often: a report by Dr H. J. Hunter in 1863/4 containing much damning comment on the housing, health and social conditions of labouring people in the countryside; and the conclusions of the 1867 commissioners on rural working class women and children where, again, there are countless depressing indictments of deplorable cottages, overcrowding, lack of decent sanitation, and harsh practices/conditions of employment resulting in endemic ill-health and every kind of human degradation. Additionally, Heath draws attention to poems, songs and ballads illustrating labouring life and lore, and occasionally cites material in local newspapers as well, most notably in his 1895 analysis of parish council elections where he quotes with approval, for instance, remarks in the *Weston-super-Mare Gazette* that:

> . . . never were the villages of the land so stirred as they are today. People of all degrees . . . are showing great eagerness to serve on the new Councils; and there is abundant evidence to show that great changes and developments in village life and its amenities are likely to flow from the infusion of new blood and new interests into the administration of the affairs of rural England.

Richard Heath's fundamental conception of the character of the English agricultural labourer, his doleful history and, most particularly, his present-day oppression, is frequently expressed, never

better perhaps than in 'The Cottage Homes of England' where he writes vehemently that:

> . . . in the process of modern civilization, the English agricultural labourer has been a constant loser. From a condition in which he might hope, by industry and thrift, to become a small farmer, he can now hope for nothing better than to perform like a hireling his day, and then to find a pauper's grave. One privilege after another has gone, until at last he is driven from the land which the toil of many generations of his ancestors has rendered fertile, to burrow with his children in the slums of some outlying village, and thence to trudge with gaunt face and discontented heart to and fro from the scene of labour, no longer sweetened by bygone memories or future hopes . . .

No less emotionally, and with the firm intention of highlighting the stark contrast between rural employers and employees, he exhorted readers of his 'Peasant Life in Dorset' to compare:

> . . . the shapely forms of the young farmers with those of the stunted young labourer, (when) the injury inflicted by compelling an immature body to such labour as agricultural work will be seen at a glance. Compare the stalwart, jovial forms of the elderly farmers with that of the rheumatic misshapen forms of the old labourers, and the evil result, not only of over-early work, but of a lifetime of poor and insufficient food and bad lodging will be manifest.

And similar sentiments are expressed again and again in these essays.

As for Richard Heath himself, he was undoubtedly much moved by what he found during his travels and his writings are thoroughly imbued with the reforming spirit of a compassionate later Victorian social commentator. Although frequently naive and simplistic in his not always consistent judgements, ever ready to express moral disapproval where he deemed it necessary and

certainly inclined to regard the history of the English agricultural labourer as a long catalogue of oppression and degradation, he can nevertheless be regarded as a real precursor of the modern oral historian. Moreover, as well as the gloom about past and present so often pervading his work, there is also a firm streak of optimism about the future. 'The light has fairly broken', he declared in 1884, and 'though the clouds keep gathering, they cannot hide the rising sun'; if the labourer is at last given power ungrudgingly 'he will in fifty years redress the evil done in five hundred.'

Richard Heath's survey of 'The English Via Dolorosa' (originally over 20,000 words in length but much reduced here) may have only scant value as history in the eyes of modern scholars, and the story it relates firmly reflects its author's personal preconceptions and prejudices: yet it remains of considerable interest both as a nice example of the genre of popular historical writing in the Victorian age and for the light it throws on the moral fervour permeating so many of the contemporary essays. Throughout 'all these long years of ignorance' (since Anglo-Saxon times), Heath declares, the agricultural poor have been condemned 'to heavy labour and grinding poverty: an ignorance, a labour, a poverty ever increasing.' Such was the tyranny of the Normans that 'well might a deep-seated ill-will exist between the oppressor and the oppressed', while 'iniquitous statutes' of labourers in the fourteenth century were responsible in part at least for the Great Peasants' Revolt of 1381. In Tudor times, moreover, legislation reflecting the rising power of the 'Middle Class' proved 'if possible (even) more tyrannical and corrupting than that more purely aristocratic', most particularly a disgraceful statute passed during the first year of Edward VI's reign. When writing of this, indeed, Heath can hardly contain his emotion and indignation:

> Robbed of their wages, and reduced to semi-serfdom by the Statutes of Labourers; robbed of their legal provision in unforeseen distress, or unprotected old age, by the confiscation of Church property for the benefit of the aristocracy; robbed by

the commercial greed of the new gentry of their little farms and of the common land, the English poor were met by an atrocious law which condemned all who did not yield submissively to their fate to feel the hot iron plough into their own breasts, and into those of their wives and children, to be reduced to the vilest form of slavery, and to find no relief except in a felon's doom.

And although this barbaric statute remained in operation for a mere two years, its repeal probably owed more to the clamour of the Norfolk rebels in 1549 than to any lessening of the 'selfish tyranny of the ruling classes.' As for the Elizabethan Poor Law of 1601, distinguishing as it did between 'wilful' and 'impotent' poor and placing the burden of relief firmly on the local community, it all too often meant in practice that the labourer 'became virtually imprisoned in his parish': in its final development, indeed, 'it came as near to the work of the devil as it is possible to imagine.' The Poor Law Amendment Act of 1834, a 'reform conceived in the hard inhuman spirit of modern science', so lacked humanity that the poor preferred to starve in their cottages rather than enter the new workhouses, for these aptly-named bastilles:

. . . lacerated their bruised souls in the only spot where feeling was left; the law tore asunder husband and wife, parents and children.

Moreover, when mounting rural discontent in the early nineteenth century produced widespread riots in southern England in 1830 – where 'night after night (the) blazing sky told that Captain Swing had been at work' – many men found themselves condemned even more arbitrarily to imprisonment, transportation or death.

When writing of his own times, no facet of English rural life more angered Richard Heath than the 'cottage homes' of many agricultural labourers. Not only did he devote a substantial essay specifically to them in 1870 but he also returned to the subject

again and again in later writings. In 'The English Via Dolorosa', indeed, he condemns their manifold inadequacies in almost lyrical terms:

> Degraded by pauperism, harried by the game laws, brutalized by drink, maddened by starvation, are you surprised that such homes produced a state of mind only to be paralleled in an old-fashioned lunatic asylum, where people are kept in cages like raging beasts of prey?

Not surprisingly, too, he vehemently confirms James Fraser's report, in 1867, that:

> . . . the majority of cottages that exist in rural parishes are deficient in almost every requisite that should constitute a home for a Christian family in a civilised community.

Clearly, the cottages of rural workers in later Victorian England varied enormously in quality; equally clearly, only a minority can be described as truly satisfactory. The commissioners of 1867 found that in Lincolnshire, for instance, an insufficiency of cottages often resulted in serious overcrowding; in Dorset the cottages had long been 'a bye-word and a reproach'; and in south-west Shropshire one commissioner reported that:

> In the majority of parishes I visited (the cottages) may be described as tumbledown and ruinous, not water-tight, very deficient in bedroom accommodation, and (possessing) in-decent sanitary arrangements.

An investigation by the *Norfolk News* into cottages in various parts of Norfolk in 1863/4 found much that was 'both shocking and scandalous'; an enquiry in Buckinghamshire in 1863 highlighted 'wretched hovels' and 'very bad cottages quite unfit for human beings to live in'; and a Berkshire commentator reported finding 'wretched pigsties of hovels' which 'destroy decency, self-respect

and love of home.' During his own travels Richard Heath was no less struck by the deplorable quality and dilapidated condition of many cottages he saw, and frequently inspected, not least the appalling 'Mushroom halls' he came across in Surrey where poor folk with no legal titles were condemned to survive in conditions 'in which it is grievous to think any English family should be reared.'

Wages, hours and conditions of work – particularly for women and children – loom no less large in Heath's recitals of his excursions into the English countryside. Throughout the nineteenth century the wages of agricultural labourers remained significantly lower than the earnings of most workers in manufacturing industry. In the south and west of England, declares Heath, agricultural labourers live on the verge of pauperism and have no hope of bettering their position. Low wages in Dorset, for instance, have made labourers there 'worse off than in any other part of the land'. Since 'the greater part is sometimes paid in kind', moreover, Dorset families are often so poor that every member must begin earning as soon as possible. Even this cannot prevent them from often running into debt, however, 'with their masters or the tally-men destroying every atom of independence or power of improving their condition.' Poverty in the Weald of Sussex has resulted in the majority of children and the elderly not getting enough to eat; low wages in Oxfordshire have long determined that wives and children must earn what they can; and even in Kent, where wages are relatively high, work is plentiful and labouring families can live reasonably well, hours can be very long and any saving is out of the question. Northumbrian peasants, too, 'enjoy good wages and frequently rise to the position of stewards'; conditions of service there are often favourable, with labourers hired by the year and 'paid alike in wet weather or dry, in sickness and in health'; *yet* the continuance in Northumberland of the ancient 'bondager' practice, whereby a farm labourer is often required 'to provide a woman whose labour shall be at the disposal of the master whenever he may require it and whom the labourer is therefore obliged to have lodging in his house', can

hardly be regarded as conducive to domestic comfort! Even more iniquitous than this, in Richard Heath's opinion, was the 'frightfully immoral system of ganging' long prevalent in the Fenlands, whereby a gang-master contracts to supply labour when and where wanted, collects a number of women and young persons together (sometimes as many as forty and even including children as young as six or seven years old), and leads them out daily to those parts of the fen where he has engaged to work. Moreover, despite the outlawing of the practice of 'public ganging' in the later 1860s (as a result of its vigorous condemnation by the commissioners in 1867), 'private ganging' (gangs employed directly by farmers on their own land) has all too often tended to take its place and ensure that virtual 'labour-slavery' remained prevalent when Heath toured the Fens in 1873.

The widespread practice of women and children working in the countryside probably aroused Richard Heath's reforming ardour and moral disapproval more than almost anything else. Labour was often hired on a family basis, particularly at harvest time when everybody tended to be roped in, and this proved more than satisfactory from the farmers' point of view since women workers were paid less than men (and children less still). This was certainly the custom in Dorset and, as a result of wives working alongside their husbands in the fields, Heath records:

> The poor little ones are locked up all day, or left under the care of some young girl of seven or eight years of age, who has enough to do to mind the baby; and, when the mother comes home, smashed crockery and sullen tempers have been the result of the family left without proper guardianship or control.

Boys in Dorset, moveover, often have to go to work at the age of eight or earlier, forced to get up with their fathers at four or five o'clock in the morning and then working almost continuously until early afternoon; as a result, not only is the boy's 'mind deadened but his poor little body is permanently injured.' In Oxfordshire, thanks to over-early employment, boys were forced to trudge about the fields:

INTRODUCTION

. . . in heavy boots on the sticky soil contract a weakness in the legs which leaves its indelible mark in an awkward gait.

Rural industrial workers fared no better. Lead-miners in Swaledale, for instance, in view of:

. . . the unhealthy nature of their employment (are) unable to work more than six hours a day. They begin at ten years of age; their lungs gradually get stuffed up with the fine lead-dust, so that as men they look very thin and sickly, and can scarcely live to be old.

Yet, when Heath remonstrated with a Kentish labourer on the morality of sending young children out to work, the response was:

. . . if his boy can get a day's work rook-scaring, the few pence he thus earns far out-weighs all the problematical advantages of a day's schooling.

A Kentish farmer was no less blunt:

It all depends on the boy's growth when he is able to work. A little chap of eight, or even less, may be useful.

Richard Heath certainly has a great deal to say about the social consequences both of brutal working practices and barbaric domestic arrangements in later Victorian rural society. Health, inevitably, calls for frequent comment. Mortality rates in villages were lower than in towns for both the young and the elderly and, as Edwin Chadwick pointed out as early as 1842, nineteenth-century agricultural labourers were among the healthiest of working men. Yet the 'stalwart, vigorous and healthy' Northumbrian peasantry are very much the exception in the annals of Richard Heath. Much more typical are 'the bleared eyes, the scrofulous skin, the ulcerated legs (and) rheumatic agonised bodies' Heath

noted in the Weald of Sussex; or the 'want of muscular development in the agricultural labourer' of Norfolk who, so a Victorian
surgeon concluded, 'has no calves to his legs and no development
of the biceps muscle of his arm.' Some places are 'scourged by
fevers', declares Heath, while others are 'decimated by consumption': everywhere 'the aged are cruelly tortured by rheumatism.'
Infant mortality, as Dr H. J. Hunter reported in 1863/4, *could* be
alarmingly high in certain rural districts (especially the Fenlands),
and, all too often, neglect by over-worked mothers might be a
prime cause. A medical officer in Warwickshire, for instance,
logged 'at least eight cases in which children left at home have
been burned or scalded: three or four of these have resulted in
death.' Even if the dangers of infant death *were* successfully
surmounted, however, the prospects of old age to come were
hardly welcoming. In a particularly poignant passage, Heath
contemplates the aged Kentish labourer drifting on to his last
refuge (the Union workhouse):

> Here he comes at last, his fine physique shattered by rheu-
> matism, his hair silvered, his cheek still ruddy as a russet apple;
> but power of work nearly gone, he is glad to break a few stones
> on the road, or, when feebler still, to do odd jobs in the Union
> grounds and to crawl about in the warm summer sun . . . His
> 'old woman', sent to dwell in a different part of the house, soon
> breaks up; while the Union is so far from his home, that his
> children come rarely to see him, and gradually forget their aged
> father, until one day they receive a summons to remove his
> body.

Many peasant families had little or no access to qualified medical
men if and when disease did strike. Hence, no doubt, why such a
'singular character' as the herbalist whom Heath met in Surrey in
1872 was able to make a living boldly advertising his practice by a
sign-board above the door of his cottage:

Worm Doctor
Professor of Medical Botany
Herb medicine prepared for every complaint
Advice Gratis

Virtually the only analgesic available in most rural homes was an opium preparation of one sort or another: Godfrey's Cordial, perhaps, or Daffy's Elixir. Drug abuse might nonetheless result. 'The unhappy natives of the Fen district,' remarks Heath, 'fill up their cup of misery by becoming opium-eaters.' Even more pernicious was the dosing of infants with opiates in order to keep them quiet, a practice also prevalent in the Fenland it seems. 'Every village has its own peculiar preparation', comments Heath:

> . . . the favourite form for infants being Godfrey's Cordial, a mixture of opium, treacle and sassafras. Each mother buys the 'Godfrey' she favours most, so that, when she leaves her baby in the morning, she will leave her bottle with the nurse. Should the nurse substitute her own, and should it turn out more potent, (the) children will sink into such a state that, in a fright, she sends off for the surgeon, who on his arrival finds half a dozen babies, some snoring, some squinting, all pallid and eye-sunken, lying about the room. Happily, he is prepared for the emergency, applies the stomach-pump, and the poisoned infants come round.

The evils of drink invariably figure prominently in any Victorian philanthropic catalogue of social ills, and it is not surprising that Richard Heath identifies over-indulgence in alcohol as a major problem in many rural communities. Not that he is unaware of the reasons for it, or even entirely unsympathetic towards those who find temptation too great to resist, but he clearly did *not* approve of:

> . . . fathers sitting outside beer-shops, like lazy hogs basking in the sun, while their children break their backs to supply the means of parental dissipation.

INTRODUCTION

A minister of nearly thirty years' standing in the New Forest is reported as declaring:

> All agree that drinking is the greatest vice of the foresters. It drags them down with remorseless grasp and is without doubt the chief evil which oppresses them.

In similar vein, drink is castigated as 'the fiend that misleads men in Dorsetshire as everywhere else', with custom favouring its temptation thanks to the deplorable practice of 'labourers receiving in some cases cider as part of their wages'; while in Devon men often take:

> . . . three pints of cider a day as part of their wages, a custom which adds to their depression by leading them to drink apart from their wives and families.

'Those who know best' report what a good thing it would be if Sussex cottagers brewed their own beer since 'all the little beer-shops would (then) be shut up and a vast amount of misery prevented.' Yet Heath does enter an important caveat here:

> Not that the peasant of the Weald is a drunkard. He is far too poor for that. It is only on club-days, and occasionally on Saturday night, that he gives way. Habitual drinking in the country is the vice of a class in a superior social position.

Immorality haunts the pages of Heath's essays, but only rarely is he explicit: more often than not his readers are left to make what they can of hints and innuendoes. Clearly Richard Heath, in common with so many other later nineteenth-century commentators, was inclined to exaggerate the prevalence of immoral behaviour: they were far too ready to equate 'immodesty' (as found, for instance, in Lincolnshire gangs) with 'immorality'; men, women and children living together in unavoidably cramped conditions were not, as a result, inevitably victims of overwhelming lascivious desire; and clergymen in particular were

altogether too ready to detect cohabitation and consequent illegitimacy lurking everywhere. Even the everyday sight of animals copulating in the fields was naively identified as a perverted stimulus to immorality! As a result of their 'wretched homes', declares Heath, 'poor girls often add shame to their wretchedness'; in Devon immorality 'is directly traced to the conditions of cottage life'; and, more generally, indifference to chastity can only result from 'the wretched sleeping-places so often the lot of labouring families.' A Surrey clergyman was convinced that 'people who live at a distance from the village always fall away in morality'; in Norfolk 'one child in ten' was said to be illegitimate; a Warwickshire surgeon reported that 'almost all illegitimacy is due to crowded cottages'; and a Presbyterian minister in the Northumberland village of Wooler informed Heath that 'illegitimacy was not uncommon', suggesting 'laxity of opinion with reference to the marriage bond' as a possible cause (although Heath himself was more inclined to highlight the pernicious influence of the 'bondager' system and the prevalence of one-roomed cottages).

Another of Richard Heath's major preoccupations was the education of agricultural labourers – or, rather, the frequent lack of it! The Newcastle commission on popular education, reporting in 1861, concluded that, although 'almost all the parents appreciate the importance of elementary education', they are:

. . . not prepared to sacrifice the earnings of their children for this purpose, and (they) accordingly remove them from school as soon as they have an opportunity of earning wages of an amount which adds in any considerable degree to the family income.

There was certainly much hostile reaction in the 1870s, from parents and farmers alike, to the Agricultural Children Act when it sought to prohibit the employment of youngsters under the age of eight and require them to attend school either to the age of twelve or until they had obtained a satisfactory leaving certificate.

INTRODUCTION

During his own travels around England Richard Heath was, on occasion, *impressed* by what he found. The New Forest, he noted, was well supplied with schools; in Dorset there was widespread recognition of the value of education as a means of helping poor children to 'throw off the yoke'; and the Northumbrian peasantry, he recorded approvingly, have such a 'profound belief in the advantages of education' that:

> . . . shepherds club together to hire a perambulating school-master, and they have their children taught Latin, and sometimes French and Euclid. In one district it is stated that there is not a person who cannot read and write.

Much more typical, unfortunately, was the defective education in Northamptonshire 'not for want of schools but owing to the indifference and want of affection on the part of the parents'; or the situation in Devon where 'unless the Vicar pays the penny the parents will frequently plead poverty or any other excuse to keep their children away from school.' A clergyman in the Fenland, an area where the 'grossest ignorance' prevails, reported that:

> . . . this year, out of twenty boys who came to me averaging sixteen years old, seven could not read at all, and ten could not write at all, while with others the power was too small to be of any practical use.

Heath himself tells of a boy he met in south Warwickshire who, despite living within a stone's throw of Anne Hathaway's cottage, had never heard of William Shakespeare! Nowhere, perhaps, did he find a greater contempt for education than among the labouring poor in Kent, where men put forward excuses for their illiteracy along the lines of:

> I can't read, and yet I can earn my living; my father couldn't read and yet he could earn his living; what good will book-learning do my son? Why, as Farmer Jones says, 'it will spoil him and make a fool of him.'

INTRODUCTION

Master and man, indeed, were all too often of one mind on this. As a Kentish farmer put it:

> A boy that is going to be a clerk is learning how to live when he is at school, but one that is to be a farm labourer is learning what is a luxury to him.

And such scorn for education, Heath concludes, ensures that 'the people here, as elsewhere, are destroyed for lack of knowledge.'

Richard Heath was a man of firm religious beliefs as well as strict moral principles. 'The writer of these pages', he tells us:

> . . . is no denominationalist, but so far as he has personal tastes and sympathies they are not with Presbyterian forms, but with the liturgy of the Church of England.

Nevertheless, he is frequently highly critical of the attitudes and behaviour of Anglican clergy in their dealings with the agricultural communities of rural England. The Church of England, he declares, is 'the most aristocratic in the world' and it is:

> . . . this characteristic of the Church of England which is mainly responsible for the degraded condition of the English rural poor.

When writing of the Weald of Sussex, for instance, he deplored 'the want of a really Christian ministry' there:

> May we live to see the day when a true priesthood in England (shall) rise to their true calling, and become the defenders of the poor. (Let) the clergy look well to it, for by some means or other the hearts of the poor are more often than not alienated from them.

The root cause of the problem, he believed, was that many rural clergy have:

. . . so closely identified themselves with the gentry as to give rise to the impression that they regard themselves as a sort of spiritual squirearchy.

As a result, although he did find evidence of powerful faith on his travels (for instance, among the Dorset peasantry), he found much superstition as well. 'Dark superstitions' still haunt the 'wild wastes' of Surrey, he declares, where the people:

. . . yet believe in witchcraft, and think that the person bewitched has the right and power to kill the witch by certain enchantments.

Reluctant though he was to admit it, Richard Heath was altogether more impressed by the behaviour and commitment of many Nonconformist ministers. When visiting the Weald of Sussex, for instance, he talked to a wheelwright who told him that most people thereabouts went to chapel; the wheelwright himself frequented a Wesleyan place of worship where the congregation sometimes numbered as many as two hundred. When asked why people preferred chapel to church, he replied:

Because they could understand better; the preaching was plainer than at church; they spoke more to the soul.

'You see,' he added, 'clergymen do it for a living.' The Northumberland peasant, Heath found, was often a man of 'considerable religious principle'; yet he too was:

. . . largely influenced by a form of Christianity that not only recognises that he is a man but that (he) can be chosen (an) elder of the church.

Nearly all the labouring people of Northumberland, Heath concluded, are Presbyterians who 'not only attend a place of worship but are generally communicants'; and, after visiting a chapel there himself, he recorded:

A more intelligent, earnest, serious congregation I never saw in my life.

Not least among the reasons why he admired the Warwickshire agricultural labourers' union leader Joseph Arch, moreover, was the fact that he was a Primitive Methodist local preacher as well.

Richard Heath ended the preface to his 1893 edition of collected essays on a clear note of optimism:

A day, as joyous as those in the past have been sorrowful, seems about to open for the Agricultural Labourer, oppressed and depressed for a thousand years.

In part this confidence about the future grew out of his knowledge of the recent emergence of unionism among rural workers. In 1872, indeed, he had visited the village of Barford in south Warwickshire (where the union leader Joseph Arch lived) and also Wellesbourne ('beneath whose now historic chestnut the leaders of the movement have found a rural forum'). The early successes of the Warwickshire Agricultural Workers' Union certainly excited him considerably:

(A) great agricultural revolution has commenced . . . From Northumberland to Cornwall, from Norfolk to Hereford, one hears everywhere the tidings of rising life. The central wave is spreading, and the adjacent counties are forming Unions; and now they talk of a congress of representatives, that they may form a National Union. The heart of old England has heaved, and every member of the agricultural community throughout the country begins to feel the glow of a new life.

By 1895 Heath was sadly forced to admit that 'several causes have concurred to disorganise and destroy the great agricultural labour movement commenced (so) hopefully more than twenty years ago'; his optimism was now fired, instead, by the successes of farm workers in the recent parish council elections. Again, it was

not to prove justified: even the limited progress chalked up by agricultural labourers in the 1894 elections was not to be maintained in subsequent contests, and, by the end of the nineteenth century, most had ceased to participate in them altogether. As Pamela Horn remarks in her splendid study of *Labouring Life in the Victorian Countryside:*

> The days of Arch had passed and most men who were dissatisfied with village life were now voting with their feet and leaving the land for good.

Keith Dockray

THE ENGLISH VIA DOLOROSA

Or, Glimpses of the History of the Agricultural Labourer

(1884)

(King) Alfred relates Bede's story of the inspiration of Caedmon the Father of English Poetry. The Divine Messenger came and awoke the Soul of this English Labourer in a stable; fitting birthplace for the first cry of the humble representative throughout English History, of the Man of Sorrows and the Acquaintance of grief.

Over its cradle bent holy women like St. Hild, saintly men like the venerable Bede, and godly kings like Alfred the Great.

If twelve hundred years ago (about the year 680) an English Labourer was capable of writing poems which would appear the prototype of Paradise Lost, what treasures must have lain hid in the souls of the agricultural poor, condemned through all these long years of ignorance, to heavy labour and grinding poverty: an ignorance, a labour, a poverty ever increasing.

To trace this Via Dolorosa is a sad work; but the poet will come who will find in it the material not only of a Paradise Lost, but of a Paradise Regained, for if he has to tell how this great mute Soul was made an offering for National wrong-doing and has to describe its suffering even unto death, he will have the joy of singing its resurrection, an event accomplished in our own day.

1

1. IN WORSE THAN EGYPTIAN BONDAGE

Those crouching figures that we see sometimes supporting the roof of a great building are fit emblems of the vast mass of the European peoples during the Middle Ages. Both in the lands under Roman and under Teutonic law, the great majority were in a state of slavery. Among the Saxons the landless man must belong to somebody, or he had no legal existence; he became an outlaw, and anyone might slay him.

This servile condition rendered him the man of his lord; he could be bought and sold together with his family and his goods and chattels; he could not marry nor give his daughter in marriage without permission of the lord; a serf, in fact, was so entirely at the mercy of his master, that where the latter had judicial authority he could torture his serf and put him to death. Outside the manor-house stood the dreadful symbols of his power: the gallows whereon to hang the men, the pit wherein to drown the women.

Nevertheless a serf could, saving his lord's right, possess property; and there must have been a certain limit to the torture that could be inflicted, since the German law fixed the highest number of blows a slave could receive at two hundred and fifty. When it was his fate to have a good master, existence was not intolerable; but under a bad one, or in times of anarchy, human imagination could hardly outstrip the fiendish cruelty of his tyrants.

The process by which the fat kine eat up the lean kine had been going on in England long before the Conquest, the old Saxon freeman losing ground before the new noble class. The Norman Conquest drove him down still lower, levelling into one common condition of serfdom, the ceorles and thraells on the confiscated estates . . .

Under the Normans all except the higher classes of villeins whose services were limited to seed-time and harvest, were bound to do the work needed on their lord's private domain. By them his

land was ploughed, dunged, and dyked, his harvests reaped, his barns filled with sheaves, his stables provided with stubble, his cattle, sheep, and pigs tended, his grain turned into malt, his nuts gathered, his woods cut, his fires kept alive with fuel. A whole army of slaves toiled for him as ploughmen, herdsmen, shepherds, malsters, woodmen, carpenters, and smiths, while the borderers scattered on the edges of the commons were bound to provide him with a good stock of poultry and eggs.

The sole reward for all this labour was the right to existence and protection. The only consolations the labourers enjoyed, were the pleasures in which they could indulge on holidays, or the mystic hopes which the services of the Church inspired. Dwelling in dark cottages made of wattles and daubed with mud, they lived on salt meat half the year, and for vegetables, ate onions, cabbages, and nettles.

How the lords fared we may judge from an account Holingshed has preserved of the Earl of Leicester's expenses in 1313. By that time there were labourers in the country working for daily wages; a thatcher in this same year received 3¼d a day. If we deduct Sundays and Holidays, such a labourer would have been able to earn about £4 a year; and as the Earl's expenses reached £7,309, less £8 16s 7d given in charity, it appears that the latter spent on his family and people an amount equal to the wages of 1825 labourers. More than half of this went on eating alone, while an idea of the revelry indulged in may be gathered from the fact that the Earl's household drank 371 pipes of wine, and burnt 2,319 pounds of tallow candles as well as 1,870 pounds of Paris candles.

Well might a deep-seated ill-will exist between the oppressor and the oppressed. It comes out in the legendary Vision of Henry I, who one night dreamt that he saw gathered round him a number of labourers bearing scythes, spades, and pitchforks, looking angry and threatening . . .

Nevertheless the labourers could work in hope, for one of their own class, a Carpenter's Son, one who had died the death of a Slave, was held to be Sovereign Lord of this feudal society. The innate royalty of the labourer was thereby acknowledged, the Christian Conscience was on his side.

And so was the course of events. The Crusades, the Rise of Commerce, the French Wars, all worked to pull down the mighty from their seats and raise those of a low degree. The Crusades brought many a baron into pecuniary difficulties, what with the outfit and the expensive tastes he acquired; so that he was glad to get out of embarrassment by selling his serfs their liberty. The rise of Commerce created great towns, and towns obtained markets at which the toilers sold their produce and thus obtained the means to purchase freedom.

The change, however, came so gradually that serfdom was a possible condition for Englishmen even in Tudor times. But the revolution had commenced three hundred years earlier, so that by the close of the thirteenth century there was a large class of serfs who had been able to commute their services into money payments, and in the fourteenth century working for wages had become common . . .

2. THE LABOURER DEMANDS JUSTICE

The stars fought in their courses during the fourteenth and fifteenth centuries to set the labourer free . . .

The Black Death in 1349 swept away more than half the population of England. Those that remained soon found that their labour had doubled in value, and the labourer became at once an important person in the realm. Parliament representing only the landlords, accordingly enacted in 1349 and 1350 Statutes by which the Labourer under pain of imprisonment and fines was bound to work at the same wages that he had received before the Plague. These iniquitous statutes acted like goads to the new life stirring in the soul of the English serf.

The first Statutes of Labourers having been disregarded, Parliament in 1360 passed a severer law. Instead of three days in the stocks, a labourer refusing to work at the old wages was to be imprisoned for fifteen days. If he fled from his service to another town or county he was to be outlawed and a writ for his recovery

4

to be sent to every Sheriff in England, and if taken he was to have the letter F burnt into his forehead for his falsity. Towns harbouring such fugitives were to deliver them up under penalty of Ten pounds to the King and one hundred shillings to the master, an enormous fine when tested by such wages as these statutes allowed: for example, 1d a day to weeders and haymakers. This Act of 1360 forbade all combination among workmen.

While these statutes if obeyed would have rendered existence by labour almost impossible, wheat at this time averaging 7s the quarter, the people managed to obtain such high wages, that Parliament in 1363 passed another Act to restrain the sumptuousness of their apparel! Carters, ploughmen, plough-drivers, ox-herds, neat-herds, shepherds, pig-drivers, deyes and all other attendants on cattle, threshers and other labourers employed in husbandry were to use no other cloth than what was called blanket or russet of the value of 12d. a yard, and to wear linen girdles suitable to their condition. The same statute restrained their diet.

Notwithstanding facts patent to all but the wilfully blind, Parliament confirmed the Statute of Labourers by several subsequent acts, relying perhaps on a clause by which it hoped to entangle its subjects' consciences: labourers were to be *sworn* twice a year to observe these impossible regulations.

What wonder that such legislation produced in pious men a horror of oaths, and in the more daring a reckless contempt of all law . . .

This discontent began to make itself felt, and came to a height during the exhaustion that followed after the Peace of Bretigny. The Black Prince died, the King was falling into dotage, John of Gaunt was unpopular in London and with the Church: all things rendered the Government feeble. A universal upheaving commenced: while the serf was striving to obtain liberty and a fair wage, the classes immediately above him thought it a good opportunity each to push its way a grade higher. Meanwhile there were some few who only sought the reign of Justice on earth, who had no personal ends in view, but who for that very reason were gibbeted in their own day and stoned and pelted with ugly names ever

since. Such an one was John Ball, the so-called 'crazy priest of Kent'. Which, however, was most crazy, the Parliaments which made laws such as the Statute of Labourers, or the Servant of Christ who preached the Kingdom of Justice? . . .

The actual cause of the explosion was the Poll-tax of 1380, and the outbreak commenced the following summer in Kent.

John Ball was in prison in Canterbury, hither therefore the people surged, and the whole town being of their mind Ball was soon set free. The men of Kent marched triumphant to London, killing all the lawyers that fell in their way, burning the houses of the stewards of the manors, and flinging the rolls of the manor-courts into the flames.

When they reached London the poorer artizans within the city rose and flung open the gates. The people proudly boasted that they were seekers of Truth and Justice, not thieves or robbers, so instead of wasting their time in rioting, they went direct to their object which was to gain possession of the king. For though the people did not love their lords they had a firm faith in the king as the fountain of Justice and the avenger of the oppressed. Sad to say it was this beautiful faith that ruined their cause. Richard II, educated in that haughty contempt of labouring-men which comes out in Froissart's courtly Chronicle, where these very labourers are called vermin, – Richard II played as false a part as any king ever played. In his eyes it seems to have been no more a crime for a prince to circumvent vile and odious rustics than to trap stoats and weasels; to catch them in his net and hang them by hundreds no worse than slaughtering wild hogs. With his pretty face he did to perfection the ingenuous young king, willing himself to become the leader of his people and to redress all their injuries. When they cried, 'We will that you free us and our lands for ever, and that we be never named or held serfs!' 'I grant it', was the ready reply, and thirty clerks were sent for, who sat hard at work, writing out charters of manumission. In the same glib manner the king stilled the Kentishmen, furious at the infamous assassination of their leader, Wat Tyler. The neck of the rebellion broken by this timely mixture of cajolery and truculence, and the

danger over, Richard quickly threw off his mask. When the Commons of Essex came to remind him of promises hardly a fortnight old, he cried out contemptuously, 'O vile and odious by land or sea, you are not worthy to live compared with the lords whom ye have attacked; you should be forthwith punished with the vilest of deaths were it not for the office you bear. Go back to your comrades and bear the king's answer, you were and are rustic, and shall remain in bondage, not that of old but infinitely worse. For as long as we live, and by God's help rule over this realm, we will attempt by all our faculties, powers, and means to make you such an example of fear to the heirs of your Servitude as that they may have you before their eyes and you may supply them with a perpetual ground of cursing and fearing you.'

And now Richard knew how to keep his word: 1,500 of these brave men were searched out in various parts of the country and hung and gibbeted as an example of fear to the heirs of their servitude.

3. A PARLIAMENT OF PHARAOHS

The boy-king was only a tool in the hands of his Council. The Council itself was powerless before the determination of the lords not to let the people go. When the royal message addressed to the Parliament that met immediately after the quelling of the Insurrection, suggested that it would be well to enfranchise and set at liberty the serfs, Parliament replied that the king's grant and letters were null and void, their serfs were their goods, and the king could not take their goods without their own consent. 'And this consent,' they declared, 'we have never given, and never will give, were we all to die in one day.'

And in this Pharaoh-like spirit they persisted. The impossible Statutes of Labourers were re-affirmed, their execution being enforced by cumulative penalties, and in case of final inability to pay, the labourer was to have forty days' imprisonment; anyone attempting to leave his place of residence without an official letter

was to be put in the stocks; all who up to the age of twelve years had been employed in husbandry must remain in that occupation, even if already apprenticed to another.

In fact, the attempt on the part of the landless labourer to free his children by apprenticing them in the towns was directly forbidden by the Statute 7 Hen. IV., c. xvii, on pain of a year's imprisonment. And not content with closing to the poor serf emancipation by way of trade, they tried to prevent him getting it through the door of learning; Parliament praying the King to ordain that no bondman or bondwoman shall place their children at school, as had been done, with a view to their entering into the Church. And the same influence induced the new Colleges at the Universities to close their gates to villeins.

To render the bondage still tighter, Parliament gave the Council the right to arrest and imprison, regardless of all former statutes, any person speaking evil of dukes, earls, barons, nobles, and gentlemen, or of any of the great officers of the realm (12 Rich. II., c. xi).

However, it was one thing to make laws, another to compel a reluctant people to give them obedience. But the labourers were isolated; each set of serfs had to settle matters with their individual lord, each particular serf to make the best of his position. The audacious, the violent, the unscrupulous, forced their necks out of the collar; the meek, the faithful, bore a double load, and sank a grade lower. The first alone received a place in history. Their growing wealth, all through the fifteenth century, rendered them an important addition to the middle class, and helped greatly to increase its power.

The impetus given to industry by the wide-spread hope of rising a step in life, added greatly to the national wealth. We have abundant proof that the poor man, and especially the small husbandman, was far better off at this period than at any other. The labourer, according to Statute, received 4d. a day, if not fed in the house, and this continued his nominal wage throughout the century. At this rate, about eighteen days' work would buy him a quarter of wheat; six days, a calf; seven or eight days, a hog for

fatting. A lamb would cost him between sixpence and a shilling; a hen, 2d.; a pullet, 1d. Eggs he could get at the rate of twenty for a penny; butter was a penny, and cheese was three farthings a pound. His garden produced no potatoes, but it gave him fat peascods, and good apples and cherries. As to his drink, Sir John Fortescue, Chief Justice in 1442, merrily says, 'He drank no water except at certain times, and that by way of doing penance.' The same authority tells us that in these days English labourers were clothed throughout in good woollens; the bedding and other articles were of *wool*, and that in great store. And if the sumptuary law of 1464 was not a malicious satire, the labourer indulged in broadcloth of which the yard sometimes reached the price of two shillings.

It is clear that the Statute of Labourers was frequently violated, and that the labourer's actual income was even better than the prices just quoted would suggest. Engaged by the year, and frequently living on the farm, he must often have saved money enough to become a husbandman himself. This position, though it involved harder living than that of the labourer, was the most happy in the realm. Too lowly to be troubled by the storms of jealousy which raged over the surface of society, he ate the bread of independence, and lived surrounded by such an England as Chaucer depicts.

A revolution had clearly taken place, a revolution which was completed by the Civil Wars in which this century closed, and which gave the *coup de grace* to feudalism. For the Day of Judgement had come for the old slave-owning baronage of Norman and Angevin England. In the Wars of the Roses it committed the happy dispatch; and at the accession of Henry VII the House of Lords had been reduced to twenty-eight members.

4. THE TUDOR KINGDOM OF HEAVEN

The Tudors and the Middle Class rise together, they symbolise each other, they are the makers of modern England . . .

But the Labouring Class reaped but little benefit from this change, the legislation in which the Middle Class interests prevailed proving if possible more tyrannical and corrupting than that more purely aristocratic . . .

In former times the chief object had been to retain the labourer in servitude, but now he was free; the point was to extract from him as much labour as possible. Thus it is that the Tudor cry is always, 'Ye are *idle, ye are idle.*' 'Go therefore now and work.' . . .

To compare the Tudor tyranny to that under which the Hebrews groaned in Egypt is to give an inadequate view of the case. That under which the poor Englishman suffered was far worse because it was practised under the sanction of the religion in which he believed. Never, perhaps, in all history has there been a race of monarchs who attempted so to mould the consciences of their people as did the Tudors. Not content with arranging the national religious services, they ordained both a catechism and a private book of prayers to be used by individuals, and in the latter they prepared a special prayer for labourers; a prayer which strings together all the texts in the New Testament which can be forced into an incentive to work.

Looked at from the position of a man well-to-do in the world, these primers were probably edifying and sometimes elevating. But the faith they undoubtedly possessed was linked in the minds of the poor with profound injustice. The same authority which taught them how to pray, refused them their liberty under terror of the stocks, whipping, and the gibbet, and more, took from them their children to be subjected to the same mingled system of drudgery and catechism, slavery and prayer. By the Act 27 Hen. VIII., c.27, the children of vagrants over five years of age were to be taken into custody and put out to husbandry and other crafts, and any such children above the age of twelve running away were to be whipped with rods.

The English outlaw has a charm for the curious reader, when his adventures are pictured in a ballad like Robin Hood, or Clym of the Clough; but let it not be forgotten, these are the primeval heroes of the history which was continued by Harry the Eighth's

Vagabonds and Sturdy Rogues. Only as the age advances, and the Chivalrous gives place to the Commercial Spirit, these unfortunate pariahs sink from high-spirited banditti – with a certain code of honour – into gangs of wolfish marauders and mean thieves.

And their numbers vastly increased by an Act, needful no doubt, but performed with the usual injustice to the poor and helpless. The Suppression of Monastic Establishments in 1536 and 1540 turned adrift 50,000 persons, most of whom were incapable of earning their own living . . .

(Now) the commercial spirit invaded agriculture. It had for some time past been found more profitable to raise sheep than corn, and arable land was largely turned into pastures. But husbandmen and small yeomen could not make this pay and were obliged therefore to sell their land. A number of little estates in the market, an ever increasing demand for wool, and laws supplying the farmer with labour at much below its real market value: here was a truly golden opportunity for capitalists; and traders of all sorts began to compete for the farms. This raised rents, and numbers of poor yeomen were soon ruined, and they and their families turned into the streets . . .

5. ANOTHER STRUGGLE FOR JUSTICE

(The) same authority that gave this country the Common Prayer Book enacted the most atrocious law against its Poor that has ever disgraced the Statute Book.

By the 1 Edward VI., c.3, Men and Women able to work, and who lived idly for three days, were to be branded with a red-hot iron on the breast with a letter V, and to be slaves for two years to the informer. The master was to feed his slave with bread and water, with small drink, and such refuse meat as he thought proper, and to cause his slave to work by beating, chaining, or otherwise, in any work or labour however vile it might be. If the slave ran away from his master for the space of fourteen days he

11

was to be his slave for life, and to be branded on the forehead or cheek with the letter S; if he ran away a second time he was to suffer pains of death as a felon. The master could put a ring of iron on the neck, arm or leg of his slave; he could sell, bequeath, or let out his slave after the like sort or manner he might do with any other of his movable goods or chattels. Any attempt to maim or wound such masters or mistresses either during or after the time of slavery, or any conspiracy to burn their houses or corn was to be deemed felony unless some person would take such offender as a slave for ever . . .

Robbed of their wages, and reduced to semi-serfdom by the Statutes of Labourers; robbed of their legal provision in unforeseen distress, or unprotected old age, by the confiscation of Church property for the benefit of the aristocracy; robbed by the commercial greed of the new gentry of their little farms and of the common land, the English poor were met by an atrocious law which condemned all who did not yield submissively to their fate to feel the hot iron plough into their breasts, and into those of their wives and children, to be reduced to the vilest form of slavery, and to find no relief except in a felon's doom.

Such wrongs could only be met by insurrection, and the people rose in the East, and in the West, and in the Midland counties. The rulers of England, the men who had done the people these horrible wrongs, now maintained their power by the aid of Italian and German mercenaries . . .

Let anyone read the story of the rebellion of the Peasants in Norfolk, as given by Holingshed, whose sympathies may be judged from the fact that he describes his poor countrymen as 'vile wretches and cruel traitors' for slaying an Italian mercenary; and such reader must be very blind, or prejudiced, if he does not see that the Norfolk men had a better cause than any that English troops were ever employed to defend . . .

The insurgents demanded a removal of the King's evil councillors, a prohibition of enclosures, and a redress of the wrongs of the poor . . .

The annals of the Poor are nearly always lost or distorted. They

have no friendly scribes to chronicle their doings, but what comes down to posterity, even when honest, is full of misconception through want of sympathy. Thus the chroniclers of the Norfolk insurrection leave unexplained its suddenness, its unity of purpose, its order, its persistent courage, above all its religiousness . . .

The immediate result of this insurrection and of those in other parts of England was the repeal of the atrocious law against so-called vagabonds and their children, passed in the first year of Edward VI . . .

(Yet) in Elizabeth's reign rogues were trussed up apace, and there was not one year commonly wherein 300 or 400 of them were not devoured and eaten by the gallows in one place or another . . .

(There) can hardly have been less than 100,000 persons sent to the gallows under the Tudors. How many were whipped until their backs streamed with blood, how many were branded with red-hot iron, or had their ears cropped, how many rotted in prison, how many died on the galleys in the Thames, how many were enslaved, no historian has told us . . .

6. HOW TO DESTROY A PEOPLE'S SOUL

(Two) statutes of the 39th and 43rd of Elizabeth became the system upon which England dealt with its poor for 230 years. It was in principle a system of Christian Socialism, but being worked throughout by persons animated by secular motives, its action was vacillating: at once feeble and hard, and, in its final development, it came as near to the work of the devil as it is possible to imagine.

The Christian Socialism of the Elizabethan Poor Law distinguished, in the most forcible manner, between the idle and industrious, the wilful and the impotent. For the one class there were stripes and imprisonment, and in the end the gibbet; for the other, relief and shelter. Everything, however, depended on the

honesty, capacity, and Christian spirit of the Justices of the Peace and Overseers into whose hands the whole care of the poor was confided. As early as 1622 we find signs that many shirked the work. In a tract of that date, called, 'Greevous Grones for the Poor', we are told, 'The poor dailie increase, in many parishes there being no collection for them, so that they are driven out of these parishes to beg, and filtch, and steal for their maintenance.'

Each parish began jealously to guard its frontier, fearing that the surrounding parishes would shift upon it the burden of their poor. This led to a series of acts which virtually imprisoned the labourer in the limits of his parish, tying him down for a third time to the soil. The place of a man's nativity being originally the parish from which he could claim assistance, it became the object of each parish to prevent any being born in its limits who might come on the rates. If a young man who had no right of settlement in a parish attempted to get married, the officials immediately sought to have him removed, lest he should have a family, some of whom might become chargeable. This deterred young men from matrimony, and the result was a large number of bastard children. That unfortunate being whom the English law pursued so relentlessly: the homeless wanderer, was still more cruelly dealt with. In the reign of James I it was enacted that a woman wandering and begging, if delivered of a child in a parish to which she did not belong, was to be liable to whipping and six months' imprisonment. Yet notwithstanding all this severity the poor were ever on the increase.

Some seventy years after the Elizabethan Poor Law had been in operation the rates had risen to no less a sum than £840,000 a year. Twelve years later, 1685, the poor were numbered at 1,330,000 heads, 400,000 of whom were in receipt of parish relief. By the reign of Queen Anne the maintenance of the poor cost one million sterling.

During the early years of the eighteenth century the rapid growth of pauperism occupied many powerful minds, but the remedies they proposed were not adopted, or quite failed to arrest its progress; so that in 1795, Mr. Fox told the House of Commons

'that the greater part of the working classes of the country were lying at the mercy and almost lay on the charity of the rich.' Mr. Fox was far from exaggerating the disease, for English pauperism was now entering an acute stage. By the end of the War it could be said to have risen fifty per cent, and there were very few of the labouring classes out of its grasp.

To estimate the full force of this steady growth of pauperism we must never lose sight of the fact that it took place side by side with an ever-enlarging commerce, with the development of the manufacturing system and the enormous increase in the wealth of the ruling classes . . .

(Early in the eighteenth century) Parliament (had) determined to try the workhouse system and by 9 Geo. I., c.7, it (had been) enacted that relief should only be given on condition of entering a workhouse; *i.e.,* that an Englishmen who fell into poverty should only be relieved on condition of surrendering what has been trumpeted forth as the birthright of every native of this country.

It was soon seen that to make this system effectual, the workhouse must be more miserable and the diet poorer than that to which the labouring classes were accustomed. Workhouses were accordingly managed by contract, and ere long they became one of those horrors, the frequent end of institutions founded on one principle and worked on another. (The poet George) Crabbe, whose profound sympathy for the poor and photographic pictures of their misery will render his fame immortal, thus describes the Village Workhouse in 1783. He is speaking of the final fate of worn-out agricultural labourers –

Theirs is yon house that holds the parish poor,
Whose walls of mud scarce bear the broken door;
There, where the putrid vapours, flagging, play,
And the dull wheel hums doleful through the day –
There children dwell who know no parents' care;
Parents, who know no children's love, dwell there!
Heart-broken matrons on their joyless bed,
Forsaken wives, and mothers never wed;

Rejected widows with unheeded tears,
And crippled age with more than childhood's fears:
The lame, the blind, and, far the happiest they!
The moping idiot, and the madman gay.

In the very year of the appearance of Crabbe's most touching poem of the Village, Mr Pitt brought in a bill repealing the 9 Geo.I, c.7, which prohibited relief to any not entering a work-house, on the ground that this provision was 'inconvenient and oppressive, inasmuch as it often prevented an industrious person from receiving such relief as is best suited to their peculiar case, and held out conditions of relief injurious to the comfort and domestic situation and happiness of such poor persons' . . .

In 1796 Mr Pitt made a remarkable speech on the Poor Laws, in which, after referring to the great abuses of the System, he laid down the principles essential to a good Poor Law. One of the most important was – Relief according to number of children.

The following year Mr Pitt brought in a bill in which he proposed to realise this principle . . .

(Although) dropped, its main proposition, the making up out of the rates of the deficiency of a labourer's income, came to be the general practice throughout the country. This suggested the necessity of a scale, and the amount a labourer ought to have was fixed, from time to time, by the price of the quartern loaf, which might vary from 6d to 2s.

By this system it was admitted that every man in the country had a right to an adequate maintenance, whether he was idle or industrious, honest or dishonest; and that he ought to receive public aid in proportion to the number of his family. English people are frightened at the word Socialism. Who ever conceived a worse type of Socialism than this?

When the Parliamentary Commission of 1833 inquired into the effect of this system, they could not find words strong enough to paint their dismay. They found the poor's rates in 1830 had reached an annual amount of six to seven millions sterling; that in some parts of the country, nearly all the labourers were paupers;

that the rascally idler was better off than the honest and laborious; the latter, one after the other, being driven to the conviction that the man who worked hard was a fool; they found, however, that employers liked the system, because it enabled them to give low wages, knowing the deficiency would be made up by the parish.

Never, perhaps, in history has there been a state of things so ridiculously immoral.

7. DESCENDING INTO HELL

(When) the War closed (in 1815), the glory of Trafalgar and of Waterloo was soon forgotten in the collapse which followed the inflation of trade, caused by the extravagance which had spent £625,000,000 in order to overthrow the French Revolution. And not only were the people of this country saddled for ever with this overwhelming debt, but the Nemesis also came in an ever-widening estrangement of classes.

The war found the farmer and his men living and working together in a somewhat patriarchal fashion; it left the master a gentleman, the labourer a pauper. The latter, no longer an inmate at the farm, lodged in some hovel and took his meals at the ale-house. But the widespread ruin the collapse produced led to the consolidation of farms in fewer hands. The separation between master and man became more complete; financial success the one end aimed at – 'buy in the cheapest market and sell in the dearest' – the one principle that prevailed. But such was the state of things that the masters were able not only to take full advantage of this law, but to go beyond it. For not only did one large farm require less labourers than the same area divided into several smaller ones, not only was the labour market abnormally increased by the stimulus given to human production by the Poor Law System, but that same system rendered the men careless of the amount of wages they received, since they knew the deficiency would be made up by the parish. Wages were accordingly given which, without this parochial dole, could not have kept the labourer alive.

17

Seven, eight, or at the highest nine or ten shillings a week, when the quartern loaf averaged eighteenpence, simply meant wholesale murder. But the screw was put on gradually, and in a few years, when bread had fallen to 11½d the quartern loaf, there were places, Northamptonshire for example, where the magistrate fixed the parish allowance at 5s a single man, 6s a man and wife, and 2s each child, whatever the family earned to be deducted from the allowance.

As 14s or 15s was the least a single man could live upon when bread was still cheaper, it is manifest that the wages which have been given to the Agricultural Labourer during the greater part of this century – 7s, 8s or the utmost 9s or 10s have meant *starvation* during the lifetime of at least one generation and a portion of two others. For be it remembered that on these miserable sums not one person, but very frequently four or five have had to live. It was only done by reducing the quantity of bread, bacon and beer, and taking in their place gruel, potatoes, suet and rice puddings, with decoctions of washed-out tea leaves. But even such fare was hardly possible under the varying prices which obtained during the Protective system. An old man told me that he remembered the time when the bread they had to eat was almost black, and so hard that they had to chop it. At such times, and perhaps many others, parents were glad on dark winter afternoons to fill their children's stomachs with fluid made of hot water and coarse brown sugar, flavoured with a modicum of milk, and putting them to bed, get rid of their cries for food until the next morning. 'No wonder,' as Cobbett said to one of his labourers, 'no wonder that you are all as thin as owlets, and that that son of yours there, who is nineteen years old, and is five feet nine inches high, is as you told me last summer, too weakly to do a man's work. No wonder that his knees bend under him, and that he has a voice like that of a girl, instead of being able to carry a sack of wheat and jump a five-barred gate.'

In Warwickshire I met two infirm men crawling like beetles along the road. After some conversation the elder of the two told me that he had brought eight children into the world and had

buried five. What they died of he could hardly tell. Decline, one died of that, he knew – they called it 'consumpted decline'. Phthisis and scrofula, as every country practitioner has known, found its most frequent victims among this famine-struck race.

The degradation of pauperism is far worse than that of slavery, and of all pauperism none surely exceeded in cruelty this which fell to the lot of the English Labourer. Pampered at first, led even into a coarse luxury, he was rapidly let down until he was treated to such degradations as being put up to auction, and his labour sold to the highest bidder, or to being made to drag gravel carts like a beast of burden.

Left in ignorance so dense that probably not one in five could read or write, was it surprising that agricultural labourers should view the introduction of threshing machines as calculated to put the finishing stroke to their ruin? When a prairie has been dried up by a long drought the merest spark will produce a conflagration, carrying destruction over hundreds of miles; so it is with a popular movement, no one knows how it began or where it will end. Thus in the autumn of 1830, Agricultural England was panic-stricken by the news that the labourers were rising everywhere, destroying machines and setting fire to ricks. The movement spread through the southern, eastern and midland counties, and even showed itself in Cumberland. Sometimes it was a mere riot with an onslaught on some poor-house, parsonage, or manor-house, sometimes it was content with merely destroying machinery, but the most usual form was rick-burning. Night after night in many parts of England the blazing sky told that Captain Swing had been at his work.

In the roughly printed booklet from whence this mythic personage sprang, he is made to say:

I am not the author of these burnings. What can have caused them? Those fires, said I, are caused by farmers having been turned out of their lands to make room for foxes, peasants confined two years in prison for picking up a dead partridge, and parsons taking a poor man's only cow for the tithe of his

cabbage-garden. These are the things that caused the burnings and not unfortunate 'Swing'.

No, these rick burnings, this machine breaking, these attacks on manor-houses and parsonages had in them nothing preconcerted. Men who in the morning had gone quietly to their work found themselves before day was out, part of a great mob, the infection seized them in a moment, and laying hold of some pitchfork or chopper they hurried on to riot in the rector's garden or break up the farmer's machine.

The contrast between the tremendous energy displayed by the Government, and the extreme feebleness of the unhappy rioters, was suggestive of the great gulf between rich and poor. Neither had the least idea of each other's real power. The greatest general England has ever had was sent down into the disturbed districts to support the Judges in the special assize held during December 1830.

Three hundred prisoners, many of them convicts expecting sentence of death, lay in the gaol at Winchester . . . When on the 30th of the month the Court met, the jury-box and the dock were filled with convicted felons The three judges in scarlet robes, supported by Field Marshal the Duke of Wellington, proceeded to condemn these poor rustics according to the cruel English law. They were brought up in batches of twenty at a time, and every one had sentence of death recorded against them. Six were actually sentenced to suffer on the gallows, twenty were transported for life, the remainder for periods varying according to judicial discretion.

The real nature of the crimes committed was shown by the youth of some of the offenders. In another part of the country a child of fourteen had sentence of death recorded against him; and two brothers, one twenty, the other nineteen, William and Henry Packman, were ruthlessly hanged on Penenden Heath on the 24th, whither they were escorted by a regiment of Scotch Greys. At the sight of the gallows one exclaimed to the other, 'That looks an awful thing.' 'Brother,' said the eldest, 'let us shake hands before

A rick burning incident, 1830.

Museum of English Rural Life.

A farmworker and his family being evicted from their tied cottage at Cherhill, Wiltshire on 10 February 1876. The family were obviously staunch supporters of the National Agricultural Labourers' Union, as the placard in the hedge exhorts onlookers to 'Read Joseph Arch'.

By permission from Cole Collection, Nuffield College, Oxford.

we die.' The younger refused at first to have the cap drawn over his eyes, saying he wished to see the people as he died. Poor heart, he knew well where there was sympathy, and expected strength from the sight.

Terrible fact! It was only by means of these lurid flames, these black corpses dangling in the wintry wind, these English slaves sent to the antipodal hell at Botany Bay, that the consciences of the well-to-do ruling classes could be brought to the conviction that there was something rotten in the social condition of the country and that the ground beneath their feet was volcanic.

The *Times* newspaper for December 27, 1830, commenting upon the Winchester trials, made the danger-signal scream in quite revolutionary accents:

We do affirm that the actions of this pitiable class of men (the labourers), as a commentary on the treatment experienced by them at the hands of the upper and middling classes; the gentlemen, clergy (who ought to teach and instruct them), and the farmers who ought to pay and feed them, are disgraceful to the British name. The present population *must* be provided for in body and spirit on more liberal and Christian principles, or the whole mass of labourers will start into legions of a banditti – *banditti less criminal than those who have made them so – than those who by a just but fearful retribution will soon become their victims.*

The Parliamentary Commission appointed in 1833 to inquire into the operation of the Poor Laws, declared itself horrified at the results of its inquiries. 'The condition of the rural labourers in too many districts was', it affirmed, 'brutal and wretched; their children during the days were struggling with the pigs for food, and at night were huddled down on damp straw under a roof of rotten thatch.'

A reform conceived in the hard, inhuman spirit of modern science was the outcome. I once read of a hospital nurse who, disgusted with the dirty habits of some miserable patient, dragged the trembling wretch half-naked out of her bed and forced her into a cold bath. Such was the humanity of the New Poor Law.

THE VICTORIAN PEASANT

The shivering labourers, accustomed to their dirty hovels, struggled long with grim famine before they would go into the Bastilles, as they named the new Workhouses. For this title there would have been no justification if honest families could have avoided their use, but that that was impossible is proved by the fact that the ordinary dietary of the workhouse fed the paupers twice as well as nine-tenths of English labourers could feed on the wages they obtained.

On a bleak winter's evening in January 1846, the Wiltshire labourers held a mass meeting in a cross-road near Goat-acre. Standing on a hurdle supported on stakes driven into the ground, the speakers read, by the flickering light of a candle or the glare of a lanthorn, their woe-begone statements. One who had come twenty miles told the story of his struggles to provide for a wife and six children out of eight shillings a week. At last he applied to the relieving officer, who gave him an order for one of his children to go into the workhouse. 'Now, fellow-labourers, is not one child as dear to you as another? I could not part with ne'er a one. I said to my oldest girl, You are to go into the workhouse. She did not like to go, and then I spoke to the others, and then I had the cries of my poor children, which were piercing to my heart, Don't send me, father! don't send me!'

Here we see the main cause why English labourers called the workhouses Bastilles. They lacerated their bruised souls in the only spot where feeling was left; the law tore asunder husband and wife, parents and children.

So these miserable people preferred to starve in their *horrible lairs,* called cottages. If you think this phrase mere rhetoric, study the Report of the Medical Officer of Health, 1864, and the Reports of the Commission on the Employment of Children, Young Persons and Women in Agriculture, 1867, and you will find that no phrase you can think of will be adequate to express the truth. Crazy, dilapidated hovels, shaking with every wind, vast numbers containing but one bedroom, in which parents and children, grown-up brothers and sisters, even grandparents and aunts and uncles, and occasionally lodgers, all pigged together, where a

whole family had to be ill of fever and to lie in the same room with a corpse, – rooms through the ceilings of which the water poured, where the walls reeked with damp, where fever lurked in the saturated floor, so that the very accent of the people seemed to have grown clammy, – such were vast numbers of English cottages up to within the time that I began to study this subject, and, by numbers of pedestrian tours, to realise the truth with my own eyes . . .

Degraded by pauperism, harried by the game laws, brutalised by drink, maddened by starvation, are you surprised that such homes produced a state of mind only to be paralleled in an old-fashioned lunatic asylum, where people were kept in cages like raging beasts of prey? Some blessed angels have been at work all over the land restraining these poor devils, binding up their wounds, sitting at their bedsides, filling their minds with a hidden hope – a hope quite undefined, but for that reason the more vast and consoling. So you may enter these hovels, and find a resignation, a peace of mind, a trust in God absolutely sublime. It is the Spirit of Jesus Christ which we have driven to dwell in the nethermost hells of English society . . .

Space fails me to speak of the innumerable miseries which rendered these miserable homes still more miserable – the toilsome journeys to the work, often many miles a day – the occupation of the mothers in the fields – the corruption of the young by the ganging system; all these causes assisted to destroy domestic affection – the one humanising influence left to the labourer amidst all his trials and temptations. When this was gone, there was nothing for him but drink, and this reacted on the home, and made its wretchedness still more wretched . . .

8. THE FIRST FAINT STREAK OF DAWN

(From) 1834 to 1872 is not a long time in such a history as we have been pursuing; but how great the change! Day had broken; the shadows were flying.

Joseph Arch, president of the National Agricultural Labourers' Union, in 1872.
By permission from Cole Collection, Nuffield College, Oxford.

In 1834, the Dorsetshire labourers, among the gentlest and most down-trodden of their class, formed a Trades-Union. The Government caused six labouring men concerned in getting it up to be indicted at the Assizes at Dorchester, under an obsolete statute made to prevent mutiny in the Navy. They were found guilty of administering an oath which this statute made penal, and were sentenced to seven years' penal servitude. Notwithstanding a burst of popular indignation, these six labourers were transported to Van Dieman's land . . .

In 1872 the South Warwickshire labourers formed a Trades-Union, and though the example soon spread through the country, thus showing itself to be a far more formidable movement than the Dorset one, not a hand was raised to stop its progress.

Few movements have been less the result of premeditation. Some labourers at Weston asked for an increase of wages; one or two of the Wellesbourne men noticed the fact in a local paper, and, talking about it to a labourer who had been in the Black country, he suggested that the Wellesbourne people should combine for the same end. They were willing, but wanted a leader. They knew a man at Barford who they thought would do (Joseph Arch): he was a day labourer, but his soul was lifted above the clods. To Barford they accordingly went . . .

(Joseph) Arch threw himself heart and soul into the work. The first thing done was to hold a meeting at Wellesbourne. From farm to farm, by word of mouth, the tidings spread, and on the 14th day of February 1872, beneath a noble chestnut, which adorns the village green, the agricultural labourers of England shook off the fetters of ages. A thousand persons or more were present, and adhesions poured in so fast to the new Union then formed that the Secretary could hardly write the names. Notices were served on the farmers asking a rise in wages to sixteen shillings a week; the demand was refused, and the labourers struck.

But their faith and courage were not severely tried, for the agricultural labourers throughout the country took up the movement, until the Agricultural Labourers' Union became a

National organisation. The labourer had boldly marched into the social citadel; he was henceforth a citizen *de facto,* and tomorrow will be so *de jure* . . .

(The) light has fairly broken, and though the clouds keep gathering, they cannot hide the rising sun. Already the pedestrian, wandering in various parts of rural England, fails to see many of the signs of the long night through which the labourers have toiled and suffered. The cottages are rapidly improving, and the labourer begins to look strong and hopeful. Give him power ungrudgingly, and he will in fifty years redress the evil done in five hundred – but on condition that he delivers himself not only from the tyranny, but also from the teaching of his old masters; that he worships 'the Suffering God' and not 'the almighty dollar.'

THE COTTAGE HOMES
OF ENGLAND

(LEISURE HOUR, 1870)

With their gable roofs of cosy thatch or of red tiles bright with moss and lichen, with their ornamented chimneys and walls of plaster laced and interlaced with heavy beams, the Cottage Homes of England, peeping out from the green lanes of Kent, or fringing the Surrey commons, or nestling in the wooded vales of Sussex, are always picturesque. They are, moreover, the one form of human habitation always in harmony with the scenery around them. In Yorkshire and in Wales their aspect is bleak as the moor or the mountain side; in Cumberland and in Devonshire they are alike built of stone; but in the north their architecture is in keeping with the stern form Nature presents among the Cumbrian hills; while in the south, covered with ivy and hidden amongst gardens and orchards, each little cot appears a poem in itself. This harmony is partly due to the fact that the same soil which produces the natural scenery produces the material of which the cottages are built. In the north wood is scarce, stone plentiful: hence the stone villages of Lancashire and Yorkshire. In the pottery districts and the midland counties clay is abundant; here, therefore, brick cottages are the rule. In Westmoreland the red sandstone is used; in Kent the ragstone, in Lincolnshire the Ancaster stone, in Cornwall granite, in Essex and Herts flints from the chalk hills, in Hampshire mud mixed with pebbles, in Norfolk and Suffolk lumps of clay mixed with straw.

Picturesque and harmonious from the artist's point of view, these cottages are in most other respects a scandal to England . . .

Crabbe, who saw things as they really were, disposed long ago of the sentimental view of the Cottage Homes of England:

Ye gentle souls who dream of rural ease,
Whom the smooth stream and smoother sonnet please,
Go! if the peaceful cot your praises share,
Go look within, and ask if peace be there;
If peace be his – that drooping, weary sire,
Or theirs, that offspring round their feeble fire;
Or hers, that matron pale, whose trembling hand
Turns on the wretched hearth th'expiring brand!

Even Crabbe's photographic painting gives but an inadequate idea of the moral misery of these pretty cots, – 'smiling o'er the silvery brooks, and round the hamlet-fanes.'

The Rev. James Fraser, afterwards Bishop of Manchester, one of the Assistant Commissioners in the inquiry made in 1867–68 into the conditions of agricultural labour (Commission on the Employment of Children, Young Persons, and Women in Agriculture, 1867: an inquiry nominally confined to the employment of women and children, but really extending to the whole subject), reports that:

. . . the majority of cottages that exist in rural parishes are deficient in almost every requisite that should constitute a home for a Christian family in a civilised community. They are deficient in bedroom accommodation, very few having three chambers, and in some chambers the larger proportion only one. They are deficient in drainage and sanitary arrangements; they are imperfectly supplied with water; such conveniences as they have are often so situated as to become nuisances; they are full enough of draughts to generate any amount of rheumatism; and in many instances are lamentably dilapidated and out of repair.

It is impossible to exaggerate the ill effects of such a state of things in every aspect, physical, social, economical, moral,

intellectual. Physically, a ruinous, ill-drained cottage, cribbed, cabin'd, confined, and over-crowded, generates any amount of disease, fevers of every type, catarrh, rheumatism, as well as intensifies to the utmost that tendency to scrofula and phthisis which, from their frequent intermarriages and their low diet, abound so largely among the poor.

The moral consequences are fearful to contemplate . . . Modesty must be an unknown virtue, decency an unimaginable thing, where in one small chamber . . . two and sometimes three generations are herded promiscuously, . . . where the whole atmosphere is sensual, and human nature is degraded into something below the level of the swine. It is a hideous picture, and the picture is drawn from life.

In the summer of 1864 a careful and elaborate inquiry was made by Dr H. J. Hunter into the house accommodation of rural labourers, and embodied in the seventh report of the medical officer of the Privy Council for presentation to Parliament. Every page testifies to its insufficient quantity and miserable quality. Summing up the results of the inquiry, the report says: 'Even the general badness of the dwellings is an evil infinitely less urgent than their numerical insufficiency,' a statement proved by the fact that in 821 separate parishes or townships in England a destruction of houses had been going on during the previous ten years notwithstanding *increased local demand for them*. 'People,' the report says, 'do not desert villages, villages nowadays desert people.'

Certain provisions of the Poor Law relating to chargeability and settlement rendered it the pecuniary interest of each parish to lessen the number of the poor residing within its boundaries. When, therefore, a parish was the sole property of two or three great landlords, 'They had only to resolve that there should be no labourers' dwellings on their estates, and their estates were thenceforth free from half their responsibility for the poor.' The Union Chargeability Act has changed all this, but the evil done remains. Other causes have doubtless been at work, but this has been the principal one. When we come to understand the

Blenheim Cottage, Brighthampton, Standlake, Oxfordshire. This cottage had a history of use as an agricultural dwelling right up to the 1930s, when it housed a carter, his wife and four children. It was declared uninhabitable in 1963. The ground floor consisted of a living room and kitchen area; the roof space, reached by stairs from the living room, contained two separate sleeping areas divided by a rough boarded partition.

Oxfordshire Museums Service

Woman in a turnip field, Hertfordshire, *c.* 1883 (Sir George Clausen). Cheap female labour was commonly used by farmers to top and tail turnips after they had been pulled up. This woman was posed by Clausen with a small hook or sickle in her right hand, preparing to chop off the turnip top. Turnip hacking was hard, cold, dirty work – it is vividly described by Thomas Hardy in *Tess of the d'Urbervilles*.
Museum of English Rural Life.

wretched pauperism into which the agricultural labourers have drifted, we can see how powerful the temptation to shift the burden of the poor-rates must have been to large proprietors. 'Agricultural labour,' says this report, 'instead of implying a safe and permanent independence for the hard-worked labourer and his family, implies for the most part only a longer or shorter circuit to eventual pauperism.'

What are the causes which have brought agricultural labour into this wretched condition?

In feudal times land was held in great masses from the Crown, and as the importance of every lord depended upon the number of retainers he could bring into the field, it was his interest to divide his estate into as many farms as he could find tenants to cultivate them, and to grant rights of common to each one over the remaining portions.

Thorold Rogers, in his *History of Agriculture and Prices in England*, says:

> In the 14th century the land was greatly subdivided, and most of the inhabitants of villages or manors held plots of land which were sufficient in many cases for maintenance, and, in nearly all cases, for independence in treating with their employers. Most of the regular farm servants – the carter, the ploughman, the shepherd, the cowherd, and the hog-keeper – were owners of land, and there is a high degree of probability that the occasional labourer was also among the occupiers of the manor. The mediaeval peasant had his cottage and curtilage at a very low rent and in secure possession, even when, unlike the general mass of his fellows, he was not possessed of land in his own right held at a labour or a money rent, and he had rights of pasturage over the common lands of the manor for the sheep, pigs, or perhaps cow, which he owned.

This prosperity continued to the close of the 15th century, when the Wars of the Roses broke out, ending in the destruction of the feudal system. Manufacturers rose on its ruin, the woollen trade

increased greatly, and large tracts of land were required for sheep-walks. This caused at the time a wholesale destruction of villages, so that, in a petition presented to Parliament in 1450, it was stated that sixty-five towns (villages) and hamlets within twelve miles of Warwick had been destroyed.

Many efforts were made to restore the former widely-spread prosperity of the English peasantry. An Act passed in 1487 forbade any one to take more than one farm, and the value of that farm was not to exceed ten marks yearly. Five or six times in the 16th century Acts were passed imposing penalties for not keeping up 'houses of husbandry' and for not laying convenient land for their maintenance. An Act of 1549 secured to small cottiers land for gardens or orchards. Another, passed in the year 1589, is peculiarly noteworthy as forbidding the erection of cottages unless four acres were attached; the object being, as Lord Bacon said of the Act of 1487, 'to breed a subject to live in convenient plenty and no servile condition, and to keep the plough in the hands of the owners, and not mere hirelings.'

And the result sought was obtained, for, towards the end of the 16th and the beginning of the 17th centuries, contemporary authorities declare that the condition of the labourers and small tenants in husbandry 'had grown to be more powerful, skilful, and careful, through recompense of gain, than heretofore they had been.'

This prosperity, dimmed for a time by the Civil War, was not seriously affected by it, for in the reign of Charles II there were, according to the best statistical writers of the time, not less than 160,000 proprietors, who, with their families, must have made up a seventh part of the whole population who derived their subsistence from little freehold estates. This second era of agricultural well-being continued until the middle of the 18th century, when, from all accounts, it culminated. Prior to the American War, the English peasantry were, generally speaking, in a comparatively prosperous condition. They were reaping the advantage of the expanding commerce of the country without any corresponding diminution in their resources.

But with the improvement and extension of modern husbandry commenced the depression and decay of the husbandmen. It was found that large farms could be managed more profitably than small ones. Thus the poor and the weak began to fall into the ranks of the hired labourer, while their richer neighbour rose in the social scale.

Few things had more helped the mass of English peasants than the freedom they had enjoyed to use the common lands. But from about the middle of the last century commenced that wholesale private appropriation of common property which has so largely helped to complete the ruin of the English peasant. Between 1710, the date of the first Inclosure Act, and 1760, only 334,974 statute acres were inclosed, while, in the century which followed, more than *seven millions* of statute acres have been added to the cultivated area of Great Britain.

In a speech made by Mr Cowper-Temple (Lord Mount-Temple), on the second reading of the general Inclosure Bill, March 13th, 1844, he said:

In former times every cottage almost had some common rights, from which the poor occupants derived much benefit; the privilege of feeding a cow, a pig, or a goose on the common was a great benefit to them, and it was unfortunate, when a system of inclosing commons first commenced, that a portion of the land was not set apart for the benefit of every cottager who enjoyed common rights, and his successors; but the course adopted had been to compensate the owner of the cottage to which the common right belonged, forgetting the claims of the occupier by whom they were enjoyed.

Had the loss of these common rights been balanced by a share in the material progress of the country, the agricultural labourer would not have been much worse treated by these Inclosure Acts than the bulk of the community, but since 1815 their wages have declined, while there has been an increase in the cost of living.

The fictitious prosperity that arose during the war only made

the subsequent destitution harder to bear. From 1815 to 1846 was a period of continually recurring distress among the agriculturalists, and the unhappy labourers sank almost universally into pauperism. Their wages fell to zero, if we may use that term to imply the lowest point to which they could fall compatible with continued existence. In different counties they varied from 7s to 12s a week. In Cambridgeshire the farmers paid 8s and beer, which made it 9s 6d, but they said it was only intimidation made them pay such prices. The labourers grew desperate, and in 1830 there were a series of incendiary fires, extending for more than eighteen months, in the counties of Wiltshire, Hampshire, Berkshire and Buckinghamshire.

But these efforts were like the struggles of a dying man, fitful, and each time perceptibly weaker. During the winter of 1845–46 the agonised sufferer was dimly seen writhing in the dark. In the newspapers of the time there were accounts of gatherings of the labourers, with their wives and children, at night, on moors and commons, under circumstances that gave a weird-like character to the proceedings. At one held near Wootton-Basset, on a cold winter's night, the speakers, one after the other, gave accounts of their own sufferings and those of their families, quite inconceivably cruel. Nearly a thousand Wiltshire peasants were present, and it was a heart-rending sight, when the moon shone out from time to time behind the clouds, and revealed the upturned faces worn with anxiety, want, and hunger.

Nearly twenty years later, Elihu Burritt, in his walk to Land's End, relates the result of a conversation he had with a hedger in Wiltshire. After detailing his own hardships, the man told him that:

> . . . his son-in-law had six children, all too young to earn anything in the field, and he had to feed, clothe, and house the whole family out of eight shillings a week. They were obliged to live entirely on bread, for they could not afford to have cheese with it. Take out one-and-sixpence for rent, and as much for fuel, candles, clothes, and a little tea, sugar, or treacle, and

there was only five shillings left for food for eight mouths. They must eat three times a-day, which made twenty-four meals to be got out of eightpence, only a *third* of a penny for each.

Thus, in the progress of modern civilisation, the English agricultural labourer has been a constant loser. From a condition in which he might hope, by industry and thrift, to become a small farmer, he can now hope for nothing better than to perform like a hireling his day, and then to find a pauper's grave. One privilege after another has gone, until at last he is driven from the land which the toil of many generations of his ancestors has rendered fertile, to burrow with his children in the slums of some outlying village, and thence to trudge with gaunt face and discontented heart to and fro from the scene of labour, no longer sweetened by bygone memories or future hopes . . .

Lincolnshire is comparatively a new country. Before this century the greater part of the lowlands was given up to the wild goose and the bittern. Even the heights were only partially cultivated. There was a large tract of land, twenty miles north and twenty miles south of Lincoln, called the Heath, a dreary waste, so vast and featureless that it was thought necessary in 1751 to erect upon it a sort of land lighthouse. The result of this state of things was that the villages were built on the high roads, while the parishes extended for miles into the rear, composed of wild moor or fen according to the district. In our day everything is changed, and the whole country brought under cultivation. Dunston Pillar, a monument of former desolation, now stands surrounded by field after field of waving grain, or of turnips set in matchless order, upon which thousands of long-woolled sheep may be seen in winter-time feeding in their netted folds. Above the neatly-clipped hedgerows rise white farm buildings, surrounded by clusters of stacks. But where are the cottages? Everything has been provided for but the human machine, by whose labour all this wonderful change has been wrought. He must find his lodging

miles away from the scene of his daily toil.

The report of 1867 says concerning the Heath district:

Two lines of villages, from four to seven miles apart, form its eastern and western boundaries, and between them there is not only an absence of villages, but almost of cottages too. The main feature of this district is that the labourers are all congregated into larger towns.

The report of 1864, speaking of North Lincolnshire, says there are 'people, women as well as men, who take an hour's walk twice a day, starting in the dark and returning in the dark, to obtain the privilege of selling a day's hard work for a shilling.' In the northern half of the Wold district, where the farms are often of 800 or 1000 acres, the villages, though numerous, are so small that there is only one room for the regularly-hired labourers; the large class of 'catch-work' men, with their wives and families, have to herd where they can. In the Fen district it is even worse. The population is crowded into small villages standing close to the high road, while the parishes stretch miles away into the Fen, and in consequence the labourer has to walk in some cases five or six miles to his work. 'At Baston,' a few miles from Market Deeping:

. . . a man had for many years walked 56 miles a week to and from his work, and all for twelve shillings. At Langtoft, two miles from Baston, a man was found living in a miserable house of three rooms, with his wife, her mother and five children. The bedroom was a garret, the walls of which, leaning to, formed a ridge at the top, with a dormer window in front. 'Did he live there to be near his work?' 'No, men have to trail a long way to work. The man was working in Braceboro', six miles from home, and came back to his family every night! He lived there because he could get a tenantable cot, and was glad of it at any price, anywhere, and in any condition.'

The Lincolnshire cottages are not as a rule bad in quality, although in one parish a farmer speaks of some as 'not fit to put a pig in', but

their insufficient quantity is the cause of evils quite as destructive of home life, and perhaps more so. Overcrowding, of course, is one of the first results, with all its deleterious consequences. A girl belonging to a family of nine children was asked 'how they all got into one small bedroom,' and she replied 'that they had to lie like pins, heads and tails, next each other.' In Grainthorpe a case was reported to the Board of Guardians, in which the father and mother and seven children were found in a room with only one bedstead, all ill of fever, no window except one in the roof. At Easttoft the incumbent writes:

> Some cottages here are dreadfully crowded, especially by the Irish. I know a case where a farmer had to send for a labourer earlier than usual, and his foreman, when he went to the cottage, could not open the door, the whole cottage being covered with sleeping people packed close together.

The frightfully immoral system of ganging, prevalent in Lincolnshire, is largely to be attributed to insufficient cottage accommodation. Mr Bramley, a farmer of more than 2000 acres of land, says: 'Want of cottages has given rise to the ganging system, and also to increased employment of women and children.' 'We want,' says Mr Little, another farmer of 1700 acres, 'all the children, as soon as they are old enough to be available.' Few cottages, few people; every hand must be pressed into service, even mothers with infants.

Depressed by dismal scenery, oppressed by noxious vapours in summer, and cold, clammy fogs in winter, eaten up by rheumatism and ague, with homes debased and brutalised, the unhappy natives of the Fen district fill up their cup of misery by becoming opium-eaters.

'All England may be carved out of Norfolk,' says an old English writer. Pasture land and arable land, heath and wood and fen, with the sea skirting two-thirds of the country; if its scenery is never grand, at least it is varied. Coke, the eminent agriculturalist,

turned West Norfolk from a rye-growing district into a wheat-growing one. His sheep-shearings were famous all over the civilised world. He taught the Norfolk farmers how to improve their stock, and his example led the way to most of the triumphs of modern husbandry. He is said to have raised his rents from tens to hundreds, and yet to have enriched his tenants as well as himself. Doubtless the same results have taken place on other Norfolk estates, so that the position of both landlords and farmers has vastly improved.

But what has modern improvements in husbandry done for the poor labourer? In Norfolk, the county of agricultural progress, his lot is worse than ever. At an agricultural dinner which took place at North Walsham in 1863, Mr W. Cubitt, the eminent agriculturalist, thus portrayed the homes of Norfolk labourers. 'They had long known,' he said:

> . . . as employers of labour, that one great source of that demoralisation of which there had been such just complaints, arose from the overcrowded dwellings of the poor. In too many instances the common decencies of life were disregarded; and if the children were not contaminated, they were sent into the world devoid of that shame which is the natural safeguard of youth. He had not lived forty years amongst the poor without seeing the evil influences of over-crowded houses. In fact, he saw it from his very door. Where was immorality bred? But too often under the influences arising from miserable and crowded dwellings.

The Rev. E. Gurdon, in a paper read before the Norwich Diocesan Work Association, stated that when cottage-building is left to speculators, instead of the comfortable, old-fashioned clay lump building, with its thick walls and deep, heavy, substantial, thatched roof, a small clay lump house, with a red-tile roof, and walls thin and pervious alike to heat and cold, is generally erected. And this is only one sample of the benefit the poor get from the arrangement of modern civilisation.

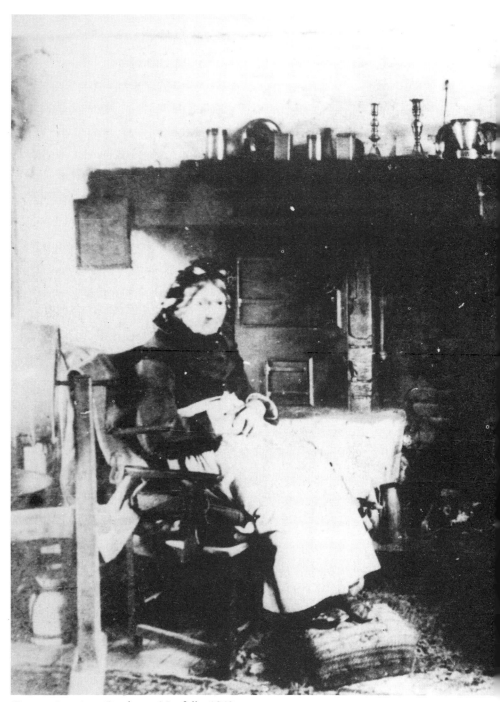

Cottage interior, Gresham, Norfolk, 1860.

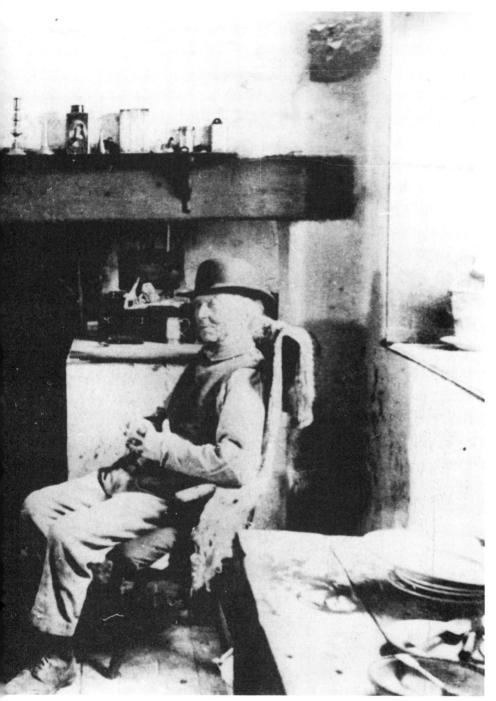

Museum of English Rural Life.

In the winter of 1863–64, the proprietors of the *Norfolk News* sent one of their staff to report on the state of the cottages in various parts of the county. The tours were made in company with Mr Samuel Clarke, sanitary inspector to the city of Norwich, and some idea may be formed of the extent of the inquiries made by the fact that the reports give in detail the condition of two hundred cottages.

The misery revealed was both shocking and scandalous. Take this picture of a Norfolk village:

> A stranger cannot enter the village without being struck with surprise at its wretched and desolate condition. Look where he may, he sees little else but thatched roofs – old, rotten and shapeless – full of holes and overgrown with weeds; windows sometimes patched with rags, and sometimes plastered over with clay; the walls, which are nearly all of clay, full of cracks and crannies; and sheds and outhouses – where there are any – looking as if they had been overthrown very early in the present century, and left in the hopeless confusion in which they fell.

The first hut entered was a fair sample of the whole. Notwithstanding the cracked clay walls, half-dismantled roof, and tottering chimney, it was occupied by a man and his wife and six children, who advanced in age from one to fourteen. The six children slept in one small, ill-ventilated chamber, and the parents in another. But these rooms were without plaster, and the sides of the roof were supported by sticks placed across – 'for,' said the occupants, 'whenever there is a little wind, the place shakes, and we lie in fear of being smothered by its falling.' It was no uncommon thing for seven or eight – in one case as many as eleven – persons of all ages and both sexes to be found sleeping in one room. And then, as would only be too likely, one or more would be ill with fever. In one case, where seven poor children slept on two stump bedsteads, five had been ill with fever for two months. Sometimes the bedroom was approached by a ladder and a trap-door, and the slanting roof was so low that only in the

middle could a person stand upright. When there were two bed-rooms, the children's roof was found at times perfectly dark. Fancy five or six little wretches creeping into the horrors of such a hole, and lying huddled up there like so many mice. Sometimes there was too much ventilation – holes in the roof – so that if rain came on, the pillows were, as one women observed, 'as wet as a pit.' Who can be surprised 'that the average duration of life amongst the industrial classes is scarcely one-half that of the wealthy'!

And this is only the physical side of the evil. With reference to its moral results, the Government Commissioner says: 'Mr Clarke, of Norwich, can tell anyone who will ask him tales of things he himself has seen, horrifying enough to make the very hair stand on end.'

(During) the last two or three years (the Commissioners have) been traversing the country in all directions – calling meetings of landowners and farmers, receiving letters from hundreds of clergymen and other parish authorities, examining persons of all classes and every condition. On the labour question, on the education question, opinions differed; but on the cottage question there was the most striking unanimity, a stream of testimony pouring in from every quarter denouncing the present condition of things as a terrible evil and a national disgrace.

In this article we propose to see what light these reports throw on the condition of cottage homes in the heart of England.

The farther north we go, the better the condition of the labourer. Thus, in the Midland Counties, the more they lie to the north, the less there is to be said against their cottages.

In Notts the condition of things which prevails is similar to that found in Lincolnshire, but in a modified sense.

The picturesque old cottages of Cheshire are generally in bad repair, but scarcity of any sort of cottages is a still greater evil. This works in a way quite destructive of the labourer's home. To ensure regular assistance, the farmer only cares to employ men who will lodge and board in the house. Married men therefore,

eating a good portion of their wages at their master's table, have only abut 5s or 6s a week left to give their wives to keep house with. Terribly pinched on such an allowance, and without the benefit of the presence and control of the father, the house soon breaks up.

In the south-west of Shropshire there is a district shut in among the hills, and cut off from the outer world by the Severn and the Thame, where the state of the peasantry is described as deplorably bad. But the Commissioner says:

> The point especially deserving of attention in this county is the infamous nature of the cottages. In the majority of parishes that I visited, they may be described as tumbledown and ruinous, not water-tight, very deficient in bedroom accommodation, and indecent sanitary arrangements. On many estates cottages are to be found belonging to the owners of the soil which are a disgrace to any civilised community.

At Bishop's Castle the Commissioner had a conversation with the vicar and others. It was stated that 'it was not at all an uncommon thing for a bolster to be placed at each end of the bed, so that all the family sleep in it with their feet towards the middle.' The vicar, going to baptize a child, found five or six children in bed with the mother.

In some parts of Herefordshire, owing to failing population and former poverty, many of the small homesteads have become labourers' cottages. Although these places are always old, and generally dilapidated, they are large and airy. Surrounded by gardens and outhouses, they have room to breed pigs, and chickens, and ducks, making all the difference between independence and penury.

The great bulk of the cottages, however, in this county, have been built by the labourers themselves on pieces of ground cribbed from the waste:

> They are generally constructed of wattle and dub, and thatched, and contain only bedroom and sitting-room. In one village many

of the cottages were found in the last stage of decay, windows broken, doors far from wind-tight, roofs not water-tight, bedrooms unceiled.

From Upton-on-Severn, in Worcestershire, comes the statement, 'Nine-tenths of the cottages are abominable; they are over-crowded, damp, and not air-tight.' Elsewhere they are described as deplorably bad and overcrowded. Archdeacon Sandford says: 'The housework often remains undone till evening, and the infants and babies are consigned to some busy neighbour, or small child, unfit for the care of other children, who ought herself to be at school.'

The same practice prevails in Warwickshire, and there, strange to say, it would appear that field-working is confined to married women. It is said that the men expect the wife in this way to help towards the support of the family. A Medical Officer of the Warwick Union says: 'I have known at least eight cases in which children left at home have been burned or scalded – three or four of these have resulted in death. I have occasionally known an opiate in the shape of Godfrey's Cordial, or Duffy's Elixir, given by the mother to the children to keep them quiet.' Another surgeon, who has practised at Knowle for twenty-seven years, says: 'Almost all the illegitimacy is due to crowded cottages. The drainage is abominable. We have outbreaks of fever which we can trace entirely to nuisances.'

Leicestershire is a county suffering from the two opposite evils of congestion and depletion. The stocking villages are over-crowded, while in the Vale of Belvoir the population is near extinction. The cottages have no gardens, and are built up close against the side of the road. 'Mushroom halls' and 'charity houses' exist largely in this county, and this is perhaps the chief reason why its cottage accommodation is so peculiarly bad. 'Mushroom halls' are cots originally erected by squatters on the edge of a common or waste, rapidly put together to avoid interference, only just serving for shelter, and patched up from time to time to keep out wind and weather. 'Charity houses' are dwellings built

expressly for or devoted to the use of the poor by private benevolence, or sometimes by the parish. Negligent administration is generally the fate of these well-meant charities. No rent being demanded, after a time the inmates frequently become the virtual owners, and sell or in various ways get rid of the property. Of course, it falls into the hands of the worst class of proprietors, as none else would purchase houses with no title.

In the close parishes of Northamptonshire the cottage supply is insufficient for the amount of labour; in the open ones the accommodation is rarely, if ever, adequate to provide for the health, comfort, and morals of the inhabitants. As an instance of the sort of building supposed to be good enough for a labouring family: 'Four cottages stand together in a village near a malt-kiln. They had gardens. A speculator bought them. He turned *the kiln* into six cottages, and built five others on the ground which had been used for gardens.' In almost all the villages of Northamptonshire instances are to be met with of overcrowding. 'A cot, measuring 16 feet by 18 feet,' the report states, 'was inhabited by a grandfather, aged eighty-four, father, mother, and eleven children – fourteen in all; and at the time the place was visited the mother of the family was engaged in washing out clothes in the only living-room.' This is spoken of as the worst case, but others very bad are mentioned.

Education is very defective in Northamptonshire, not for want of schools, but owing to the indifference and want of affection on the part of the parents. This is attributed to the demoralisation resulting from bad cottages, and to the poverty of the people and consequent want of hope.

> Bedfordshire is very inadequately supplied with cottages. They are few and small, and their condition is often a mere precarious holding together of rotten materials; the stitch in time has not been applied, and there are hundreds on which no repairs can now be bestowed with advantage.

This was the state of things in 1864. In 1867 Mr Culley reports that in about half of fifty-five parishes of which he received descriptions,

the cottage accommodation was either mixed, bad and good, or generally bad – so we take the above as descriptive of the cots in such parishes. Of one district it is said:

> Most of the men are intemperate. The causes are the aggregation of cottages in the villages, the wretched condition of the cottages, the entire absence of a proprietary considering themselves in any way responsible for the moral and physical well-being of their tenants, and, lastly, the very defective legislation about public-houses.

In Buckinghamshire the labourer's home is no better than elsewhere. Here is an interior drawn by a landowner at Coleshill:

> Look into a cottage in Bucks. You see a want of furniture, scanty bedding, perhaps the remains of a quartern loaf, and a mug smelling of beer. The family, not having a good meal of victuals once in twelve months, do their work (except piecework) accordingly without a will. As a rule, they are honest and well-conducted, but their enemies are want of economy, ignorance, and the beer-shop.

In the autumn of 1863 the *Morning Star* published a series of articles, entitled 'Rural Life in Buckinghamshire'. Mr Culley mentions that in seven of the worst parishes exposed in these articles there has only been improvement in two. Of cottages in other parts he speaks in such language as 'very wretched dens', 'wretched hovels', 'very bad cottages, quite unfit for human beings to live in.'

In the 'Burnham Magazine' of May 1868 were some strong remarks about the cottages in that town, ending thus: 'Human nature caged up in them must become degraded, and when these homes are emptied from the sheer impossibility of living in them, the beer-shops of course are filled.'

Oxfordshire is a thoroughly agricultural county, and in its farming arrangements still maintains some old-fashioned ideas

and practices. Boys are still lodged at the farmers' houses, and instead of looking to factories and mines for an improvement in their position, they aspire to be grooms, and girls to go out to service. The boys are employed on the land, as they are in most other parts of the country, too early, and, trudging about in their heavy boots on the sticky soil, contract a weakness in the legs, which leaves its indelible mark in an awkward gait.

Oxfordshire cottages are not so bad as those of Beds or Bucks; but in treating of Oxon and Berks Mr Culley attributes the loose morals of the female population to the overcrowding of cottages.

From Berkshire come a series of denunciations. The Rev. W. J. Butler, Wantage, says: 'Wretched pigsties of hovels destroy decency, self-respect, and the love of home. I could mention frightful results from the present system of dwelling-houses.'

Speaking of the Union of Newent, in Gloucestershire, a union comprising eighteen parishes with a population of 12,500, Dr Fraser says:

> The physical, social and educational condition of the labouring classes appeared to me to be low. Many cottages which I saw in the parishes of Newent, Linton, and Taynton, are simply unfit for human habitation . . . In Linton I was informed very few of the cottages have a staircase; the bedrooms are reached by a ladder or steps. The cases in which the roof – particularly when it is old thatch – is so utterly unsound as to be unable to resist anything like a downpour, and where people's bedding, in consequence, constantly gets deluged, are too numerous to mention.

Mr Cattle, a surgeon practising at Newent, took Dr Fraser a drive one afternoon through his district, and showed him some of the worst of these dens; and he says that:

> . . . speaking generally, anything more deplorable than the way large masses of the population in the neighbourhood of Newent, in Kilcote, Gorsley, Linton and on Glass House Hill,

are housed cannot be conceived. The state of their homes tells on the physical condition of the people. Many of them never wash; the flannel undervest is perhaps only taken off when it is worn out. The dietary is correspondingly low – many families have nothing but bread from one week's end to the other.

He speaks of the depression that he felt on his return from the drive, in which he had seen type after type of social life almost degraded to the level of barbarism.

The charges these Reports bring against the cottages in East Anglia and those in Mid England are, upon the whole, true of those in the southern counties; and of the metropolitan counties the same dark tale is told.

In Essex Dr Hunter found that a destruction of houses had been going on in twenty-two parishes, without arresting the growth of the population, so that in 1861 a large number of persons were squeezing themselves into a smaller number of houses than had been the case in 1851. At Great Chesterford he describes some of the cots as 'pictures of misery.' At Little Chesterton were 'plenty of tumble-down houses with most wretched thatches.' At Wendon were 'some most melancholy cottages; the crumbling clay exposed the ribs, and none but the poorest materials seem used.' At Little Hallingbury the floors were of large pebbles set in concrete, which of course busy little fingers were hard at work day by day pulling out. Washing such floors must have been out of the question – a pail of water would leave them as full of pools as a bad road on a rainy day.

In Surrey the commons are skirted by cottages of the poorest description, originally built by squatters out of the waste. In course of time some have been sold, and so rebuilt or repaired as to become decent habitations, but numbers may be found only containing one bedroom and one sitting-room, totally destitute of drainage, and in a wretched condition. Those who live near such commons must have often heard – 'they have the fever on the common', that is, the 'scarlet fever'. Even the pretty,

comfortable-looking Surrey towns have their dark spots, and these are just the habitations of the poor labourer – Epsom, for example. Of Godstone it is said, 'We have many cottages unfit for human habitation; they are small and crowded, without ventilation or drainage, outhouses, gardens, or water-supply.' At Farnham the Commissioner saw a cottage in which a man and his wife and ten children lived. The whole family slept in one room, divided by a wooden screen, carried partially across. There was only one window to supply light and air to the whole room on both sides of the screen.

From the neighbourhood of Maidstone, in Kent, we get evidence similar in character to that concerning Norfolk:

> Cottage accommodation is generally miserable, especially as to bedrooms; no decency can be observed. The sitting-rooms are too often stone or brick floored – draughty, cold, wretched places, from which the father and grown-up sons are only too glad to escape to the warm public-house near. The sanitary arrangements are horrible, and, in short, the cottages of the working man are so curiously contrived as to sap the foundations of morality, religion, and health.

In East Kent it is said many of the cottages are quite uninhabitable. What, then, must be the misery of the Cottage Homes of England, when, in the face of such evidence, the Commissioner says, 'and yet it appeared to me that they were better in Kent than in any county I have visited'?

When in these reports we continually read such remarks as: 'Our cottages are better now', 'There is not much to complain of now', and find the whole matter spoken of as 'the evil growth of many generations', we become conscious of a continuity of misery, under which generation after generation has dragged out a painful existence. William Cobbett thus described the homes of the peasantry:

> Look at these hovels made of mud and of straw; bits of glass, or of old cast-off windows, without frames or hinges frequently, but

merely stuck in the mud wall. Enter them, and look at the bits of chairs or stools; the wretched boards tacked together to serve for a table; the floor of pebble, broken brick, or of the bare ground. Look at the thing called a bed, and survey the rags on the backs of the wretched inhabitants, and then wonder, if you can, that the jails and dungeons and tread-mills increase.

If after years of effort on the part of some landowners, the above description is scarcely now an exaggeration of certain parts of the country, how universally true must it have been before the national conscience was aroused on the matter!

Pent-up city folk often envy the fresh complexion and the stalwart frame of the farmer or country gentleman, while they wonder how labourers who breathe the same air have such a feeble and dejected look. Who can wonder, when he once knows the secret of those 'Black Holes,' miscalled bedrooms, in which they nightly inhale draughts of poisoned vapour?

One of the most evident results of bad dwellings is physical debility. One surgeon in Norfolk 'observes the want of muscular development in the agricultural labourer: he has no calves to his legs, and no development of the biceps muscle of his arm.' Another notes the blanched and unhealthy-looking condition of the children in a particular locality. Some places are scourged by fevers, some decimated by consumption – everywhere the aged are cruelly tortured by rheumatism.

'There is a want', writes Lord Sydney Godolphin Osborne:

> . . . of physical energy, of what I may call labour pluck, a deadening of mind and body force. They may work up to what they are worth as regards the value of what they do in the labour market, but even this is done after a very listless fashion. They form farm machinery in the mass, but the motive power is weak.

In the south and west of England agricultural labourers live on the verge of pauperism, and have no hope of bettering their position:

A labourer who is ill one day, or whose child is sick, as a matter of course applies to the parish doctor, and a week's illness always sends him to the parish. Even the best and most industrious labourers are discouraged from joining friendly societies lest it should interfere with their right to come upon the rates. And too often the management of these societies is calculated to make them think that it is far wiser to rely wholly upon parish relief. In hundreds of cases, after years of patient self-denial, and of saving against a day of trouble, the poor labourer has been sent on the parish because there is nothing 'in the box of his club', or because he and others were getting old, and were likely soon to come on its funds, the younger members of the club having dissolved it and reconstituted it without him.

Sickness and want of work bring many labourers into debt against their will, and the system of the tally-men with whom he deals is so tempting as to render it with many a confirmed habit.

The reports frequently refer to the indifference to chastity, attributing it to the wretched sleeping-places so often the lot of labouring families. 'The rage for beer' is described as such that if a man gets an extra shilling it goes in drink, while mop fairs, club festivals, and harvest homes are usually scenes of intoxication. What with the overwhelming force of a propensity, the result of a habit of many generations, due largely to wretched cottages and the abominable little beer-shops which are spread like devil-traps over the countryside, the labourer has no chance. 'If the Queen means to do any good to us,' said a poor wife to Mr Culley, 'she had best begin by putting down *them alehouses; they makes gentlefolks' fortunes,* they do; look at this, captain; and they won't put them down, but the Queen might, or, leastways, shorten their hours. It's Saturday night till twelve o'clock, and they ain't well out o'church on Sundays till they're in again. Them alehouses is our curse, they are.'

Human nature gets used to the circumstances around it, and nothing at last becomes so painful as a change. Thus the labourer

gets used to his wretched cot, and dislikes the change involved in his removal to a better one. A great landlord complained that he had given a very good cottage to a labourer, and found it was not appreciated at all. The tenant put his apples in one room, did not inhabit another, and would put his pig into another, if allowed to do so. Another landlord said: 'If you built a palace, and furnish it to match, you would scarcely induce the people to leave these places into which you would hardly put a pig to live.' Could any sadder proof be given of the moral depression into which the men have fallen on whose labours these great landlords live than this clinging to wretchedness, this habit of living in misery?

'In the eye of the moralist,' says Dr Fraser, 'the most malign aspect of poverty is in its power to generate the loss of natural affection. Poverty is emphatically hardening – at any rate, in its influence on the natural man.' In Cambridgeshire the children go to work as young as six years old; many at seven or eight. The reason appears to be in many cases that the parents compel the ganger to take the little one on condition of getting regularly the labour of the bigger child of the same family. But what is to be expected of people who see their families suffering under such wretched physical evils, and are themselves depressed and disheartened by them? 'For,' says the report:

> . . . the formidable difficulty of all is not the apathy of their parents, but *their poverty*. It is impossible for men with large families to look beyond the present hour. To be warmed and filled is to them the one great object in life, and to talk to them about improving the minds of their children, while they are unable to provide those things which are needful for their bodies, must seem to them like mocking.

Can a mother forget her suckling child? Think of the Lincolnshire babies, drugged by their mothers with opium; of poor Betsey B — who did not remember how many babies she had had. Think of mothers driving their poor little weeping children out to work before it is light, threatening to beat them if they do

not go. Think of the fathers sitting all day outside beer-shops, like lazy hogs basking in the sun, while their children break their backs to supply the means of parental dissipation. 'Without natural affection.' This is a result of a wretched home. And what can come of such a home? The poor girls often add shame to their wretchedness. In Norfolk one child out of every ten is illegitimate. The boys grow up to be young ruffians, who care for nobody. If they are wild, they will turn poachers, and perhaps get hanged for killing a gamekeeper, or they will be picked up by the recruiting sergeant; or if they are steady, they will continue to tread the same weary round as their father, and, unless these things be not speedily altered, perpetuate this misery to future generations.

These reports do not give any direct statement as to the religious condition of the agricultural poor, but we note that the greater part of the information is obtained through clergymen, and that its tone is, as a rule, depressing, carrying the conviction that religion is at a very low ebb indeed in our rural districts. The conclusion to which an Oxfordshire clergyman has come may fairly be accepted as descriptive of the condition of things throughout the country:

> I am satisfied, from observations which I have made during a period of thirty-five years passed in the ministry of the Church, that before our teaching and preaching can have the effect we look for, we must house the labourer in a better manner.

Devonshire cottages look quite idyllic, standing among the gardens and orchards of that picturesque county, but the report describes them as being, except upon the estates of a few landowners, in a deplorable condition. In one place they are spoken of as 'wretched', in another as 'ruinous hovels', in a third as 'damp, dark, unhealthy holes'. Usually the walls are made of 'cob', a concrete formed of mud, straw, and pebbles. The roofs are of thatch, but too often open and out of repair. The usual form is a kitchen and back room, with two bedrooms above; small cots of only a kitchen and a bedroom are comparatively rare. The

interior of these cots is cheerless enough. Enter one, and it will be found dark and dingy for want of light – no bright coal fire, but a grate with a solid front, into which are dropped the roots that have been grubbed up for fuel. The floors are of concrete, or paved with slate, occasionally nothing but earth, and at times very rough. Mount the stairs to the low-pitched bedroom, and you may sometimes find such holes in the floor that your legs are in danger of slipping into the chamber below. According to Dr Hunter, the people say they feel oppressed and heartless about furnishing their rooms or keeping them tidy. Sometimes they only use two of the rooms; of the rest, one will be turned into an ash-bin, the other into a store-room for potatoes, or into a general receptacle for rubbish. An occasional show of crockery suggests that, under happier circumstances, the Devonian labourers could make themselves bright and cheerful homes.

One secret of their depression is the empty larder. They rarely get butcher's meat, but eat coarse, brown bread, washed down by too much rough, sour cider. If moderately well off, their usual diet is bread in milk and water for breakfast, bread and cheese for luncheon and dinner, and potatoes and bacon for supper. Everywhere there is depression and hopelessness, owing partly perhaps to the damp, humid climate, partly to a decay of the prosperity which once distinguished the western counties, but mainly to the fact that they are miserably housed and under-fed.

Women work to some extent in the fields, but no one will allow that it has a demoralising influence. The men receive three pints of cider a day as part of their wages, a custom which adds to their depression by leading them to drink apart from their wives and families. Immorality is directly traced to the conditions of cottage life. Little value is set on education, and unless the Vicar pays the penny, the parents will frequently plead poverty or any other excuse to keep the children from school. In one district – probably a sample of others – the boys are described as a rough, coarse lot. 'There is a marked class of lads,' says the clergyman writing:

> . . . from the ages of fourteen to twenty and twenty-four, who are most difficult to handle, shifty in their work, ignorant. Very few

can read or write, and they are utterly regardless of authority. 'Juvenile rowdyism' is on the increase, and is a marked and bad feature in our present social position, full, to my mind, of future evil.

In the annual report for 1868 of the South Devon Congregational Union, a missionary, whose work lies about Dartmoor, gives the following instance of belief in witchcraft, as significant of the condition of the people:

A poor man suffering from an internal complaint had been sent to the Torquay Infirmary. His disease completely baffled the skill of the medical men there, and also of others whom he had consulted. But this occasioned him no surprise. He was quite satisfied that he had been 'ill-wished', and all efforts to shake this conviction were fruitless. In conversation one day he said, 'he was better, and able to do a little work again.' I asked him how it came about, and the following was his account of the matter: 'I knew all along it was not God's affliction, and now I have proved it was not. A man came to me and said, "I think you are bewitched, and I will tell you what to do. Take a lump of salt, and put it into the fire at twelve o'clock at night, and if it gets hard you are ill-wished." Well, I did so, and sure enough it did get hard, and then I knew what was up. After that I got some pins, and threw them into the fire, and while I was burning them there was a such a noise on the outside of my door that I was frightened. I did this for three nights, and after that a woman near me was taken ill, and I got better, and since then my wife has been cured in the same way – and after that you mustn't tell me there is no such thing as ill-wishing.'

To pass on to Dorset. There the cottages have long been 'a bye-word and a reproach.' Much has been done, and still they remain more ruinous and contain worse accommodation than in any county the commissioners visited, except Shropshire. Several villages mentioned and described in the evidence are said to

contain many cottages unfit for habitation. 'I saw', the commissioner says, 'whole rows of cottages abounding with nuisances of all kinds. Remonstrance is generally disregarded, and the state of filth in which many parishes are left calls aloud for active interference.'

The Dorset cottage is usually built of mud, with a thatched roof. Many have only one bedroom; three is a luxury to which few can lay claim. Enter one: a more dreary place it would be difficult to imagine. There is no grate, but a huge open chimney, with a few bricks upon the hearth, on which the miserable inhabitants place their fuel – sometimes nothing but clods of peat, emitting wretched acrid vapours. Owing to the low open chimney, the house is constantly filled with smoke, rendering the ceilings, where they have them, black and dingy enough. Dr Aldridge stated at a meeting of the Farmers' Club at Dorchester, in January 1867, that:

> . . . the cottages at Fordlington were so bad that he ventured to say that they would not put their animals in such places, and yet they were occupied by families of five or six individuals. In many of these cottages one could not stand upright, and the smoke, dirt, and filth together made a state of things not to be equalled in St Giles's.

Around these wretched hearths the poor family crowd on a winter's night, stretching out their hands and feet to gather what warmth they may. But some are so poverty-stricken that they can only afford to light a fire at meal-times; often their wet clothes can never be dried, but are put on damp again the next morning; for fuel is very expensive. One woman stated that it cost them £2 in the winter for firewood. Here is a case mentioned in the *Labour Circular,* Feb.1868:

> E.,10s per week; wife and six children. Son, 3s 6d per week; total income, 13s 6d; no grist or allowance; rent, 1s 6d, leaving only 12s a week to support and clothe eight persons, a little more than 2½d *a day* for each member of the family.

No wonder there is a 'want of labour pluck' in such people, a deadening of mental and physical force. No wonder that such

circumstances send the father to the public-house; no wonder that the mother, disheartened at the difficulty of keeping her smoky, dilapidated house decent and clean, gives up the task in despair.

Frequently, however, the home does not get the benefit of her presence, the custom prevailing in Dorsetshire of hiring a whole family. Thus the wife goes to work as well as the husband, and takes her place in the barn, or in the field, or beside the threshing-machine. The poor little ones are locked up all day, or left under the care of some young girl of seven or eight years of age, who has enough to do to mind the baby; and, when the mother comes home, smashed crockery and sullen tempers have been the result of the family left without proper guardianship or control.

But they are so poor that every member of the family must earn a crust as soon as he can. Boys of seven or eight go out to work – nay, sometimes they begin as early as six. Their poverty, again, and the unconscionable way the farmers have of paying their wages fortnightly, or even monthly, causes them to run into debt with their masters or the tally-men, destroying every atom of independence, or power of improving their condition.

One advantage they have – larger allotments than in any other part of the kingdom, and to most cottages ample gardens are attached. And here, if they had the energy, they could add considerably to their domestic comfort. If every penny was not of immediate consequence to them, they could cultivate these plots of ground to great advantage . . .

To conclude, however, with a brighter picture, one that will show that there is nothing in agricultural labour of itself to depress a man, or to prevent his realising domestic happiness.

The Northumbrian peasantry are described as stalwart, vigorous, and healthy, independent yet courteous, provident and sober, with a profound belief in the advantages of education, and considerable religious principle. They enjoy good wages, and frequently rise to the position of stewards. Enter one of their cots. It is often but one apartment, lit up by a single window, with

nothing but a concrete floor, and some are unceiled, or only have a partially ceiled roof. In one corner stands a large bedstead, the family heirloom, completely shrouded by white dimity; while a box-bed, closed in the daytime, is the children's resting-place at night. The stores of bacon overhead, the butter, and cheese, and meal in the half-open cupboard, the variety and whiteness of the bread and cakes on the table, attest the truth of the good wife's assertion when, with simple pride, she assures her visitor 'that they are not poor.'

The mahogany furniture, bright with hand-polish, the display of crockery and ornaments, the easy comfort of every arrangement, seen in the dancing light of a brilliant coal-fire, all tell of good housewifery and ample incomes. Every fire-place, too, has its set-pot and oven, both being in constant requisition, for they have plenty of meat. Yet the good wife will tell you that they had a 'sair' fight for it before the children earned anything, for, if there was a point on which they were determined, it was that the bairns should not go to work unless they spent at least the autumn and the winter in getting a little schooling. Surprising indeed are the facts related, showing the belief both parents and children entertain of the value of instruction. Shepherds club together to hire a perambulating schoolmaster, and they have their children taught Latin, and sometimes French and Euclid. In one district it is stated that there is not a person who cannot read and write.

On a winter's evening the family circle gather round the cheerful fire, the women knitting, the father mending shoes – an art nearly all acquire – while one of the younger ones reads for the benefit of the whole group.

Notwithstanding such a high degree of domestic happiness as these facts suggest, the report speaks strongly concerning the miserable accommodation many of the Northumbrian cottages afford. Formerly they were mere sheds, without window frames, partitions, grates, or ceiling; the unfortunate tenant had to bring all these things with him, so that if the weather was wet he frequently found a great puddle on the earthen floor.

Even yet there are cots to which this description exactly applies,

and the miseries the inhabitants have to undergo, especially with their taste for the comfortable, must be great. Under any circumstances it must be extremely 'confusing', as one woman mildly put it, to have to perform all the operations of bedroom, parlour, and kitchen in one apartment, and quite distressing when any member of the family is sick.

The 'bondager' system peculiar to Northumberland, by which every farm labourer is bound to provide a woman whose labour shall be at the disposal of the master whenever he may require it, and whom the labourer is therefore obliged to have lodging in his house, does not conduce to domestic comfort. So favourable, however, are his other conditions, and such is the superiority of his character, that these two circumstances – a miserable cottage with only one room, and a stranger lodging with him – do not prevent the Northumbrian peasant possessing a decent, happy home.

No doubt something is due to the fact that he comes of a race which has dwelt for generations on the battle-field of English history, developing a power of struggling with and conquering difficulties. Something also may be attributed to the climate. The average mortality in the Glendale Union, one of the largest agricultural districts in Northumberland, from the year 1851 to 1860, was only fifteen per thousand, whereas the general average of Great Britain is twenty-two per thousand. And again, to the favourable conditions of his service, he being hired by the year, and *paid alike in wet weather or dry, in sickness and in health.* And perhaps more than to any of these causes, though they all work together to the same end, he owes his comparatively happy position to his superior education.

Thus the great exception of the Northumbrian peasant destroys the theory that evils attending the lot of the English labourer are mainly due to his miserable, unhealthy cottage. His material wants are signs rather than causes of the evil that besets and ruins his life. That evil must be sought in a circumstance with which these reports do not deal, a condition into which they make no inquiry. Yet, after all, nothing is so important to men as their religious environment.

The Northumbrian peasant is largely influenced by a form of Christianity that not only recognises that he is a man, but that, without ceasing to be a labouring man, tending sheep, or following the plough, he can be chosen, and is chosen, if found worthy, an elder of the Church. The labourers in most other parts of England have been regarded as a helot race, born to be hewers of wood and drawers of water – brothers and friends in much the same sense that horses and dogs are brothers and friends. That this is no unfair view of the lordly way English gentlemen have of looking at the labouring classes is amusingly illustrated in these very reports, one of the Chief Commissioners giving it as his opinion that the cause of the happy position of the Northumbrian labourer compared with the southern labourer is 'that he is better educated, and hence is both mentally and physically *a superior animal*.' The writer of these pages is no denominationalist, but so far as he has personal tastes and sympathies, they are not with Presbyterian forms, but with the liturgy of the Church of England. All the more he is bound to point out the superior educative power of the Presbyterian to the Church of England system, as seen in the higher form of the manhood and womanhood of the people under its control.

The reason is clear – the one is a democratic religion, the other the most aristocratic in the world. It is this characteristic of the Church of England which is mainly responsible for the degraded condition of the English rural poor.

THE KENTISH
WAGGONER

(GOLDEN HOURS, 1872)

Each county or district seems to afford to the student of agricultural life in England a different problem. Here in Kent we have the labourer and his family all earning high wages; from one end of the year to the other there is plenty of work for husband, wife, and children; they are rich, as farm labourers go; and yet, when the time of trial comes, they are no better off than their brethren in less favoured parts of the land. When they are sick they go to the parish, when they are old they come to the workhouse.

The solution of the problem is not far to seek. The Kentish agricultural labourer shares a delusion common enough in every class of society, that there is some wonderful talismanic power in the mere possession of the coin of the realm, which will bring a man all he really needs . . .

'Enlighten', said a Kentish farmer, 'a labourer *reasonably,* but don't let it be only book-learning. A boy that is going to be a clerk is learning how to live when he is at school, but one that is to be a farm labourer is learning what is a luxury to him. It all depends upon a boy's growth when he is able to do work. A little chap of eight, or even less, may be useful.'

In this the labourer and his master will be found of one mind. He is not unwilling to send his children to school if you can only show him that they can earn more money by it. But if his boy can get a day's work rook-scaring, the few pence he thus earns far out-weighs all the problematical advantages of a day's schooling.

It is this contempt for learning, unless it can be rapidly turned

into money, which causes the agricultural labourer in Kent, notwithstanding good wages and plenty of work, to remain at the same dead level as his less prosperous countrymen. The people here, as elsewhere, are destroyed for lack of knowledge.

If we trace the life of one of these Kentish labourers, we shall see how thoroughly his material interests and those of his family are sacrificed. . . . Let us take as a type one of the better class, a waggoner, a man, we will suppose, with every advantage in character, health and regular employment.

Commencing life by a moderately regular attendance at the national school up to seven or eight, he is, as we have seen, soon made useful as a little scarecrow. After he has been employed in odd jobs off and on for a year or two, he is entrusted with an old gun or a pistol, with which he amuses himself popping at the birds. From November till May, Sundays included, he follows this monotonous employment, unless perchance his father should volunteer to do duty for him that he may go to the Sunday School. What a vacuity of mind must result from standing about day after day in the same fields, surrounded by the same objects – objects, too, concerning which the poor lad knows nothing save their outward shapes; and such wearisome, protracted labour undergone at this tender age stunts the body as well as the mind.

If, however, he is a waggoner's son, he will soon get more congenial employment as a 'mate.' For a waggoner's son is carter-bred, and as used to horses as his brothers and sisters. The atmosphere of his home is redolent of the stable. The horses are the one object of thought, of talk, and of interest to father, mother, and children. Speak to a waggoner about his team, and you have won his heart; ask the poor worn-out mother about her husband's horses, and her face will brighten up, and in the midst of her cares and hard work, she will find time to dilate on the merits of Captain, of Violet, or of Jerry. Visit them when the day's work is over, and the whole family are gathered round the hearth, and the never-failing topic of conversation will be the horses.

As a babe the first words he lisps are the names of the horses.

A young labourer, Dartford, Kent, 1862. The smock was standard working clothing for the farm worker, the tankard was probably a studio prop, but the hat has an incongruous air. Perhaps the photographer's own hat had been appropriated by the youngster for the occasion.

Munby Collection, Trinity College, Cambridge.

Does he cry – he is taken to see 'Prince' or lifted up to pat 'Diamond'. He no sooner learns to walk than he finds the way to the stable, toddling with the rest of the family after 'dadda', as he spends hour after hour cleaning and baiting his charge. Thus, from earliest infancy, he is receiving a technical education; he hears of nothing, thinks of nothing, talks of nothing but of that one business by which he is to live; the stable becomes playroom and schoolroom combined; all his ideas centre in it and gather round it; and when in due course he becomes a mate, he displays at once an inborn and inbred faculty for managing horses.

And the life thus commenced continues with unvarying regularity to the end of the chapter. Once a mate he has to be up at five o'clock in the morning; his work is not over until ten at night, and during every hour of the day, except when he himself is eating, he is with the horses, either in the field or the stable.

Of course such hours are outrageously long, and would indeed be insupportable if it were not for the society of the horses. Efforts have been made to shorten a mate's daily work, and in one place it is reported that by an arrangement of staying longer one day, and coming later the next, the hours are *reduced* to twelve!

Moreover, under this system, all about the boy are as ignorant as himself. Whether he lodges with his father, or the waggoner with whom he works, it is about the same as far as his stock of ideas is concerned. From all parts of Kent, even from employers themselves, comes the same tale. One employer says:

> I have not a well-educated labourer, male or female. They may some of them be able to read after a fashion, but there is not one of them that writes well enough for a stranger, unused to them, to read off (what they have written) at first sight.

A lady who takes much interest in 'waggoners' mates' says:

> Many, if not all, have been to school, but have forgotten nearly all they learnt. They have generally lost all desire to improve themselves. I know seven men in one hamlet who cannot read.

A clergyman at East Church speaks of 'the heavy, overworked, weary young men, who scarcely know their alphabet.'

The only possible means of preserving the little knowledge they have is to be found in the evening school. But such a school rarely prospers in a purely agricultural district, simply because those for whom it is intended are too tired to come to it. After a long and perhaps wet day's work, it is not in human nature to quit the warm fireside and the family supper to goad the poor bedulled intellect into tiresome effort. Warmth, indeed, may sometimes attract a poor lad, who cannot get much of it at home. 'Let me sit by the fire, and I'll do a jolly good sum, and no mistake about it', said one such boy to a friend of mine, a teacher in a Kent night-school.

While these schools can never supply the place of regular and daily instruction, they may and do keep alive the desire for better things. My friend quoted above sometimes enlivens his lessons by reading a little tale, and finds those most acceptable which describe a higher state of society than that to which the boys are accustomed:

'I wish I was a gentleman', said one boy.
'What would you do?' he was asked.
'Sit in front of the fire and eat bulls-eyes', he replied.

There is another occupation which stands much in the way of the young waggoner becoming a very zealous attendant at the evening school. He may forget his letters, but he never forgets the art of love-making. He finds that he can soon earn what to him seems a good bit of money, and his thoughts naturally turn to settling in life as his fathers did before him. . . . With a certain prospect of getting a living as long as his health lasts – and he never has ache nor pain, he is scarcely likely to trouble himself much with this consideration – he does not wait to save enough to buy furniture or even clothes, but as soon as he has man's wages he takes his lass to church, and launches on the troubled sea of matrimony.

THE VICTORIAN PEASANT

Two rooms in a small row content him, and there is always some benevolent broker willing to supply the necessary furniture. Then as to clothes, his credit is good here also. Every one knows him, and that he is not likely to run away just as he has taken himself a wife. Our young waggoner is so ignorant that he cannot be expected to look beyond his nose in this or in any other particular unconnected with the management of horses. His duties to a possible posterity, or to society through them, are considerations quite beyond his 'tether'; all he knows is that he will be more comfortable. And who can blame him if the description given a few years ago of the domestic comfort he enjoyed when lodged on a farm still be true? An essay by the Rev. E. O. Hammond of Sundridge, addressed to the Sittingbourne Agricultural Association in 1856, thus describes his lodging:

> He returns home after a long day spent in the service of his master, generally fatigued, often wet since the morning. Here and there, but not generally, there is a fire accessible where he may restore his frozen circulation, and do something at least towards drying his wearing apparel. When a little comfortable, he may take a candle and amuse himself according to his taste. Ordinarily there is *no fire and no light* for the farm servant when the toil of the day is done. If there is a fire for his use he must light it himself, or if candles, he must either buy them or economise his stable allowance of five for two nights. Not infrequently he will sacrifice his supper to go straight to bed, on which, having first deposited his *boots* to prevent them from freezing, he ensconces his person between a pair of sheets that defy all the colours of the rainbow for a hue that will match them. The stench of the chamber is intolerable in many cases, and no wonder, under the occupation of stable and labour-stained men and clothes, the men varying in number from three or four to nine or ten in a room on very large farms, and sleeping in most cases two in a bed.

A Kent woman is no more accustomed to idleness than her husband; so, yoked together, they enter the mill, and commence to tread the weary round, hoping for nothing better than permission

67

Harvesting at the East Kent Hop Gardens, *c*. 1901.

to tread it to the end of their days. The good man has now to be up every day in the year between three and four o'clock in the morning. At six he comes home to breakfast, and not only must this be ready, but by eight all the work in the house done, for then the wife too must turn out and do her share of outdoor labour.

For in Kent, with its hop-gardens, its cherry-orchards, and its market-grounds, there is always plenty of work for a waggoner's wife all the year round. In the early part of the year there is pole-shaving, pole-butting, and dibbling beans. Then comes couching or weeding, thistle-spudding, hop-tying, and thinning the mangolds. With summer-time comes fruit-picking. Then Kent is seen in its glory. All the cherry-orchards are full of active, merry groups, some on ladders, some laden with baskets, all busy and hard at work. Then comes harvesting, followed quickly by the great work of the year, when every one – mother, sisters, brothers, and even the baby – all go out from morning till night into the hop-gardens, and pick as much as their fingers can. At last the circling seasons end with duller work – picking up potatoes, couching amongst the sown wheat, and pulling up mangolds and turnips.

Thus a Kentish wife is pretty well occupied, and she only stays away from the field when absolutely obliged to do so. For it is an understood thing that she and her children are to give their labour to the farmer whenever he needs it. Cottages, when they are on the master's land, are sometimes let subject to this arrangement, so that any objection on the part of the woman would lead to the eviction of the family. But they do not object. On the contrary, they seem rather to like it. 'I think', says one:

> . . . it is quite right. Women ought to go and do women's work, and help their husbands, and not stay at home. I have taken my daughters out at six years old, hop-tying. When I was eight years old I tied three acres myself. They would give me a dinner every day that I should keep up. I was very quick at it. Now I can't do so much but I and my daughters tied five acres this year. I go to ladder-tying too.

Only she did not think she was fairly paid. 'I go and do more than a man would, and yet they give a shilling instead of half a crown.'

Thus the money flows in from all sources, the family purse gets replenished, and should the father continue in good employ and have no serious illness they may be said to do moderately well.

The ordinary wages of a Kentish waggoner are about fourteen shillings a week. A correspondent of the *Field* newspaper, an agriculturalist in East Kent, in a letter which appeared in that paper this year (1872), says that in his locality, the Isle of Thanet, some farmers pay fifteen shillings a week, that he himself pays threepence an hour, and gives the average earnings of his men last year:-

	£	s	d
46 weeks at 15s or 3d an hour	34	10	0
1 week, hay-cutting	1	4	0
5 weeks' harvesting	9	0	0
	44	14	0

– which is nearly seventeen shillings a week all the year round for the father's earnings alone. In addition to this, the wife will earn from two shillings to half a crown a week, while the bigger children will be getting from three to seven shillings a week.

Food in an average family of half a dozen children will probably come to sixteen or seventeen shillings; for, working as they all do, from morning till night, it is necessary that they should live well. And this in fact is the great and beneficial result of the Kentish agricultural economy. Supper is the social meal of the day; and the honest waggoner, when he sits down after all the toils of the day, comes to it with an appetite as capacious as the omnivorous giant Jack of bean-stalk fame had the honour of dining with. He will commence with a large beefsteak pudding, and finish up with a basin full of bread and milk or several cups of tea. As to the boys who work, each one rivals his father, the bigger one perhaps outdoing him altogether. As a result the men are stalwart, the

women rubicund. There is a harmony in the appearance of both land and people. It is a well-nurtured land, and the people are a well-nurtured people.

But here it ends. Ignorance, notwithstanding high wages and good living, robs them of all the higher benefits they might obtain from their prosperous circumstances, and renders them as truly dependent as are the rest of their class.

The great drawback of their lives is their unceasing, protracted labour, the compulsion put on their wives to turn out into the fields, and the temptation offered to make use at the very earliest age of the money-making power in the children.

Had they knowledge, they would find out that a little combination among themselves would soon shorten the hours of labour without lessening the wages. So too they would see clearly that a wife's services at home are worth vastly more than she can earn abroad, especially if there is a young family. Had they knowledge, they would never dream of putting forth such an excuse for their negligence as this: – I can't read, and yet I can earn my living; my father couldn't read and yet he could earn his living: what good will book-learning do my son? Why, as Farmer Jones says, 'It will spoil him and make a fool of him.'

This ignorance not only works to oppress the poor waggoner, but also to oppress the ratepayers. If a man was well-educated, if he had read a few books that had nothing whatever to do with his daily toil, he would feel it a disgrace and degradation to ask for charity when he had the whole world open before him in which to earn a living. Such a man must utterly break down under the combined influence of sickness and poverty before he could ever descend to apply for parish relief.

But the Kentish labourer has been educated under the 'mind your own business' system, and knows of only two alternatives – to work in his native fields, or live at the expense of his native parish. The agricultural worker's position is an anomaly in the nineteenth century; it is a relic of feudalism *minus* all its advantages. He has been taught that his own position is that of the serf who tills the land; to want more education will only unfit him for

Workhouse inmates, photographs from *Country Life*, 28 October 1911. The sexes were segregated at the workhouse; even married couples were parted, irrespective of the circumstances.

Country Life Library.

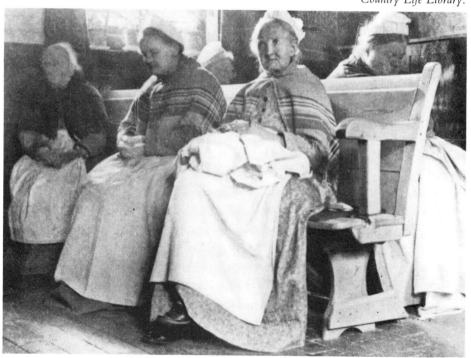

his post. 'I am content,' he argues; 'I will do my duty to the land, but when I can't work then the land must do its duty to me.'

He has not risen out of serfdom, and the doctrine that he is to learn nothing but what will fit him to follow the plough will keep him there for ever. If so, we may expect an ever-increasing pauperism. Even now parish relief is his anchor of refuge. The club is convenient in its way, but would never maintain itself if it were not held at the 'Red Lion', and brought weekly visions of foaming pewter pots, and long clay pipes, and roaring songs, and loud thumping of delighted hob-nails. But he knows it has an ugly habit of casting off the older members, so he does not trust it, but drifts on to his last refuge, the Union workhouse.

Here he comes at last, his fine physique shattered by rheumatism, his hair silvered, his cheek still ruddy as a russet apple; but power of work nearly gone, he is glad to break a few stones on the road, or, when feebler still, to do odd jobs in the Union grounds, and to crawl about in the warm summer sun. . . . His 'old woman', sent to dwell in a different part of the house, soon breaks up; while the Union is so far from his home, that his children come rarely to see him, and gradually forget their aged father, until one day they receive a summons to remove his body Then they go, and with some lamentations and some slight twinges of conscience, bring the old waggoner back again to the spot which gave him birth and bury him . . .

SURREY
COMMONS

(GOLDEN HOURS, 1872)

Very few, even of those who dwell in Surrey, have any adequate idea of the number and extent of its commons . . . (Yet) one could easily count on the inch-to-a-mile ordnance map more than a hundred commons or heaths having distinct names. Indeed, the western part of the county is a series of commons. . . . This sort of land may, in fact, be said to be the characteristic feature of Surrey . . .

(Today) the only persons to whom the common is of use are the poor cottagers, who dwell upon it, and who can turn out a cow or a few sheep, some geese or ducks, and watch their property all day long with their own eyes. It is these people who appear to be, and, as a matter of fact are, the real commoners now; although, when the question comes to be legally dealt with, and an enclosure takes place, they are as completely put out of court as any stranger would be. For few of them can produce, as one boasted to me she could, 'papers', proving their title to the holding. In the majority of cases they were originally squatters with about as much 'legal' right to the land as the gipsy who settles for the night on a village green. It was a notion held among the peasantry in olden times, that he who could in one night erect a 'Mushroom Hall' or a 'now-or-never', without hindrance from the officials of the manor, had obtained a copyhold right to the land. Thus frequently it happened that labourers, and sometimes travelling tinkers, or basket-makers, would set up a few hurdles in a night and enclose a piece of land. If no interference ensued, a wall soon took the place

of the hurdles, ere long it was roofed in, and thus arose many of those wretched little hovels, in which it is grievous to think any English family should be reared . . .

The sort of building put up on these encroachments was about equal to an ordinary tool-house in a gentleman's garden. One I saw and sketched on Epsom common contained two apartments, and I was informed by the man residing there that the old lady to whom it belonged brought up twelve children in it. He himself lived there with eight children. His case was an illustration of the numerous accidents to which the agricultural labourer is liable. Twelve years ago he had had his foot crushed in a wheel-rut, rheumatism had seized the leg, and had at last taken possession of his whole body, so that he had never been able to do a day's work since. His wife set to work bravely, sometimes leaving home at five in the morning to stand at the wash-tub all day. The baby, five months old, had already become so resigned to its hard life, as to be willing to go to bed and to sleep when it grew dark without a whimper. The father said he could not read or write, but he sent all his children to school, for he 'knew the miss of it', and he told me with a glow of pride that the schoolmistress said that the little bright, intelligent girl by his side was the best scholar she had.

The house he said had 'common rights', and possibly it had, as it was evidently an old one, and might from its mere continuance for sixty years have itself become a freehold, and turned the privileges it had taken into legal rights. On this common, through the kindness of the late lord of the manor, every poor cottager had permission to turn out ten sheep; while upon another I found the lord doing all he could to encourage the people to keep cows, but it did not appear that in either case many avail themselves of the opportunity. There are no doubt some cases where from exceptional causes the people make good use of their common, but as a rule the majority are too poor to take advantage of their situation. A cow or a sheep implies food and housing in winter, and they have neither the means to purchase the one nor the convenience for the other.

Perhaps the most general use made of the commons is to cut the

fern, to make litter for the pigs, and to get firing for the house. In some places coal has superseded the necessity for seeking much of the latter, but in the more remote parts wood and turf is the only fuel known. With fires made from them cottagers still smoke the bacon which they hang up their chimneys. In seasons when fruit is scarce, the blackberries and other wild fruit found on these commons afford quite a little addition to their year's income.

Fowls are not much kept. They, too, cannot live solely on the land, and are a constant source of ill-will where there are neighbours. Geese and donkeys are characteristic features of every Surrey common. Notwithstanding the objection to the former, they are found everywhere. Not that they are always the property of the cottagers; in some cases they only watch them for others. Bees are much kept in some parts, and produce fragrant honey, feeding as they do on the wild thyme and marjoram, and the purple-blossomed heather.

Since the Inclosure Act has been passed, a clearer idea has obtained of the legal aspect of the question, and accordingly on some commons the freeholders have succeeded in entirely stopping the cottagers from exercising any privileges whatever. On other commons, where the cottagers are numerous, it would be impossible to do so without force. I know of one common where few of the persons who use it could probably prove their legal right to do so. As the common-driver told me, he could rise up any morning and drive off all the cattle and sheep on it, but he is not likely to attempt it. This common adjoins another belonging to a different manor, and yet the sheep of people living in one wander at their own sweet will over the boggy slopes of the other.

In the middle of the latter common I found a poor woman, living in a very comfortable cottage. Her husband was a labourer, and they had brought up a numerous family on 2s a-day, but it did not appear that they had ever thought of making any use of the common. And yet she told me of one man who had about 200 sheep which he turned out every day. Of course he had no right, or at least no right to pasture for one-tenth part of the number . . .

The fact is, the majority of the lords of the manors do not care

to stop these encroachments. They know they can make no use of the commons themselves, and they have no wish to play the part of the dog in the manger.

And this leads me to speak of those for whose advantage these extensive wastes really exist.

There is a class of self-willed, determined, acquisitive sort of men, to the production of which common life is especially favourable, because it gives freedom from all restraint; permits the development of peculiarities without hindrance, and in the doubt which hangs over the character and extent of its rights, gives a stimulus to such natures to get all they can. These are the people who make a living out of the commons.

I got into company with such a man on a walk I made to a common in the north-west of the county. . . . At last I heard a cart coming along, and, begging a lift, found myself seated beside a little jolly, apple-cheeked man, who was carrying bread from a neighbouring town to the very common to which I was bound. He had commenced work as an agricultural labourer at eight years of age, and had, since he had been a man, worked at 14s a week. Now, however, he lived on the common, and sold beer and grocery. As we passed along he remarked that, had he known what he did now, he would have had a bit of land.

'How?'

'Built on it,' he replied, 'asked no one.'

'Couldn't the waste not yet enclosed be turned to account?'

'Not for wheat, but,' quoth he, 'if I were the parish of C — I know what I'd do with it. I'd enclose it, and take all these 'ere paupers, that are doing nothing, and make 'em plant trees upon it, and then work in tending 'em.'

He was evidently well-to-do, and spoke with a sort of contemptuous pity of those who inhabited the miserable cots we saw huddled together in little groups on various parts of the common . . .

Upon another common I met with a still more singular character. Over the door of a cottage, standing in a large garden on the side of a common, was this sign-board:

THE VICTORIAN PEASANT

Worm Doctor.
Professor of Medical Botany
Herb Medicines prepared for every complaint.
Advice Gratis

The owner thereof was a shrewd, taciturn old man, of the American rather than the English type. He had been a soldier, and had stood guard over Napoleon in St Helena, and was there till the captive emperor died, leaving the island on the day of the funeral. He told me some interesting facts about Bonaparte, but I was more anxious to talk to him about the art he practised.

How he came to be a herbalist was on this wise. When a boy he had suffered so from chilblains in the winter that his hands were of no use to him. One day he saw a herb in the hedge, and wished to pluck it, but his father told him it would 'pisin' him. Genius, however, was not to be restrained, so he gathered it, rubbed his blains with the berries, and to his joy they departed, never to trouble him again.

Ever since that time he had been a believer in the wonderful potency of herbs, and had scraped together such knowledge as a shrewd man, who had lived in various countries, must have many opportunities of acquiring. His garden was full of marvellous herbs and ordinary kitchen stuff, growing together in happy confusion. Pointing to one, he told me it was worth its weight in gold. Speaking of what disease each herb was good for, he assured me that he had cured one young man of the King's evil, but it had taken him months to do it.

The house he lived in was the inheritance of his wife, and whether by worm-doctoring, or by his native *savoir faire*, I cannot say, but the old stocking was so full that he was about to purchase the adjoining plot of ground for £300.

Such characters, perhaps, serve to maintain a spirit of independence and self-reliance among the class to whom they belong. 'I'm a Hindependent', said one of them to me; and it was true in every sense. He was evidently a man of independent means and independent views. He declared himself an independent in religion, and he was equally so in manners.

79

But it does not follow that because a few hardy natures flourish on these wastes, the majority can do so. We have seen that where the strict letter of the law is understood and enforced, they can be deprived of their imagined rights, and that when they are permitted and even encouraged to make use of them, their poverty prevents them doing so.

To all, however, there surely remains one great advantage – the situation. To live on the edge of a breezy common, where the children can scamper about all the livelong day, would seem to many a parent, compelled to bring up his family in the close street of a city, an advantage impossible to over-estimate . . .

One evening this summer I was passing over a common not twenty miles from London. It was a wild spot, broken up by pools of water, and skirted by tall trees, amongst which the little cots hid themselves. The great red sun was sinking over the woods which crowned the western height. As every sight was beautiful, so every sound was pleasant. The tinkle of the sheep-bell, the soft 'baa' of the lambs, the merry voices of the boys playing at cricket in one corner, the sudden blow of the ball, all was suggestive of rural poetry.

But look a little longer. Try to cross the common, and dry as the weather is, you will find your feet continually sinking into the mud. Look at those pools; they are black and stagnant, and emit a smell like the vilest sewer. Pass along the skirts of the common where these miserable little cottages stand, and you will find a Styx-like ditch, widening in one part into a filthy pond. Around this pond the children are playing, and upon one of the planks which cross this rivulet of death sits a mother and babe, while, stretched along another, sprawling flat upon his stomach lies, a father.

I asked a man if the place was healthy.

'Oh, dear no,' he replied; 'we've had the scarlet-fever bad enough, eight or nine died. My son lost his only child, a sweet, engaging little thing; it's near broke the mother's heart.'

Well might the poor fellow ask me for a bit of 'bacca', the only disinfectant the unhappy people knew of. He said they had no

drainage, but spoke of the cottage we were looking at as having a great pool behind, where they threw their chamber stuff, and all their slops, and only emptied it as the garden wanted manure.

But while evils of this kind are more or less local, there are moral disadvantages incident to the very nature of all common life . . .

Nothing brutalises human beings so rapidly as withdrawal from the influences of society; and when the morality of a common is said to be comparatively good, as I am told in some cases it is, I think it will be found that the cottagers to whom the statement refers live in small villages, not in isolated dwellings. When this is the case, a standard of morality is maintained among them, according to the ideal of those who, from position or character, are their guides and leaders.

But, as a rule, life on a common *is* an isolated one. And when this is the case, to quote the testimony of a clergyman living in the neighbourhood of the extensive commons in the south-west of Surrey, 'people who live at a distance from the villages always fall away in morality.' A minister who has laboured for the last ten years on very extensive commons in the centre of Surrey speaks of their morality and religion as being in the lowest state. The young people of both sexes are very corrupt – little virtue, in fact, is to be found anywhere; much drunkenness prevails, and a disposition to live without regular employment. The corruption of the young is mainly due to want of regular employment and gross ignorance. They often do not go to school at all, but spend their time wandering over the common gathering wood, or wild fruit.

In such places they are, practically, of the same religion as their forefathers, 'the *heathens*'. The dark superstitions which once held sway over every part of rural England still haunt these wild wastes. The people yet believe in witchcraft, and think that the person bewitched has the right and the power to kill the witch by certain enchantments. My friend assures me that such opinions not only prevail, but that he has known them acted upon in several cottages . . .

SUSSEX
SHEPHERDS

(GOLDEN HOURS, 1871)

(The) South Down villages are amongst the quietest spots in the world. You see a cluster of lowly habitations built of flints or boulders, with little gardens stocked with roses and wallflowers. The cottages are mostly thatched, and look wonderfully cosy. Then amongst the tall elms or ashes – and they are tall in these sheltered spots, mighty giants – stands the old farmhouse, an ancient, high-roofed, gable-pointed building, surrounded by barns and stables and haystacks, with circular pigeon-house, all suggestive of a quiet patriarchal life . . .

What curious people live in these out-of-the-way places! Wandering through a village . . . I came on a farm in ruins. The last time I walked to this place it was at this spot I had talked with an old man, an ancient worthy who had fallen in every way into the sere and yellow leaf. He had evidently gone, for his house had fallen into sad decay. The broken windows, the wilderness garden, the barns unthatched, the rafters naked, seemed to suggest some melancholy tale. Perhaps his heirs had quarrelled, perhaps he was the last of his race, and there was no one to care for his honour or his house.

Stepping across a stone stile, I lifted the latch, and found myself in a kitchen with a large old-fashioned hearth, and I looked up at the sky through its chimney, blackened with smoking many a side of fat bacon. In one corner were some rickety stairs, up which I crept into a small, low-pitched bedroom. I opened the back door, and looked upon what was once a little fruit-garden. Through

another I found the dining-room, and then up the front staircase into bedrooms, sad and dreary and tenantless.

I descended, and opened an outer door, expecting the same desolation, when I found a room, bright and cheerful, paved with red bricks, clean as the cleanest floor. All around seemed tidy and furnished. An old man, with a face like a russet apple, sitting cosily by a little fire, did not seem at all surprised at the intrusion; so begging his pardon, I turned it off by asking him to whom the ruined house belonged. Laughing at the idea of its being in Chancery, he told me that it was the property of an old lady who had too much money, and therefore chose to allow her houses to go to rack and ruin rather than let them.

The cheery little man hobbled off his chair, and came and stood at the door. Amongst other things he told me that an able-bodied man in these parts could earn thirteen shillings a week, a carter or a ploughman fourteen shillings, with his rent free into the bargain. On this he thought they might do well if they did not visit the public-house. Said he, 'My wife and me, we scratches together about eight shillings a week, and we do pretty comfortable.' Then he made a little money by selling manure, which he collected off the roads, and for which he got three shillings a cart-load. But he had children doing well, and perhaps they helped a bit. One son had been on a man-of-war five-and-twenty years, and now had a pension of twelve shillings a week; another daughter was married to a pensioner who kept a beer-shop, and was doing a good trade; so that if it was not for the 'rheumatics', the old man would have been quite happy, and contented with his lot.

I asked him about the church, which was very picturesque, and evidently well cared for in every detail. He said, 'Our parson do love the church, he do.' Thinking this suggested ritualism, I asked him if the rector was a High Churchman. 'Oh, dear no,' he replied, 'he be very *low*; you can't hear him at all unless maybe you sit close by.'

Pass through one of these villages on a summer's afternoon, and 'all around is silence'; but return at evening, and at each cottage door groups are standing, while on every road one meets the

labourer homeward bound. But Saturday is the evening to see the village wide awake; then all the world is out. It was on one such evening I was returning from Angmering across the meadows, when I passed an old man, blear-eyed, and clad in blue smock. He was seventy-five years of age. Early in life he wished to emigrate; but his father would not let him, lest people should say that he had wanted to get rid of him. He worked as a hedger in winter, at half-a-crown a day; and in summer by the piece, at odd jobs, making about the same. Sometimes he made only four days' work. He did not think much of benefit clubs, because the parish took advantage of them to lessen a man's allowance when he was sick. He greatly objected to steam ploughs and mowing machines, because they lessened men's work. We passed a field where the clover was all tossed about by the rain, and the old man said, 'Perhaps it's my poor foolish way, but I think the Supreme Being has done this for the benefit of poor men.' Railways it was a mistake to suppose took up much of the country; it was gentlemen's estates, where they enclosed the best land, and planted it with shrubs, that he disliked to see. 'Vanity pleasures', the old labourer called them.

On Saturday night in a village inn be warned, ye pedestrians, especially if it be haymaking or harvesting. It was not Saturday night when I tried to sleep at the inn at Findon; but it was the haymaking season. Hour after hour passed away in songs, always followed by the delighted thumping of hob-nailed boots. As the small hours drew nigh, the riot seemed to grow worse . . .

Higher and higher I mount over the soft green sward, until I reach my goal – Chanctonbury Ring. As I wandered round its base a panorama such as one sees nowhere else lay spread out before my eyes. Here, like a living map, the verdant weald, intersected by a thousand hedgerows, stretched for many a mile, dotted with leafy parks and dark umbrageous woodlands: while from among the trees peep the towns and villages, each nestling around its ancient church, the whole scene closed in by the forest ridge which rises far off, crowned with dark fir copses.

In the centre of the ring is an open space, soft with *débris* of a

hundred autumns. The giant elms stretch out their long arms and shade it from the sun; while those around send up their branches heavenwards. On one side is a wood of pines, through which the wind moans mournful as the roar of the waves on the sea-shore.

Beneath their shadow was an old shepherd tending his flock. He was an old man – seventy-five years of age, he said; but he looked much younger. His hair was only partially grey, and his honest face might have been quite handsome, had it not been for a rather Hebrew nose which the winds of sixty years had coloured into a bright red. He was a man of character, and spoke in a strong, decided manner, but with no roughness . . .

But when I tried to learn something about the way a shepherd was paid he would give me no direct answer. Perhaps he thought it beneath his self-respect to do so; or maybe it was his Sussex breeding, so that he naturally fenced with any question which he deemed important.

In former times the shepherd had an interest in the flock. Shepherds kept their own sheep amongst those of their masters. . . . Many, too, had their own little bits of land. 'Shepherds' Acres' is still the name attached to some pieces of ground, but they are all absorbed into the larger properties. The possession of property, however small, gives a permanent character to a family, so that there were shepherding families on the South Downs who, if they had consulted the parish register, could have traced their ancestry as far back as the times of the Stuarts.

The old shepherd of Chanctonbury Ring was not, however, a hireling. He knew every sheep in his flock personally, and thought the sheep knew him. He had been 'sixty years on the Downs, Sundays and week-days, and had his health, sure, thank God.'

During the present summer (1871) I found my way into the cottage of a Southdown shepherd, who had pursued his calling for well-nigh seventy years. Old H — was a fine intelligent man, with a forehead large enough for a professor, arched, characteristic eyebrows, and a mouth full of humour. In came his ancient comrade, Peter, an honest and true-hearted old worthy. They both complained sadly of the change in the position and prospects

Shepherd Smith of East Dean, Sussex, *c*. 1865. Shepherds were the aristocrats of the farm labour force, and a good deal of mystique surrounded their ancient craft.
Ian Serraillier.

The sheepwash at East Lavant, Sussex.

Ian Serraillier.

of the shepherding life now-a-days. They corroborated the fact that a shepherd was formerly allowed to keep his own sheep among the flocks of his master, and instanced the case of one shepherd who, if I remember right, possessed as many as seventy sheep, all bought out of his own earnings. Now the masters objected even to their keeping a hog.

Forty or fifty years ago a shepherd's wages were seventeen or eighteen shillings a week; at present sixteen or seventeen is the highest amount he can get. Everything is dearer now than then, except bread . . .

Peter had to pay two and sixpence a week for his cottage, and it had, I think he said, no garden.

Old H — had been in one situation where he never went home to his dinner from year's end to year's end, Sundays and Christmas Day included.

Winter was bad enough, what with wind, and rain, and cold; but summer was worse. It was anxious work to keep the sheep from straying, but the great trouble was to keep the flock free from their terrible enemy, the blow-fly. This miserable insect lays its eggs in the wool of the poor sheep, and the maggots become alive in four-and-twenty hours, and begin at once to feed on their victims. Directly a sheep is 'struck', as they call it, the only remedy is to shear it at once, for if not quickly relieved it will faint from exhaustion.

These men were respectable in the best sense, yet they evidently thought it no degradation to take the parish money. At the basis of all their thoughts about life lay quite unconsciously communist principles. They had a right to live; and if they, by hard labour, could not keep themselves and their families, then the parish was bound to step in and provide whatever was necessary. Therefore it appeared to them that the increased strictness of the parish now-a-days in giving relief was an additional element of hardness in the poor man's lot. In former times, they said, every man who had more than three children received a gallon of flour per week from the parish for each additional child; now nothing is given, except in the case of absolute need.

They had both gone to work when about seven years of age, and had never had a day's schooling in their lives. Peter could read a little, but old H — could not read at all. They could scarcely ever go to church . . .

SUSSEX COMMONS
AND SUSSEX SONGS

(GOLDEN HOURS, 1871)

(In) ancient times the vast woods, which then existed all over the country, supported thousands of swine. According to Doomsday Book, in Essex alone there were nearly a hundred thousand hogs. Still more must this have been the case with the (Sussex) Weald, which at that time was covered with forests. Now, however, the breeding of pigs is a comparatively unimportant addition to the produce of the farm; and where it is carried on to any extent, acorns are used sparingly, since it is averred that acorn-feeding produces a pebbly sort of bacon. So that the acorn harvest, once so important, has dwindled into a gleaning of the roadsides by the unemployed people. However, they get a shilling a bushel from the farmer for what they find, showing that great quantities are still devoured by the Sussex pigs.

In the south-eastern portion of the Weald, taking the parishes Heathfield, Warbleton, and Waldron as a centre, a large proportion of the labourers and small farmers keep from eight to sixteen brood-hens, and breed chickens for the fatters. They live chiefly in remote places away from the villages and hamlets, their favourite spots being the light, dry soil of the commons, and the higher grounds clothed with heather and short grass. Their special aim is to obtain large broods early in the spring, in preparation for the London market, the price of spring chicken being twice or thrice as much as can be obtained at other seasons.

Some idea of the importance of the business to this part of the Weald may be gathered from the following statistics furnished

me by the vicar of Heathfield. In 1864, 163 tons, 5cwts 7lbs of fatted chicken were sent up to London from Heathfield by one carrier, being 101,547 fowls fed and fatted in the three parishes of Heathfield, Warbleton, and Waldron. In 1867 and 1868 the quantity somewhat diminished; in 1869 and 1870 it rose to 181 and 191 tons, or 105,887 fowls.

Between thirteen and fifteen thousand pounds has been paid annually to the fatters by this one carrier, besides the sums received direct from the London salesmen. The quantity this year (1871) it is estimated will reach 200 tons. To these numbers may be added about half as much again, sent up to London by a different route, besides the poultry sent to Brighton and Hastings. The estimated price of the chicken sent by both routes from Heathfield to London is £25,000 per annum.

In this part of the Weald, and along the Kentish border, hop-picking is the great business immediately the wheat harvest is over. Hop-picking is carried on in Sussex in a somewhat more Arcadian fashion than in the neighbouring county, into which Whitechapel and the East of London pours itself during the season.

One evening I slept at a little inn at Rotherfield, and listened to some very curious singing going on in the bar-parlour. The songs were given to solemn tell-tale tunes, sounding in the distance very much like a recitation of the Athanasian Creed. Next day I had a talk with one of the singers, a miller, who was said to know more songs than any one else in the district. He had never seen them in print, but would try to write out a few. Here is one he gave me in praise of the hop-bine:-

A song and a cheer for good English beer,
That froths in the foaming can;
The beer and the bine in union join
To gladden the heart of man.
When the Spring appears, the bine it uprears,
Its circuline race begins,
Till it reaches at length its beauty and strength,
And waves in the summer winds.

Chorus – So long may the hops in their beauty stand,
    And still be the pride of our native land.

And so on for four stanzas more.

In the woodlands a very important branch of labour is the felling and preparing timber for the market. St. Leonard's Forest covers a tract of 9000 acres, in the cross-roads of which it is easy to lose the way, especially after dark. A sawyer, who had lived thirty-five years in the forest, told me that he could remember when it was far more extensive than it is now. Oaks are mainly raised, and some exist of an enormous size. Certain of them are quite famous.

The poverty of the people he described as excessive. He had no idea how they managed, but supposed they must be half starved. Throughout the Weald the labourers add a little to their income by working in the woods during the spring. They are employed by the timber merchant, and the job lasts about a month. They work by the piece, and their business is at first to fell the timber, and then to strip it and set up the bark. The whole of this work goes by the name of 'flawing'. 'Faggoting the lop' and scraping and 'hatching' the bark are different operations. A man can earn by 'flawing' two-and-sixpence to six shillings a day; women and children do the scraping. In some parts felling timber goes on all the winter, from November to March, and if a woodman is clever he gets from twelve to fifteen shillings a week. In autumn a good deal of wood is cut for other purposes – as, for instance, making gunpowder. Near Uckfield I met a man driving a cart laden with black alder, going to be used for this purpose . . .

Thus it would appear that a clever and industrious man on the Weald, who has his wits about him, can find something to do all the year round; and according to the report of the Agricultural Commission such a labourer can earn an average sixteen shillings a week. However, the labourer will tell you that there are important drawbacks not taken into account, such as having to provide his own tools in connection with the hopping work, and, if it is a wet season, firing, night after night, to dry his wet clothes.

Moreover, this estimate supposes a man not only to be industrious but *clever,* and must therefore be taken as the maximum of wages to be earned in the Weald. Besides, it does not take into account accident or illness. The regular day-wage varies from twelve to thirteen shillings and sixpence the week, and the amount is made up by extras, earned by piece-work connected with the hop-gardens, hay-making, and harvest. The wife generally helps at these seasons. At hop-picking and tying she can earn about £4.

No doubt among rural labourers, as amongst every other class, there are rich and poor. The rich are those who just pay their way, the poor those who are ever on the verge of pauperism. The rich are the rare exception, the poor the vast majority. When the family is young, and there is only one pair of hands to supply the food, it constantly exists in a state of semi-starvation.

Thus, at Mayfield, in the depth of winter, I went into a cottage, where I found a mother and eight children – four boys and four girls. They had only eighteen-pence each a week for meals. The children were having their dinner, which consisted of a dole of bread and cheese.

Happily there is much fellow-feeling among labouring families. If any one gets down very low, those who are well off come to the rescue. Here is a verse of a song the miller gave me. It may be called 'A Poor Man's Song'. Its note is sympathy produced by a past and a too probable future experience.

Oh come, come to the ingle-side,
For the night is dark and drear;
The snow is deep and the mountains wide,
Then stay and rest thee here;
My board is simply spread,
I have a little food to spare,
But thou shall break my wholesome bread,
And have a wholesome share.
For while the faggot burns
To warm my cottage floor,

Cottages at Singleton, Sussex.

Ian Serraillier.

In the garden behind Butcher's Lane cottages, East Dean, Sussex.

Ian Serraillier.

They never shall say the poor man turns
A poorer from his door.
Then come, come to the ingle-side . . .

Where a labourer or his wife is idle and improvident, the sordid misery into which they sink is something beyond belief. In Rotherfield I went into one cottage where a woman sat in the grimy chimney corner, trying to make a kettle boil over a few sticks of wood. Two little girls were hanging over the dying embers, for it was miserably cold. The mother took us upstairs, where there were two compartments. In the first, a sort of landing, the parents slept on a miserable bed almost on a level with the floor. In a small outer-room was a little shake-down on which the children slept. Not a chair, nor a table, nor any other article of furniture, was in the room. In the parents' sleeping-place the wet came in, so that the woman said one night she was wet through. She had had ten children, but had only reared two. One boy died when he was nine; the others had died mostly of decline and galloping consumption – slow starvation, in fact! For this miserable habitation they paid two shillings a week. It had, however, a garden, in which they raised cabbages. Her husband earned, on average, ten shillings a week all the year round.

As a rule, the Wealden peasant is provident. Some men subscribe as much as £8 or £9 a year to clubs; £1 for support in illness, and £7 to £8 is expended for clothes. The general arrangement in the hop districts is that the man's wages pays for rent and food, while that which the women and children earn goes towards clothes.

But provident or improvident, there can be no doubt that the majority of children and old people do not get enough to eat. The old people have a peculiar complexion arising from poorness of blood, in some cases breaking out into sores. I was told that there is widespread hereditary consumption in East Sussex . . .

I met with a poor boy near Cross-on-Hand, who had been paralysed since he was eighteen months old, in his leg. His body was not fit for any work, but his mind had grown. He told me

that in arithmetic he had gone as far as vulgar fractions, and now he longed to draw. Yet those who exercise the Christian ministry in the Weald complain of the apathy and stolid indifference of the people, of the rowdyism of the boys, and the immorality of both sexes. From all I heard, it would be difficult to exaggerate the latter evil. Let no one suppose, however, that they are peculiarly corrupt. It is poverty, ignorance, and a low state of public opinion which is at the root of the evil. I saw a kind little woman, at the risk of losing other employment, attending upon a poor old bed-ridden couple, who were being eaten by vermin, and had no one else to care for them. She had had two illegitimate children, but from the way she spoke of the fact it was believed that she only regarded it as an inconvenience.

The people are very clean, as a rule. The men generally wear black smocks, and the women are neat and tidy in their dress. The interiors of the cottages are black from the smoke of the wood fires; but the floors and seats are scrupulously clean. Although I saw some miserable dwellings, Sussex cottages may be described as, on the whole, roomy and comfortable. Sometimes they are old farmhouses converted into two or three different tenements. In many parts of the Weald are to be found picturesque examples of ancient farmhouses and cottages, laced and interlaced with great beams. Some have been restored, and are carefully preserved by their enlightened proprietors, but they cannot restore the stalwart yeomen who were once their inhabitants.

Most of the old cottages have a large open chimney, with a pedestal of bricks in the centre of the hearth, on which a log of wood or a few sticks burn daily. Suspended above by a chain hangs a kettle, or the *pot-au-feu*. In front you may often see the settle or *bist*, as it used to be called in Sussex, a grand old bit of furniture, telling of better days. In the wall at the back of the hearth is an iron plate with two handles. This is the cottager's oven, and here they bake their bread. Those who know best say it would be a good thing if they could brew their own beer, and then all the little beer-shops would be shut up, and a vast amount of misery prevented.

Not that the peasant of the Weald is a drunkard. He is far too poor for that. It is only on club-days, and occasionally on Saturday night, that he gives way. Habitual drinking in the country is the vice of a class in a superior social position.

The Wealden labourer is inclined to be suspicious, and will fence unnecessarily with a simple question. In some places he will exhibit a certain independence of spirit, which would probably be more common if life were a little easier with him . . .

WEALDEN LIFE
AND CHARACTER

(GOLDEN HOURS, 1874)

(Of) the depth of superstition, ignorance, immorality, and poverty which prevails in the Weald of Sussex, it is impossible for me to give any adequate idea. I will relate a few facts in illustration of these points . . .

In a parish contiguous to Mayfield the clergyman told me that an old woman came to him, and having informed him that her little grand-daughter was ill, she said in an insinuating way, 'I think, sir, it 'ud do her good if she were to have a little of the sacrament wine.'

In another Wealden parish a minister said that it was his impression that not more than half of the population could read fluently; a few of the remainder very imperfectly, the rest not at all. On a jury, on which I think he said he had occasion to be prsent, composed of farmers, most of whom were well-to-do, only six could write their names; on another, only one witness out of five could write.

Passing over Crowborough common, I came upon a little cot not much higher than a man, and about ten or twelve feet in length. I looked in at the open door, and found it papered with odd bits of paper, and ornamented with a sheet of the *Police News*. My tap aroused a recumbent figure on a bed, which just filled up the whole of one end of the cottage. The gruff voice assured me that its owner was not ill, but merely taking a rest, as he worked hard all the week. He was a sweep, and lived here alone with his boy.

Grimes was not sullen, but very genial. He came and sat on a stool in front of an old fireplace, all burnt out and rusty. He could not read, nor his boy either. What was the use? His father and mother hadn't been able to read, and yet they pulled along, and went to America. He hadn't been able to read, and yet he had pulled along; indeed, he was in such repute, that if I was to offer to sweep his chimney ever so well, his customers wouldn't have me. What more, then, could his boy want than to be trusted and believed in, and allowed to sweep these same chimneys, until he in his turn could make the next generation of boys do it for him?

From what he said, it appeared that boys still climb chimneys in this part of the country. He had a machine, but it was impossible to clean some chimneys; they had such ledges and such windings, you couldn't nohow get at the soot unless a boy went up. He didn't believe in boys being ill-treated; had heard of pricking boys behind, but didn't believe it. You must be very good to boys to get them to go at all. It was no use larruping them, or they'd sulk and refuse. When you'd taught them their trade, then if they put on you, you might larrup them.

If I were to relate the statements I received on the subject of morality, I feel sure that I should be accused of exaggeration. Suffice it to say that as regards the relations of the sexes, public opinion can scarcely be lower in any part of England.

I observe from the Report of the Agricultural Commission in 1868 that in some parts of West Sussex the demoralization was attributed to habits of drunkenness on the part of the labouring classes. This is not true of the Weald; the people really have no money to spend on drink.

Poverty, miserable cottages, and the want of a really Christian ministry – these are the causes of much of the degradation to be found in the Weald of Sussex.

To realize the poverty and the wretchedness of their homes one must live amongst them, not as a mere bird of passage, or a summer visitor, or a gentleman resident, but as one of themselves. One must pass up and down the Weald in winter-time and in rainy weather, note how they have neither cisterns or drainage, how

therefore they suffer from thirst in the dog-days when all the springs are dry, and have floors swamped when the rainy season sets in, while the house-filth oozes out from a slit in the wall to trickle into the garden or wayside gutter. One must go into the cots themselves, blackened with ages of wood fires, and breathe the reeking smoke and foul air, see the mother and children cowering over a few poor sticks smouldering on some bricks under the great chimney. . . . One must see the children eating bread and butter for dinner, and drinking the hot wash they call *tea*; one must note the bleared eyes, the scrofulous skin, the ulcerated legs, the rheumatic agonized bodies – one must see these things and a hundred others for oneself to realize the depth of their miserable poverty.

The benefit caused by any fresh industry which will give employment to a few hands, and thus bring a little runlet of the vast wealth of the outlying world into this impoverished district, may be seen in the villages which form the parish of Hurstmonceux. In this neighbourhood about twenty persons find profitable employment in making the flat baskets so much used for agricultural purposes – such, for instance, as bringing potatoes from the field. Many are sent over to France, the Hurstmonceux makers having established a reputation through one of the first of their number obtaining a prize at the Exhibition of 1851.

In speaking of Sussex commons, I have described how, in Heathfield and its neighbourhood, chicken-fattening has grown up into a large trade. The men who collect the chickens from the cottages which fringe the edges of the numerous commons, or which lie hidden in out-of-the-way lanes, are called *higglers*. You can scarcely traverse any road in this locality without meeting one of them – lean sinewy men or youths, carrying an enormous wicker cage, full of chickens, on their shoulders, and a stout staff in their hands. Trudging along at one pace, they bear the burden of life in a brave though somewhat moody fashion.

Even among those who are better off, one is oppressed by a sense of the poverty of the Weald. The fires of wood and small-coal, the inferiority of almost every article of diet –

everything, in fact, repeats the same sad tale. However, this very poverty seems to tell in favour of the few tradesfolk to be found in every village, for it has prevented a rush of competitors. Unlike the poor labourers, who are wholly dependent on the goodwill of the employers of the district, most of the tradesmen can afford to be independent of individual customers. As to the artificers – the builder, the wheel-wright, the carpenter, or the smith – they are, generally speaking, masters of the situation, and can not only charge what they choose, but do their work how or when it suits them best. This enviable position produces a sort of crabbed independence, an illustration of which was given me in the character of one parish which was thus graphically sketched by its rector: 'The people here wouldn't care twopence for a duke.'

The more prosperous such people become, the more this disagreeable phase of character predominates, until the whole atmosphere becomes laden with petty jealousies, wounded self-love, and outrageous egotism, working up here and there into rancorous life-long animosities.

No mere formal religion, however perfect in theory, can do anything to prevent or heal this strife. People who are of the same blood or dwell under the same roof, or go to the same church or chapel and pronounce *Shibboleth* in exactly the same way, can still be sullen foes. Nothing but the true spirit of the kingdom of heaven can make a man at once independent and sympathetic; and such characters can be found in every sect and form of Christianity, and in the present disjointed state of Christendom unconnected with any denomination.

And they may be met with even in these dead Wealden towns. I know one, a smith, a type of the soft-hearted Sussex man. His wife, a pale, sickly woman, with the sad smile of the permanent invalid, is constantly at work, either attending to the shop or to the tribe of small children, whose presence both she and her husband seem to imagine constitute their greatest earthly happiness. Added to this, she is ever assiduous in helping her neighbours, nursing the sick, and promoting the good of the little Christian society in which both she and her husband find a

continual spiritual stimulus, making and keeping them what they are . . .

Near Waldron I met a bright, happy-faced boy, seventeen years old, who told me that he had worked ever since he was nine; left school then and went to service – first for fourpence a day, then for sixpence, then for eightpence, then for eighteenpence, then for two shillings; now he works in the fields, has eight shillings a week, and will shortly be raised. Some had lately gone from those parts to New Zealand, but he did not care to emigrate as long as he had two hands and there was work to be done. He went to a night-school in winter, and gets on there a good bit; has a few books – 'The Negro Servant', and a book about 'Noah's Ark', and 'The Tower of Babel', which he has read over and over again.

This boy had worked ever since he was nine. Sufficiently young, but in his case it appeared to be domestic service; not as I had seen just before I had met him, a child of that age actually employed in the fields. He was a little fair-haired boy, and came running to the side of the field to ask the time. He told me that he had to work from six in the morning until six in the evening, with an hour at twelve o'clock for his dinner. His job just then was pulling up a red weed in the corn. He had worked for three summers, and only went to school in the winter. I parted with him and his three little sisters at the gate of their father's cottage, where they had all come to welcome him home to his dinner – not of meat, but of gooseberry pie.

There are doubtless many parishes in England in which no voice is ever raised against the cruel wrong done to a young child in thus making him work eleven hours a day. But where a voice is raised to rebuke the parents who sell their children into slavery, and the farmers who buy their labour, whose voice is it? Whose is the counter influence that can come with any weight against parental influence, against the exigencies of the sole employer, the exigencies of stern want? Only his who can claim them for God, who can remind parents and employers that these children have minds and souls which have a right to knowledge and education – the much-abused parson! . . .

May we live to see the day when a true priesthood in England . . . shall rise to their true calling, and become the defenders of the poor, and the oppressed, and the suffering in EVERY class against their foes!

But let the clergy look well to it, for by some means or other the hearts of the poor are more often than not alienated from them.

Not far from Cross-in-Hand I had a talk with a wheelwright, who was at work in his shop by the road-side. Most of the people thereabouts, he said, went to chapel. He went to a Wesleyan place of worship, where the congregation sometimes numbered two hundred people. 'Why did the people prefer chapel to church?' 'Because they could understand better; the preaching was plainer than at church; they spoke more to the soul. You see, clergymen do it more for a living.' 'Do not people think it a benefit to have some one in the parish to whom they can always go?' 'Never knew anyone who did', was the answer. 'The clergyman here is not bad to people when they are sick, but,' continued the wheelwright, 'I would not go to church for that sort of thing; it must end bad. What'll such people do when they come to die?'

This prejudice against the clergy on the part of those who are just beginning to realize their power to think and act with independence, arises from the fact that the rural clergy, as a class, have so closely identified themselves with the gentry as to give rise to the impression that they regard themselves as a sort of spiritual squirearchy.

When they shall have the courage to descend from their high social position, and to claim no status but a heavenly one; when they shall become willing to be regarded quite as much as labouring men as squires; when, in fact, they shall absolutely refuse to take any particular position in the social scale, but shall claim equality and fellowship with all, then they will be in a fair way to recover their influence with every class, and to find it tenfold greater than it has ever been.

If, too, the rural clergy would recover and retain their influence as pastors of the whole flock, they must strive in a spirit of deep sympathy to understand the real faith and character of those

amongst their parishioners who dissent from the National Church.

Throughout Sussex the hyper-Calvinists are the most numerous body. Their churches were no doubt founded to maintain the same creed as that once held by the greater number of Baptist churches, a creed of which particular salvation was a distinctive point; but while the greatest part of the denomination had become so affected by the modern evangelical revival as to sink and almost lose sight of this doctrine, the Baptists of East Sussex, coming under the influence of Huntingtonianism, have continued more and more to magnify its importance, until, like Aaron's rod, it seems to have swallowed up everything else. In most villages they will be found to have a chapel, the minister of which is not unfrequently himself a farmer or a labourer. At Buxted the pastor of the chapel proved to be an ancient labourer in a dark smock, a truly simple-minded, good old man.

While I was staying in an ancient Wealden town, a large new Calvinistic chapel was opened, creating for the day quite an unwonted excitement. The building was well filled, one might almost say crowded, by a respectable body of worshippers, mostly farmers, their wives and children, many of whom came long distances in chaises, waggonettes, and carts.

The preacher in the morning was one of the most eminent holding their peculiar views. It was evident that he knew that the people he had to deal with were a desponding race, entertaining the most melancholy ideas concerning the fate of mankind in general, for his sermon was entirely devoted to an attempt to assure as many individuals among them as he possibly could, that, come what might to the bulk of men, they at least were safe . . .

In the evening the minister of the place preached. He was a farmer, and lives miles away from his charge, but amongst these people the minister's office appears to be chiefly that of preaching. Every elect soul, they believe, has its appointed teacher, and every teacher has his appointed work. The former must go any distance to hear the right man; the latter any distance to do the right work. Thus in the course of this sermon the speaker spoke of having

himself gone to hear a certain preacher, with the conviction that what HE said would settle his fate. He came home with the joyful assurance that he was *safe*. So with reference to a preacher narrating his own experience. He said that poor souls listened and said, 'That is just how I feel. If that man goes to heaven – and I am sure he will – I shall go too.' . . .

Calvinists are not the only Dissenters in a Sussex village. There are those who represent a more modern style of Nonconformity. From the pulpits of their chapels may almost always be heard sermons in harmony with what is widely known as Revival preaching. Its favourite text is, 'For God so loved the world, that He gave His only begotten son, that whosoever believeth in Him should not perish, but have everlasting life'; and its favourite hymn, 'Just as I am, without one plea.' This ministry, when exercised by a gentle, loving-hearted man, has calmed many a troubled heart, and such scenes as the following seem to suggest progress towards a real unity.

It is Sunday evening, the service is over, and the majority of the congregation have gone. The forms and seats are pushed back, and the little table at which those who led the singing usually sat, is spread with a small white cloth, a bottle of wine, a large wine-glass, and a small plate of bread. The communicants gather round – old and young, poor and better off. Boys are there of eleven or twelve years of age, and one little girl about eight, two or three of the small maid-of-all-work type, making the number of the young an unusual and interesting feature. The pastor sits down among them, and reads the passage, 'Ought not Christ to have suffered these things, and entered into His glory?' Then singing and prayer and eating the bread, singing and prayer and drinking the wine, another hymn, the offertory, and benediction. Thus concludes this great act of Christian worship, in all its parts perfectly harmonious and beautiful, because the spirit which pervaded it was one of true adoration and love.

And yet such men, working day by day in God's name, and for the love of Christ, cannot be recognised and encouraged, because, providentially, they have been brought into the work by other

channels than those of the Established church; while, on the other hand, they must be quite cast out of the synagogue, because they do not make election the beginning, middle, and end of all their sermons.

In the presence of such ignorance, superstition, immorality, bigotry, and consequent suspicion and disunion, how can we be surprised that Romanism is replanting itself in the Weald? Although at present no effort is made at proselytising, it would be idle to suppose that the Jesuits have chosen this locality wherein to build two noble orphanages, and to found a nunnery on the site of an ancient archi-episcopal palace, without any ulterior purpose of propagating their faith among the people.

The nunnery is contiguous to the parish church, and being a restoration of the ruins of the palace built about the same period, the two buildings will, in course of time, seem to belong to each other. The great hall, a fine apartment, which formerly possessed an open roof, has been turned into a chapel. On the walls have been placed a series of beautiful bas-reliefs representing the stations of the cross. Two figures of Jesuit saints SS. Stanislaus and Alphegius – stand before the altar, apparently guarding it. The nuns call themselves 'the Sisters of the Holy Child'.

The orphanages being in lofty positions, are visible for miles around. They have both been built at the expense of the Duchess of Leeds, and are said to have cost, the one £15,000, the other £20,000. I made a pilgrimage to one and found its arrangements all that could possibly be desired. The door was opened by one of the brothers who acts as cook; another brother was sent for, who very courteously showed me over the building. I was taken into the chapel – a plain building with an altar decorated with flowers, and a statue on one side of St. Joseph and the Child, on the other of the Virgin Mary. She was also surrounded with flowers; it had lately been the feast of the Assumption. My cicerone told me that a Dutchman named Reinkens was the founder of their fraternity, and that they were called *Xaverian Brothers,* after St. Francis Xavier, and were a branch of the great Ignation Society.

He took me into the dormitory – a vast apartment which

seemed to extend the whole length of the building. It was divided by a number of arches down the centre, filled in to about the height of a man's breast, so cutting the dormitory in two without lessening the quantity of air. The elder boys slept on one side, the younger on the other. When they enter the room for the night, each boy stands at the head of his bed, and taking hold of the white counterpane, folds it up. Then, at a given signal, they all kneel down and say their evening prayer. These acts, and every other, are all done by rule, the whole company being directed by a single brother, who stands on a step by one of the arches.

In the schoolroom the boys appeared seated at desks, or standing in a half-circle. They were reading out of a lesson-book, the subject being *'The Third Foe to Salvation – the Flesh.'*

In the upper part of the building was another large apartment, and used at present as a play-room, but intended for another dormitory, but as yet the orphanage only contains fifty boys, whereas it is constructed for two hundred.

The brothers, I think, were ten in number, and are liable to be removed and sent elsewhere at any time. Their vows are the three ordinary ones – poverty, chastity, and obedience. Their chief work is educating the young, and they have such faith in their system that this brother said that if a boy six years of age were placed in his hands he would undertake to mould him according to his own will. When the boys grow up they are rarely devoted to the priesthood. On the contrary, they are sent into various secular stations abroad, or in England. Carpentering, tailoring and baking are taught in the house. But they are educated not only for artisans, but some even enter the liberal professions. One was already in the Ordnance Survey, and two were clerks in London. They all wear a brown holland skeleton suit in summer, and a corduroy one in winter. A friend asked one of the boys, who was working in the garden, how he liked it; he gave no direct answer, but replied in this characteristic fashion – 'If I were to speak against the orphanage, should I not be an ungrateful boy?'

Faith still lingers in the Weald, genuine and powerful. 'I never saw such beautiful death-beds as I have seen in Sussex,' said a

clergyman to the writer. Among the cottages I visited was one in a drear, dilapidated row. I entered. It was a large, bare room, with a brick floor. I was invited, however, to ascend the staircase, and there in the upper room lay a pale, intelligent woman. She had been ill for years, and was so weak that she could not speak, spelling out all she wished to say by means of a large alphabet. She had had a bad husband, and was now partially supported by the parish. On her bed were a number of religious papers and tracts, which she gave to every one who came, so that there was not a house in the town without one. It was easy to see that she was carefully tended by those who loved her. A little lad sat by her bed-side – a neighbour's child, she said. An atmosphere of calm, peace and love reigned around. The Divine light shone all the brighter for its bare, poverty-stricken surroundings.

A SOUTHDOWN
VILLAGE

(GOLDEN HOURS, 1874)

(Ere) long Alfriston appears in sight – a cluster of grey-brown houses all comfortably snoozing together. Behind rises the Down, to the left a large motherly church, grey and weather-beaten, built in the form of a Greek cross. This little but most ancient town stands immediately on the bank of the Cuckmere, and to reach it we must cross the meadow, now bright with buttercups; and traversing a long and narrow foot-bridge we enter the town up a side lane.

Thirty or forty years ago Alfriston possessed tanyards and tallow-chandlers' factories, but now they are all gone, and nothing remains to occupy its inhabitants but agricultural labour. . . . The decay of Alfriston is an instance of the results of this common evil: the blindness, the vice, engendered by poverty. Ignorance dense and dark seems to have settled on the place. 'More immoral than any part of the Weald', such was the testimony of a resident. Neither church nor chapel seemed to have much power for good. The chapel was the ugliest, most dismal-looking building in the town. Little or no interest could be aroused in the people, save when some homely preacher in a smock came and talked to them in the language of hyper-Calvinism. Why does this dreadful doctrine so commend itself to these poor souls? Is it not because it represents God as dealing with the universe just in accordance with their own experience of life? – the great mass left to rot on in blindness, misery, and corruption, while a favoured few are lifted up into health and wealth, and the enjoyment of all kinds of happiness.

One day last summer we saw this chapel decked out in a way that proved that even old-fashioned Dissenters were beginning to believe that repulsive ugliness was not a necessary adjunct of pure religion. It was the anniversary of the opening of the chapel, and some joyous hearts and tasteful fingers had adorned its naked walls and heavy galleries with floral wreaths and posies.

The old meeting-house was well filled, for the preacher was one who not only had a message to deliver, but was endowed with that gift of eloquence which, like sweet music, steals away every heart. The little inn-yard was crowded with vehicles, showing that preaching has not yet lost its power to attract men.

This was not by any means the first time this little inn had been made busy by such an unusual class of customers. In fact, it may lay claim to be called a house of call for the religious. It dates from the early part of the sixteenth century, and is believed to have been used by the pilgrims on their way to the shrine of St. Richard of Chichester.

For three centuries there was no name so popular in Sussex as that of the good Bishop of Chichester, Richard de la Wyche. Divested of the superstitious wonders with which his memory afterwards became associated, it is certain that he was in many respects a model bishop. Although he exercised his rule with a certain quaint, fatherly severity, he was always full of sympathy for the poor and suffering among his flock . . .

(In) this mediaeval inn, sacred to such old Catholic memories, the theological food dealt out to the modern wayfaring guest is not simply Protestantism, but Calvinism of the extremest type. The evening we spent under its hospitable roof, we had no friends but the books which loaded the window-sill of this little parlour. They were mostly hyper-Calvinistic magazines; nevertheless we found one which proved to be interesting. It was the life of a man struggling towards light amongst people of these views, and who himself subsequently became a minister among them. For a long period he appears to have been in great and distressing doubt as to whether he was among the saved, but he relates how much this doubt was removed by the text, 'We know that we have passed

from death unto life, because we love the brethren.' What a lesson Joseph Tanner, the hyper-Calvinist preacher, here teaches Christian people! And the answer will be that of the old Scribe – 'And who is my brother?'

This little Plantagenet hostel is old – the grey weather-beaten motherly church is older – but Alfriston contains a symbol older than either, telling of a better welcome than the hostel can afford, of a larger unity than the Church dares to speak of. In the centre of the village, beneath the shadow of a tree, is an old stone cross, a relic of those days when men were taught as much by the eye as the ear; but still, if we rightly think of it, witnessing to us of the same great truths as it did to them; above all, witnessing that there *is* a great uniting power in the world, able, if men will only permit it, to reconcile them to God and to one another. This cross has indeed a peculiar right to stand there as a symbol of that great reality which alone can turn the hearts of the fathers to the children, and of the children to the fathers, binding all the generations in one; far from its steps the same old story has been repeated age after age by friar, Reformer, Puritan, and, latest of all, by an Independent preacher, one George Gilbert, an old soldier, whose earnest appeals resulted in the erection of the ugly little meeting-house, about whose anniversary we have been speaking . . .

PEASANT LIFE
IN THE NEW FOREST

(GOLDEN HOURS, 1892)

(Whatever) may be the exact truth about the origin of the New Forest, it is certain the Conqueror much enlarged it, absorbing the lands of many Saxon owners; and, above all, greatly increased the severity of the Forest Laws, executing them with fierce rigour.

The cruelty and injustice of these laws is one of the main points in English history, and did more than anything else to turn the Norman barons themselves into the champions of liberty. We cannot, therefore, be surprised that in the New Forest itself they excited the bitterest antagonism. Within the memory of some living, almost every man in the New Forest was a poacher. To kill the king's deer was looked upon as no sin. In early times it had worn the mask of patriotism, but though the halo had long departed, public opinion was affected by the tradition.

Even in recent times quite a system of snaring the deer existed. Sometimes hooks were baited with apples; sometimes the fawn's hoof was pared, or a thorn thrust into the foot, in order to keep the doe in one spot until the poacher wanted to kill her. Thus the foresters were never without 'mutton', as they called the venison. If one house had not a supply, another had some, and community in lawlessness made them very neighbourly.

Stretching down almost to the seashore, and from its very nature well adapted for the commission of every dark deed under the sun, with a public opinion thus demoralized by ages of oppression, the New Forest was just the place for smuggling to take root and to flourish. At the close of the seventeenth century

the narrowest commerical policy prevailed in England, so much so, that during the war with Louis XIV, trade with France was entirely prohibited. The rapid decay of most of the ports on the Channel soon ensued, and many of the inhabitants took to smuggling. Even great capitalists embarked in it, and illicit trade became so extensive that all the efforts of the Government during the whole of the eighteenth century were insufficient to place any effectual bar in its way, much less to put it down. On the Hampshire coast the smugglers grew so bold in their impunity, that at times as many as twenty or thirty waggons laden with kegs, and guarded by two or three hundred horsemen, each horseman bearing some two or three tubs, would come over Hengistbury Heath, making their way in open day past Christ Church into the Forest. The demoralization of the district became so thorough that at one time a gang of desperadoes took possession of Ambrose Cave, on the borders of the Forest, plundering the whole country, and murdering upward of thirty people, throwing their bodies down a well.

Boat-building went on in many a barn, and the foresters had fierce fights with the coast-guard, defending their ill-gotten booty with 'swingels'. Sometimes they had the worst of it, and then in their flight they would pitch the goods into one of the numerous ponds with which the Forest abounds, returning some subsequent night to haul them up again . . .

Happily the temptation to smuggling and poaching has ceased to exist – in the latter case by the withdrawal of the deer in 1851. It is still true that there are men in the Forest who partially support themselves by stealing game, but the general tone of public morality has so much improved that one who has lived amongst them as a minister nearly thirty years, affirms that, if drink were put aside, he does not believe that there is a more decent, orderly and honest community in the kingdom.

What a fact for the advocates of the abolition of the Game Laws and of ale-houses! Here is a population for eight centuries a lawless race, made so because their rulers cared more for the preservation of wild animals than they did for the moral elevation of the human

beings committed to their charge. The deer abolished, the laws concerning them a dead letter, and the demoralized people rapidly return to law-abiding ways.

Eight centuries of deer-stealing, one might have supposed, would have so ingrained poaching into the nature of the forester, that their removal would have only driven him to seek a new channel for the gratification of his propensity. But such has not been the case with the greater part of the population; and it is fair to argue that, just as the forester has learnt to be honest now the deer are gone, so would he learn to be sober if that infinitely more demoralizing influence was removed, namely, the existence of ale-houses.

All agree that drinking is the great vice of the foresters. It drags them down with remorseless grasp, and is without doubt the chief evil which oppresses them. Such, however, is the force of custom in this particular, that some of their employers help to make them careless workmen and improvident parents by paying them their weekly wages in the village tap-room.

While, however, the abolition of the deer has greatly elevated the tone of public morality in the Forest, it has without doubt increased the hardship of life to the labouring portion of the community. For it is manifest that life with plenty to eat is a very different thing from life with an empty stomach. Formerly it was meat every day, and as much as they liked; now it must be something very different, seeing that the ordinary wages of a New Forest labourer vary from ten to twelve shillings a week. A carter gets a shilling more, and is allowed a house and garden rent-free.

Under the old state of things the harshness of the law was somewhat balanced by a number of privileges enjoyed by the foresters, such as the right of pasturage, and of getting wood, turf, and fern out of the Forest. It was found, however, that great abuses had crept in, and in 1848 the rights of the foresters were defined. As is usually the case in these legal arrangements, to those who had was given, while to those who had not was taken away that which they had. The result is that the poorer foresters have now no privileges whatever, except that of picking up the fallen

pieces from the trees and pulling up the furze stumps, locally called 'blacks', after a fire.

Those, however, who put in their claims, and could show anything like a title, seem to have retained their right of pasturage, and many are thus enabled to keep a horse or a cow. Some keep asses, and some rear a few of the ponies, which are now as much a feature of the Forest as the deer formerly were. Pigs also can be turned out during masting-time, to eat the beech-nuts and acorns. Wood, too, can be bought for fuel.

Moreover, the neighbourhood of the Forest presents so many opportunities whereby a shrewd and industrious man may fairly increase his income, that it does not appear that the poverty of the district is anything like so severe as it is in many other parts of agricultural England.

From autumn to spring is the time for felling the larger timber. First the fir, then the beech, lastly the oak. In the spring the young trees in the enclosures, locally called 'flitterns', have to be thinned. Then comes the hay harvest, and the turf, and fern seasons, while all the year round there is work of some kind going on – making fresh enclosures, cutting brambles and brushwood, hedging, ditching, and draining.

The wood-cutters work in companies of six or eight, under the eye of an overlooker, who has frequently been a workman himself, and so practically understands the setting out of the work and its management. These overlookers are answerable to the inspectors, of whom there are eight; they in turn are subject to the Deputy-Surveyor of the Forest, who resides at the Queen's House in Lyndhurst.

The labour is very severe, and the men often have to walk some miles to their work. Their average wages are twelve shillings a week, and even if they work by the piece, they are not expected to earn more. Cutting and peeling the oak is paid by the piece, stacking up the wood by the fathom, faggotting by the hundred.

The work, however, only employs a limited number of men, and these not entirely; so that there are many other occupations pursued by the foresters.

Charcoal burners, New Forest.

Museum of English Rural Life.

Charcoal burner's hut and family, New Forest.

Museum of English Rural Life.

Some of course find enough to do tending their cattle, ponies, and pigs. Others, who go by the name of 'broom-squires', make brooms from the heath, and sell them in the neighbouring towns; some purchase wood, which they hawk for firing; while the very poorest use their right to collect the dead sticks in the Forest to make them into bundles, and sell them as 'Match' or 'Farthing faggots'.

In these various ways a labourer in the New Forest may make, upon an average, fourteen or fifteen shillings a week all the year round. Such an estimate, however, implies intelligence; but since we know this is not a gift possessed by the majority of any community, we may judge that life here is not quite so easy as such a sum might lead an economist to expect.

There is a class of small farmers in the Forest, such as have elsewhere sunk into the condition of labourers, but whose position is here maintained by the benefits accruing from Forest privileges. Some farm as few as five acres, for which they pay a rental of about £12 the year, and do all the work themselves, with the assistance of their wives and children. As they are obliged to keep a couple of horses, they use them when unemployed in doing job-work. They keep one or two cows and a number of fowls, and once a week the farmer's wife carries the produce of their little farm to the nearest market-town for sale.

One other occupation has been carried on in the Forest from the earliest times, and still flourishes, at least in the neighbourhood of Lyndhurst. Everybody has heard of Purkess, the charcoal-burner, in whose cart the body of Rufus was conveyed to Winchester. Nearly eight centuries have rolled away since then, and charcoal is still burnt on the same spot and in the same round ovens; but what is even more wonderful, as showing the unchanging habits of the foresters, is that descendants of this same Purkess, or of his family, are still to be found in the woods and in the village of Minestead.

The cottages in the New Forest are beyond the average. There are some miserable dwellings at Beaulieu Rails, belonging to squatters, which are merely mud huts; but elsewhere they are very comfortable. At Beaulieu every cottage in the parish belongs to

Lord Henry Scott, and has a living-room, scullery and pantry, and two or three bedrooms, with good water supply and thorough drainage. Each cottage has a pigstye, and at least twenty perches of garden. The rent charged is only a shilling a week; the average rent for a cottage throughout the Forest is £4 per annum.

The appearance of a New Forest cottage, with its warm cosy thatch spreading in all directions, and its old fruit-trees trained over its sides, standing in its own little orchard or garden, is suggestive of comfort. Bees too are largely kept, and find an untold harvest of honey in the heather bells. Bee-keeping is an ancient custom in the Forest; it is recorded in 'Doomsday' book that the woods round Eling in those days yielded twelve pounds of honey every year. Mead is still made and drunk, as in old English times . . .

Nothing sweeter, nothing more charming, can be imagined than the appearance of a New Forest village, seen as I saw Minestead, on a bright autumnal morning, the blue smoke curling gently heavenwards from its brown thatched roofs, as they peeped out here and there among the trees. Not a jarring note could I hear, not even the clang of the blacksmith's hammer or the woodman's axe; all was silent and still, nought save the happy voice of children playing in the 'boughy' dells, a sound which rather increased than disturbed the deep repose of the scene . . .

Passing through Minestead, I went into a cottage; it was very small, but neat, and its sanded floor gave it a fresh and bright look. The biggest thing in the house was the great chimney. A fire was burning on the hearth, lying on flat iron bars, with two ancient fire-dogs in front; a tall clock ornamented the room. The old dame said they no longer burned turf, for her husband had never put in his claim which he ought to have done, and so they had lost their right; but she did not think it was much of a loss, since they had had to pay heavily for cutting and carting turf; and besides, it took up so much room. Coming out, I noted the beautiful form of the pitchers in use in the Forest, and saw the same make again in Dorset.

On I wandered, down lanes laden with blackberries, and on the

outskirts of the village sketched two of its cots. They were good types of all the rest; and thick thatch coming deep down over the upper windows gave the appearance of two ill-matched eyes peeping out from under heavy humorous eyebrows . . .

Leaving Minestead, I crossed Squire Compton's Park, where the cottages, models of beauty, comfort and picturesqueness, stand in their own little grounds in the midst of their lord's larger ones. They were occupied by the labourers on the manor, and were let to them according to size, from one to two shillings a week. On the outskirts of the Forest, near Lyndhurst, I came on a little hamlet, and seating myself on some logs of wood which lay on the corner of the sward, watched its life. Before me on one side of the road stood a row of blind-eyed, brown-bonnetted cots; then a wheelwright's shop, where the furnace was burning and the hammer twanging; next a smithy, where the horse stood quietly while the farrier tapped his shoe; last of all, an old cot under the shade of a large tree, with a man on a ladder mending the roof. Opposite was a little road-side inn, with wondrous attractions both for the waggoner and his horse. In the inn-yard were stacks of fern and hay, the former being used for litter, as straw would be elsewhere. Along the edge of the grass, a couple of black sows, followed by their numerous progeny, went nosing about with a most unsatisfied grunt, while a company of geese with nervous quack-quack strutted over the green.

It is quite possible that in the less frequented parts of the Forest one might meet with uncouthness and suspicion, but for my part, I found them not only civil but friendly; and this experience is corroborated by those who know them well, and who protest against a character for unusual rudeness being ascribed to them. One gentleman who has lived amongst them thirty years assures me that he has never received a rude answer but once, and that was from a stranger.

Much, no doubt, has been done by the schools with which the Forest is well supplied. Probably, too, it is they who have driven the old superstitions away, and scattered the mental twilight which for so many ages pervaded these leafy solitudes . . .

PEASANT LIFE
IN DORSET

(GOLDEN HOURS, 1872)

It is, I suppose, an undisputed fact that the Dorset labourer has worked for generations at a lower money wage than any other member of the agricultural community. I suppose, too, it is an undisputed fact that the cottage in which he has been compelled to live has long been a byword and a reproach. I know that the question of wages in Dorsetshire is embarrassed by a number of so-called privileges, and by opportunities of extra earnings; nevertheless, there can be little doubt that the labourer in Dorset has been, and still is, notwithstanding the rise in wages which has taken place in some districts, worse off than in any other part of the land.

So wretched indeed has been his lot, that Sir Charles Trevelyan is probably within the truth when he says, 'The state of our southern peasantry is worse than the present state of the peasantry in the greater part of Ireland.'

Many people no doubt console themselves with the belief that such a condition of things is not so hard as it seems, considering what dull, coarse-minded clodhoppers the people are who have to endure it. As a matter of fact, however, natures of the gentlest mould may be met with perhaps as frequently among 'dull clodhoppers' as among the classes above them in the social scale.

The peculiarity in Dorset is that such natures are not so much the exception as the rule. The Dorset peasantry are gentlefolk by birth. It is not that veneer which the most thorough scoundrel can easily assume, but that native inbred refinement, that perception

of beauty and fitness, which is almost, if not quite, a divine gift . . .

Dorsetshire may be divided into three districts. There is the highland, running through the centre of the county, and forming its back-bone; the vale of Blackmore to the north, mainly laid down in grass land, and occupied by dairy farmers; while to the south of the chalk hills stretches for many a mile vast tracts of heath, much of which is uncultivated, and upon which are to be found most of those wretched cottages for which Dorsetshire has earned such an unenviable notoriety.

However, some of the worst cottages in the county are in the neighbourhood of Dorchester itself. Nothing can well exceed the description of those in the village of Fordington, as given in the Government report of 1867, and I saw enough as I passed through the village last autumn to enable me to testify against the place.

The villages in Dorset have a very grave, sombre appearance, and the cottages are built in rows, and mostly formed of stone or 'cob', with no front gardens; and if it were not for the cosy-looking thatched roofs and the two dormer windows peeping out underneath them, these Dorset villages would look as stern and as bleak as those in the north country. But the thatch covers the whole village – at least, all those portions that are contiguous, like some beneficent natural growth, spreading its protecting arms over everything. No form, however unexpected, or ugly, or unusual, is left out of its embrace; it undulates gently over them all, and brings cottages big and little, outhouses, barns, pigsties, all into one harmonious whole, and may be regarded as emblematic of the unity of the society dwelling beneath it.

'Cob' is mud covered with a thin coating of plaster. Cottages built of this material are very snug and warm in winter, and cool in summer. The old cottages are mainly built of it, and are often very large and roomy. I went into one, in an old tumbledown row in Stowborough. The cottage itself was perhaps twenty feet wide. Its sole inhabitant was a good dame, the old schoolmistress of the village. The floor was sanded and furnished with tall chairs and an ancient escritoire, which had come from Corfe, some thought

from the castle. On the old hearth were a couple of fire-dogs. In another part of the house was a stack of 3000 peats, her winter's supply. Every poor cottager about this part burns peat, so that there is a turfy smell pervading the air. They can get 1000 peats for about three shillings, but to those who have to employ others to do the cutting, carting, and unloading, it costs ten times the money. The good old dame's school had been one of the ordinary stamp, but she had conducted it for forty years; and when she gave up, the parents and scholars had presented her with a large illustrated Bible, as a testimony to their gratitude and respect. The greatest trouble she had was that her landlord wanted to pull down the old house, the home of her fathers, and build a new one. And this touches a chord which is very common amongst the rural poor. For the old house is full of sweet memories, and if you destroy it, you destroy the only joy left in life for the old – to dwell in the thought of the past . . .

Here is an account of how the family of an ordinary Dorset labourer lives, given by the good wife, and reported by the Commissioner, Mr Stanhope:

We have brought up ten children and have never had sixpence from the parish. My husband had 8s and his cottage and garden. We mayn't keep a pig, but instead of this master gives us 6d a week for the wash. Sometimes, master's glad to sell us some of the meat. In the last three years we have got perhaps seven or eight bits in this way. We have bought a bit at Christmas, when the children are here. We buy a little pig-meat; we use it with the potatoes. At harvest we have some cheese, but not at any other time. We don't often get potatoes. When we had ten at home, we could not live on the bread we could buy. We'd get a little rice if the potatoes wasn't good. My children never used to drink much tea. I'd mix them a little broth (bread, hot water, pepper, and salt). At harvest and hay time we get money to buy cider.

Another woman, the wife of a shepherd, who had lived at Blandford twenty-seven or twenty-eight years, stated that she had

had twelve children, seven of whom were living at home with them then. They lived on potatoes, bread, and pig-meat, but often sat down to dry bread. They never had a bit of milk. They had learned to drink cocoa at harvest, which is doubtless a great improvement on cider. The husband had 10s a week, and a house to live in, because he worked on Sundays. They had a piece of potato ground near the house, but, as she pathetically observed, "taters, 'taters, every year they don't turn out very much.' They bought their own firewood, but had to draw it themselves. Sometimes their wood will cost them £2 for the winter. At one time they only had two bedrooms, and when all the family were young, thirteen or fourteen persons would be sleeping in them.

I am assured, however, that remarkable care may often be noticed among them to avoid the ill effects of overcrowding, such as sending out the young men at nights to lodge with neighbours; and that in some cases, where too many have occupied one room, it would be difficult to trace the slightest symptoms of want of modesty. But this, as my informant tells me, depends almost entirely on the character of the parents. However the fact may be, that it should be possible at all under the circumstances speaks well for the innate delicacy of the Dorset peasant.

In the neighbourhood of Dorchester the cottagers kill a pig now and then, but they too commonly, if not mainly, live on bread and cheese and potatoes. . . . But what better fare can be hoped for with wages such as the Dorset peasant gets – wages too of which the greater part is sometimes paid in kind? Many farmers keep a running account with their men. There is the grist-corn, that is the barley or second wheat, which they sell their labourers at the market rate. There is skim-milk, wash for the pig, the occasional bits of dead meat; and in the Vale of Blackmore a quantity of beer and cider; so that when the time comes for the settlement of accounts the labourer finds he has very little cash to receive.

It is a miserable system, liable to great abuse, only working well under masters who are both prosperous and generous. As to prosperity, the modern farmer is driven by high rents and heavy taxes to closer dealings with his men than was the case with his

predecessors; he cannot afford to be so generous as they were. In those days there was a community of feeling between the farmer and his men which made such a system work satisfactorily for both parties. The patriarchal idea still held sway in rural life.

Nevertheless the Dorset peasant speaks well of his employers, is amenable to his parson, and has a good word for the squire. He is neither sad nor suspicious. He makes the most of his joys, and bears his sorrows as best he may.

Thus in 1847, after the potato famine, when the people were suffering much more than usual, so that they were thankful to buy undressed flour and pea-meal, the children were as bright and merry, and the people as cheerful as under ordinary circumstances.

Like all simple, true-hearted natures, they are very susceptible to love and friendship. Walking down the road in twilight, or meetings in the woody hollow, are institutions as faithfully observed by the young men and maidens here as elsewhere.

Most frequently the fair is the place where the attraction is first felt. Then the young labourer, arrayed in his holiday costume, is emboldened to try his fortune, and overcome the shamefacedness so natural to him . . .

It is perhaps in dress and behaviour one sees more than in anything else the gentle breeding of the Dorset peasant. On Sunday the men mostly wear tidy coats of black or blue, with tall beavers, while the women are simply but neatly attired . . .

Not that there is less gaiety or mirth in Dorset than in any other part of England, but, as far as I could learn, it was wholesome mirth. Indeed, the love of joking, play of wit, and sharp but kindly repartee, the ready appreciation of irony and of principles conveyed or hinted in a playful manner, is quite a striking feature in Dorset character . . .

Feast-day is an institution vigorously supported by bell-ringing, fifes playing, horns roaring, drums beating, and boughs over every door, while from the country all around the people come flocking in.

Club-day, too, is an important anniversary, when the members, bearing their great flags, walk in procession to the church, where

Mr Goodman, the rector, preaches them a sermon. . . . However, the church is no match for the public-house, and dinner and drink soon make too many of the members heedless of the exhortation (to spend their evening like their morning), and so, 'stark mad with pweison stuff', the evening of a club-day presents a sad scene in many a cottage home, for drink is the fiend that misleads men in Dorsetshire as everywhere else. Unhappily, custom favours its temptation, labourers receiving in some cases cider as part of their wages. No doubt both masters and men are under the belief that it helps them to work better.

Mr Bailey Denton gives a striking instance of the prevalence of this opinion in Dorset, and how signally it was refuted. In 1852 he was employing Dorset labourers on some large drainage works in the county, at the rate of wages which were then given – 7s and 9s a week. Convinced that labour so poorly paid was hardly worth having, he induced some north countrymen to migrate south, promising them a minimum wage of 18s a week. When the Dorset men learnt what the north countrymen were getting, they were filled with a spirit of emulation, and commenced drinking a greater quantity of beer, that they might be able to work as hard. But they soon saw their error, when they found that their competitors were living on good bread and meat, while they were half starved on bread, tobacco, and bad beer or worse cider. After a while they became convinced that a little butcher's meat was worth all the beer in the world, and under this diet became so efficient that Mr Denton was enabled to reverse the experiment, and take the Dorset men to do work for him in Yorkshire.

With all their poverty, and the absolute necessity that every child in the house should do its utmost to add to the family purse, Mr Stanhope, the Government Commissioner, says:

> I noticed with pleasure the great desire for instruction among the labouring poor in this county, one proof of which may be found in the fact that the proportion of parishes with night schools is unusually large. In Dorset there are forty-four night schools in 100 ecclesiastical districts; while, in Kent, where the

labourer is so well off in a money point of view, there are only twenty-six in an equal number.

But night schools can do but little when a boy goes to work at eight years of age, or frequently earlier, getting up with his father at four or five o'clock in the morning, and stumping about over the fields from six until two with no cessation excepting little halts for meals. Not only is his mind deadened, but his poor little body is permanently injured.

Compare the shapely forms of the young farmers with those of the stunted young labourer, and the injury inflicted by compelling an immature body to such labour as agricultural work will be seen at a glance. Compare the stalwart, jovial forms of the elderly farmers with that of the rheumatic, misshapen forms of the old labourers, and the evil result, not only of over-early work, but of a lifetime of poor and insufficient food and bad lodging, will be manifest. Add to this that they suffer from a want unknown to the northern labourer – a good fire. At Milton Abbas the vicar says, 'Fuel is so scarce that the families as a rule never have a fire at meal-times except in winter.'

All these things combine to depress a naturally sensitive people, and to render them the victims of oppression both earthly and spiritual.

Education helps them to throw off the yoke, and every clever lad naturally thinks of emigration as the only possible cure for the terrible hardships he must endure if he stays at home. As a poor mother said, 'They like to be good scholars, because it helps them to get away.'

Education, too, frees their minds from still darker evils which oppress them – belief in omens, witchcraft, ghosts, etc . . .

Sunday gives the poor toiler an opportunity of cultivating those human affections without which life would become bestial. It is the only day when families and friends can meet . . .

The Dorset peasant's faith in God is simple and childlike – God has promised, and he will perform . . .

Nevertheless poverty and a sensitive heart are no protection

against the snares of Satan; on the contrary, it is just because he has a sensitive heart that the Dorset peasant is all the more easily crushed and rendered reckless by adversity. Periods of semi-starvation and wretched cottages drive such natures into vice and practical atheism. At whose door lies the sin?

Is this the practical result of modern social economy? If so it is a system by which the poor get poorer and the rich richer; a system, the evil effects of which are more manifest in the country than in the town, since it is evident that the small landed proprietor, the small farmer, are every day losing ground, while the great landed proprietor and the large farmer are every day adding to their domains and increasing the acreage of their farms . . .

Thus the poor are made poorer, while, still worse, the very lands of the poor – the *common* land – is taken from them – enclosed; for whose benefit? The large proprietors again. They get the lion's share, while the poor man gets nothing at all. Not possessing any freehold land of his own, the privilege he has enjoyed for ages of pasturing his cow, or feeding his geese or ducks, goes for nothing . . .

NORTHUMBRIAN HINDS AND CHEVIOT SHEPHERDS

(GOLDEN HOURS, 1871)

Notwithstanding the miserable condition of a large number of our fellow-countrymen who follow 'the painful plough', there yet remains, even in England, a peasantry concerning whom a Royal Commission has given the following report:

> They are very intelligent, sober, and courteous in their manner. This courtesy, moreover, is not cringing, but coupled with a manly independence of demeanour. Crime is almost unknown in agricultural Northumberland.

During this present summer I sought to find out, as far as I could, what it was made the Northumberland peasantry so superior. I visited Wooler and its neighbourhood, walking along the base of the Cheviots as far as Rothbury, and during my rambles I took every opportunity of conversing with the people, and learning from their own mouths the true state of things.

First of all, the conditions of agricultural service in Northumberland are peculiar. The *hind,* an old Saxon name implying a household servant, is hired by the year, his term of service commencing on the 13th of May to the same date on the following year. Something like statute fairs are held about Lady-day in Wooler, Rothbury, Belford, Alnwick, and Morpeth, at which the hinds are hired. Unmarried hinds and domestic servants are, however, engaged only a few days before they go to a place.

Cottages are provided expressly for labourers on a farm, and

Women field workers, Glendale, Northumberland, *c.* 1900.

Museum of English Rural Life.

'The Stone Pickers' (oil on canvas, Sir George Clausen, 1887). The removal of surplus stones from fields and meadows was a back-breaking job usually allocated to female labourers, who worked for half the male wage rate.

From the collection at the Laing Art Gallery, Newcastle-upon-Tyne.

Reproduced by arrangement with Tyne and Wear Museums Service.

their use considered as part of the wages. They are the property of the laird, as the landlord is called; are built by him, and included in the farmer's rent. Wages are paid mostly in kind, and perhaps the best idea I can give of what this means is to quote a statement given by the post-master at Wooler to the Commissioner, as to the value of wages paid in this fashion:

Cow (its keep)	£8	0	0
House	3	0	0
Coals (carrying from the pit)	1	5	0
Potatoes	4	0	0
Oats	6	0	0
Barley	4	16	0
Peas	3	0	0
Wheat	2	0	0
Stint Money	5	0	0
	£37	1	0

A hind can, if he prefers it, get paid in cash, but taking all things into consideration he can by this system make from fifteen to eighteen shillings a week.

But there is one great drawback. The hind has to provide a woman to work for his master as required. The hind has to give the 'bondager' – for such is the ugly title, evidently a relic of serfdom – yearly wages amounting to £12 10s, besides food, and lodging, and washing. As he only receives £15 for her work, it is clear that he only gets 50s for her lodging and maintenance all the year round. It frequently happens, however, that the bondager is his own daughter, and this leads to his making a bargain for the labour of his whole family . . .

Wooler is a little town, with one long street branching out into two or three ways at one end. It has a number of inns, but all but two were very small, and none appeared to do any business. It was market-day when I arrived, but the sole additional excitement consisted in the entry about noon of a dozen or twenty squires and

farmers, who walked or stood about in groups conversing with each other.

There were a few quiet shops in the street, one a bookseller's. Everything in the way of stationery sold there was of the cheapest description, showing that the owner catered for a class who were not disposed to spend their money on mere luxuries; but on the counter I saw works, which certainly argued an enlightened public in Wooler and its neighbourhood. . . . That same afternoon a number of boys running out of school overtook me in the fields. Three of them almost immediately stretched themselves on the grass and recommenced summing. The English Presbyterian schoolmaster at Wooler told the Government Commissioner, Mr Henley, that he had four boys in his school learning Latin – one the son of a gamekeeper, another the son of a shepherd, a third the son of a skinner of sheep, and the fourth the son of the widow of a railway porter. Two others learnt French and Euclid, one a shepherd's son, and the other a hind's.

At the beginning of the last century, the country round about here was almost in a state of nature, now there are few parts of England so well cultivated. Turnip-growing is the work to which the Northumbrian farmers devote their best energies. Thousands of acres are planted here along the base of the Cheviots, upon which, when its verdant herbage begins to fail, the sheep are fed. It is curious to note, as one may frequently at this time of the year, a party of women and boys turnip-hoeing, and all working in a line, with one man as overseer directing them. To a stranger unaccustomed to such a sight it unpleasantly recalls old scenes in the sugar plantations of Jamaica or of South Carolina. But with such a people as the Northumbrians anything like slave-driving is quite impossible. The arrangement is the result of systematic farming, the application of the rules of the factory to the field.

Just outside Wooler is Humbleton Hill, an outpost of the Cheviots, and famous for a fierce border battle, described by Shakespeare. The hill itself is wild and picturesque, with great boulders of granite scattered all amongst the fern. . . . When at last I reached the top, the wind blew so fiercely that I was glad to

shelter myself behind a great cairn which had been raised there. . . . In my descent I came upon an old man carrying home a bundle of wood. He appeared surprised when I told him that I understood labourers were better off in Northumberland than elsewhere. He said that they reckoned, when they had taken everything into consideration, that they did not get more than 12s a week. He had never been married, but had lived in his old and miserable cot for twenty years.

'Why had he never cared to marry?'

'Because,' he replied, 'a woman in Northumberland's not worth house room. Why, you see, sir, she's out in the field all day, and knows nothing about housework . . .'

He had made up his mind early in life, not only on this account, but because he would not bring a woman and perhaps a family into the bargain into misery.

'Men and women lived disagreeable, for there was nothing like poverty to make them quarrel.'

Here was the other side of the question, though some will, no doubt, think he was a cynical old bachelor. But his face had nothing sour in it, and I could not but admire the manner in which he accepted his hard fate. He assured me he was quite contented; and although it seemed hard to believe, there was no reason to doubt that he meant what he said.

Next morning I started for a ramble over the Cheviots, but soon lost my way. However, I came upon a couple of cottages, and was allowed to enter one to have a look at its interior. The tenant was a widow woman, who lived there with her three sons and two daughters. One son was a labourer, the other worked in a quarry, while the third went to school. Both daughters worked in the fields, one serving as the bondager. The mother complained that working in the fields affected the health of one of the daughters.

The house consisted of one room and a loft ascended by a ladder. Downstairs were two box beds, which I sketched, as they afforded a good example of this essentially Northumbrian practice. In this particular instance they were without sliding doors or

even curtains, as is elsewhere frequently the case. They had begun to entertain some ideas of the benefit of ventilation.

Things looked very comfortable, as doubtless they were not badly off, with four grown-up young people earning their living. They kept a cow in winter-time; it had formerly come into the house, but I understood the practice was discontinued. While sketching, in came a strong, good-looking youth, about eighteen or twenty. The labourers have a good long rest in the middle of the day, an hour and a-half, or two hours. They live well, 'eat a vast of meat', although it is principally bacon. Their bread is made of barley and pea-meal mixed. This, with a good basin of porridge and milk, forms their breakfast. To judge from the number of dealers in tea and tobacco, no village, however small, is without one. I infer they drink a great deal of tea and coffee, and this is corroborated by the reports, in which medical men continually express their regret at the growth of this practice, since they believe it to have an injurious tendency.

From thence I wandered over the hills, trying to get into the right track, until at last I came on a shepherd's cottage, where I again inquired the way. Here, too, I was heartily welcomed. The shepherd was at home, and while I attempted a sketch of the interior of his house, he told me freely the conditions of his service.

But first of all, let me describe his home. Its exterior looked dreary enough, seen in the rain. I passed through a little stone passage, and then into a larger apartment. Here were two box beds as in the former house. There was no ceiling, but canvas had been drawn tight over the rafters, so that the great beams came under it. The sides of the house were of rough stones, of the same make as the dykes. Paper had been put over them to give it an appearance of comfort, but the wind got between it and the wall, and made it wabble to and fro. A spotless deal table stood beneath the window, upon which the good-wife was kneading her bread. When it was made it went into a large oven, which formed part of the usual range found in most Northumbrian cots, and which is put in by the tenant himself. By the side of the window was a

looking-glass and a little case of shelves containing the crockery, all tastefully arranged. As I talked with the shepherd, he kept rocking the cradle, a curious little box on rollers.

His conditions were as follows. When he entered into service he was allowed to purchase a number of sheep at his master's expense. When he was married, he began with thirteen; now he has forty-two. He also has a cow, and kills perhaps two large hogs in the year. Cow and hogs, as well as sheep, are well provided for by the master. Besides this, he supplies him with thirteen barrels of corn, each barrel containing six bushels, and fifteen hundred yards of potatoes, and a house to live in. Coals he buys himself, but they are carted by his master to his door. He makes his income out of the wool of his sheep, and the sale of his lambs. He was going to Alnwick Fair with the latter on the following Monday. His eldest boy was twelve years old; he worked in the fields with the women, turnip-hoeing in the summer, and went to school in the winter.He had a taste for drawing, and had ornamented various parts of the room with his little efforts. His parents said they hoped, if they were spared, to give him another season or two of schooling, although they had four other boys and a little girl.

The shepherd, whose house I sketched, always went down to Wooler on Sundays, to the Presbyterian Church, as his father had done before him for fifty years.

He took me to see another shepherd, who lived in a new house built by the Earl of Tankerville. It was as comfortable as anyone in the world could wish; two large rooms, with every convenience; a capital stove, good oven and boiler, all put in at the laird's expense; a roomy dairy, a cowhouse with stalls for six cows, a stable for the horse, and a place for the dog. Nothing was forgotten. I can imagine no life, on the whole, so healthful and so hopeful as that of a Cheviot shepherd, if the old conditions of service can be maintained, and such cottages built for him.

It is, however, one full of anxiety, and sometimes of great peril. During the winter months they are liable to terrible snowstorms, in which not only the flock but the shepherd himself has been

known to perish. The mariner is hardly more weatherwise than the shepherd, but the most experienced shepherd is unable to foresee the extent and fury of these pitiless storms. Sometimes they come with hardly any notice at all, or after warm weather sufficient to delude all but the most canny into the belief that the winter is over and gone; at other times the skies will gather and lower for hours, but none can tell in what quarter the storm will break. In sheltered parts of the hills the shepherds erect stone walls in the form of a circle, roughly built of boulders, and about four feet high, as places of refuge for the sheep when a storm comes on. Happy is the shepherd who can gather his sheep, and fold them into such a 'stell', for if they get scattered after the storm has set in, they will, of their own accord, seek the nooks and gullies – the very spots where the snow-wreaths accumulate, and get buried at the depth of many feet. When this occurs, the shepherds go and search for the lost sheep with long poles, with which they probe the snow, but in the white, wavy, trackless drift they would have little chance of success, if it were not for the help of their invaluable dogs. The intelligence of these sagacious animals is an ever-renewed cause of wonder; without them, it is not too much to say, a district like the Cheviots would be a desert . . .

In the interesting blue books . . . we have some surprising proofs given of the determination of these shepherds to obtain instruction for themselves and their children.

Anthony Dagg, a shepherd of Linbriggs, on the Cheviots, the father of eleven children, about twenty years ago hired a schoolmaster at his own expense. After a year or two he took his master and two other shepherds into partnership. The school is now attended by thirty-one children, and there is not at the present time a person in the district who cannot read and write. The schoolmaster moves from house to house among his four employers, receiving board and lodging during fourteen days for each scholar.

Near Bellingham a few shepherds on the hills keep a schoolmaster between them, and later commissioned their schoolmaster to procure for them Virgil, Horace, and Caesar.

THE VICTORIAN PEASANT

In the winter-time the parents will send the bigger boys into lodgings at Wooler, that they may have further advantages in the way of education. In the school belonging to the English Presbyterians the master speaks of having two sons of shepherds, one learning Latin, the other French and Euclid.

Perhaps the secret of this mental energy lies in the deep religiousness which characterises them as a class . . .

Leaving Wooler, I bent my course southwards along the base of the Cheviots, preferring bye-roads, because they brought me through more villages. The system of building cottages on the farms makes villages scarce, and one would be inclined to think there were no people in the land, so rarely does one meet even a solitary wayfarer on the road . . .

At Ilderton I came on a long row of cottages, mere plain, substantial little dwellings, each with a window and a door, cold and dreary-looking enough in the pelting rain. I found one where they kept a shop, and sold small groceries, and, entering, ventured to ask them to make me some tea. The house consisted of the one room, which served as bedroom, sitting-room, kitchen, and shop in all. Yet it was a really comfortable little place, as clean as one could wish, and the box-beds hardly looked stuffy. Pictures, not at all bad, adorned the wall; one was a large portrait of John Bunyan. On the table was a volume of Spurgeon's sermons, and a book by McCheyne. There, too, was the tall clock, without which a cottage would never seem furnished in the north.

The good woman, with just a slight tinge of coldness at first, took off the great pot of nettles she was about to boil for the pigs, and hung up the kettle. It seemed to boil in no time, and soon she made some excellent tea. Then she sat down, and began to knit away as if for her life, while her eldest daughter was busily engaged in numberless domestic duties, doing it all so pleasantly as if it were no effort. The youngest daughter it seemed had not reached the age for labour, and it being too wet to go to school was busy with a piece of fancy-work.

The mother said they were not obliged to provide a bondager, like most other people. There was a church at Ilderton, but only

two or three families went; the rest were Presbyterians; she should like to hear Mr Spurgeon preach; she had read his 'John Ploughman's Talk', and thought he seemed to know all about agricultural life.

On I went until I reached Wooperton, where I was invited to rest by the postmaster. His home was the pink of neatness, but then he was an old bachelor. However, he gave a very different account of Northumbrian women to my old cottager. He had known women who had worked in the fields who were very clever with the needle, and good managers; still, he believed it a bad system for domestic life. There was, however, a true simplicity of character about these labouring girls. He spoke of some who would not look at a man in a superior position; were he worth hundreds, they would refuse him. He believed they were very happy. . . . The people, he said, came on Sabbath for miles to their chapels in Wooler, Branton, and Glanton; but on sacramental days, which only occur three times a year – in March, July, and October – every one makes an effort to be present, and then the chapels are thronged.

Next day being Sunday, I had an opportunity of going to the chapel at Glanton. A more intelligent, earnest, serious congregation I never saw in my life. There was scarcely a listless or stupid-looking face among them all, the greater part being men between eighteen and fifty. The service was in no way attractive; the hymns were the Scotch paraphrase of the psalms, and the singing at times dragged heavily. But these people have a religion in which they believe, and which they themselves support. They do not go to church to receive a loaf, or a dole of flannel or money; on the contrary, they are expected to believe it is more blessed to give than to receive, and every Sunday round from pew to pew goes the collecting-box, and few, I venture to say, let it pass without a weekly offering. Nearly all the labouring people, shepherds and hinds, are Presbyterians, and not only attend a place of worship but are generally communicants. In Wooler there are three churches of this denomination, with 600 communicants, another with 300, and at the third, which is called English

Presbyterian, there are about 200. Most of their children are sent in due course to be catechized by their ministers . . .

Before I left Wooler I paid a visit to one of the Presbyterian ministers. He endorsed all I had seen of the domestic life of these noble people. The bondage system, he said, was not so strict as it used to be. He spoke of the blot on the fair name of Northumbria. Illegitimacy was not uncommon, but he did not think it much due to field labour; the cottages, no doubt, were a source of evil.

The prevalence of this particular vice is attributed by others to the laxity of opinion with reference to the marriage bond, arising from the frequency of border marriages in former times; but it does not seem necessary to go far for a cause in the presence of the bondage system, carried on in connection with one-roomed cottages.

At Eslington, close to Lord Ravensworth's mansion, I went into a cottage where seven persons – a father, mother, grand-mother, two grown-up sons, and two other children – all slept in one room, and that room was not weather-tight, since daylight could be seen through the boards which formed the ceiling. They had given up the box-beds because of the 'varmint', and had two four-posters, and a fold-up bedstead for the sons.

In this case the mother acted as the bondager, and the grand-mother did the housework. Surely such a domestic arrangement is bad enough in itself; how much worse, if in addition they had been obliged to receive a stranger into the family, and that a young female. To a stranger it must be a matter of astonishment how such enlightened people as Northumbrian employers can allow such a system to continue a single day, did we not remember that there is not an evil which had afflicted and oppressed mankind but it has found its ablest apologists amongst truly benevolent men, whose interests, unfortunately for their own clearness of vision, were wrapped up in the maintenance of the institution.

It would be a great mistake to suppose that when we speak of seven people sleeping in one room in Northumberland, it comes to the same thing as it would be in other parts of England. We must remember that the house consists of only one room, and is

therefore large and comparatively high. This fact, and the good living and air the whole family enjoy, renders it innocuous to health. Both sexes are physically strong.

It is well known that in all athletic sports the north countrymen excel. Perhaps there are no such leapers in the world as the borderers. At Glanton I witnessed the Great Northern Games, and nothing surprised me so much as the height over which the natives leaped. In the flat-racing, hurdle-racing, and wrestling the professional athletes from Scotland and elsewhere came off conquerors, but the leaping was hotly contested by the natives, some vaulting with the aid of a pole over a stick between ten and eleven feet high.

With the more serious sports were mingled others of a lighter nature – the Highland fling, donkey-racing, and a curious game at which the boys played blindfolded, and each armed with a bag of coloured dust. The fun consisted in a man, who kept ringing a little bell, leading them all a wild-goose chase, while they, on their part, tried to beat him with their dust-bags, but more frequently falling foul of each other. Of course this excited much merriment, otherwise the proceedings were conducted with the utmost decorum. There was very little laughing, occasional outbursts of enthusiasm in the way of applause, especially of little knots interested in the success of a friend. Otherwise there was no undue prepossession, and the strangers got their full due. All classes were represented, but the greater part were so dressed that had it not been for a covered stand devoted to the gentry, it would have been difficult to say who was who in such a respectable assembly.

I cannot conclude this paper without relating one more incident which occurred in my last walk in Northumberland. Being tired, I came to a lone cottage, which had, however, the inscription, 'Licensed to sell tea and tobacco', over the little porch. I looked in, and asked them if they would make me a cup of tea. This they readily agreed to do, and going to their store, I soon had everything I could wish. While refreshing myself, my eyes wandered over the room, which served alike for parlour, bedroom, and kitchen, the groceries being kept in the lean-to. Box-beds had been discarded for two well-appointed four-posters, very different from the gaunt

skeletons, with drabby shawls doing duty for curtains, one sees so often in southern cottages. But what struck me most of all were the books. . . . I was not surprised to learn that these people were good Presbyterians, and staunch believers in the value of education. The father was taking his rest after his midday meal, reading the newspaper, and I fell into converstaion with him and his wife. They told me that their children, a boy and a girl, had to walk every day six or seven miles to school at Whittingham, but they did not speak of it as a hardship, or as an excuse for neglecting to send their children. As to the young people themselves, they evidently loved learning all the more since it had cost them such an effort to obtain it.

It was in the churchyard of the parish where they went to school that I met with the following inscription:

SACRED TO THE MEMORY
OF
JAMES MITCHELL, TEACHER, BRANTON
Son of William and Mary Mitchell
Who died 15th August 1853, aged 26 years

He was a young man of cultivated and refined mind,
well aware of the importance of his profession. He
discharged his duties efficiently, gained the
affections of his pupils, and the respect of all
who knew him. 'Having kept the faith', he died in
the full hope of attaining a 'crown of glory'.

All honour to the land that honours the schoolmaster! What can give to England's peasantry the intelligence, the self-respect, the self-reliance, the home comfort which makes Northumbria a land of Goshen in our agricultural Egypt?

Changes wide and deep may be in store for us, but this we know – they will all be delusive without the aid of the schoolmaster . . .

A YORKSHIRE DALE

(GOLDEN HOURS, 1872)

(Shut) in by two long ranges of opposing cliffs, rising at times to the altitude of nearly 2000 feet, Swaledale has preserved longer than elsewhere the interesting and often valuable customs of the fore-elders. The ancient town of Richmond, at the entrance to the dale, is its only direct communication with the outer world. . . . The only public conveyance in the dale is the carrier's cart, which jogs to and fro from Richmond to Reeth, a village about half-way up the dale.

The little company with whom I rode to Reeth consisted of an old daleswoman and her daughter, and a woodcutter who sprang up soon after we left Richmond. He was an independent sort of a man, as indeed I found all the dalesmen to be. There is a practical equality among them, arising from similarity of position and education, which shows itself in many ways. Farther up the dale, I was told, the servants sit in the same parlour as their master and mistress, and call them, with the simple familiarity of friends, Tom and Mary.

The woodcutter was very talkative. He was employed in cutting down small, or 'spring-wood', as he phrased it, used for the purpose of making supports to the cuttings in the lead mines. He was paid 4d a dozen, but the dozen was reckoned in a curious way. Twenty-four small sticks, or one pole of ten feet, were alike regarded as equivalent to a dozen. He found employment nearly all the year round, and was evidently not badly off. He thought there were not many poor people in the dale – that is, people in

want. On the contrary, many poor-looking men were very rich, and had hundreds of pounds in the bank. Those who live near the moor can feed their stock for nothing, live in the barest manner, and save little by little. (Indeed) their frugality and prudence too often degenerate into mere avarice and selfishness. The woodcutter spoke of one man, worth £2000, who hired himself as a day-labourer to his brother, because by doing so it cost him nothing to live. I was told of another man who lived at the rate of about £20 a year, and suffered all the anxieties of the wealthy miser. 'No one', he was heard to say, 'knew what it was to sleep on seven thousand pounds' . . .

Peaceful, indeed, would be the lives of these dalesmen, if it were not that their chief industry – lead-mining – is subject to much fluctuation. Reeth, the centre of the mining district, is a bleak and rather dismal place, surrounded by lofty hills . . .

In Reeth and its neighbourhood I conversed with some of the miners. When the veins are exhausted, the mining companies offer them a large percentage to search out fresh veins; but when they are found, they reduce the amount rapidly, as they know that labourers will then come flocking in. This makes the work very precarious. One man told me that he had earned by a single job as much as £60 or £70, while at another time he had not earned more than eighteenpence in eighteen weeks. When in regular work they average nine or ten shillings a week, taking the whole year round. Owing, however, to the unhealthy nature of the employment, they are unable to work more than six hours a day. They begin at ten years of age; their lungs gradually get stuffed up with fine lead-dust, so that as men they look very thin and sickly, and can scarcely live to be old.

In a walk in the neighbourhood of Reeth I met one – a gentle, intelligent man. His complexion was pale and yellow, but through it shone a genial, shrewd, and far from melancholy expression. He was returning home from the mine. He had to walk two hours to his work, and two hours back – a distance of five or six miles each way. He worked in the mine his own time, and spoke well of the masters. Sometimes the miners descend shafts twenty-four

fathoms deep; these shafts are supported by woodwork, and the men have to climb up and down them. In the levels they work by candle-light, and go in by a very narrow tunnel on a tramway. They never have explosions, as in coal-mines, but the air is close, and when they come out they feel dizzy for a bit.

In addition to his earnings at the mine, he farmed three acres, on which he kept a cow — selling the milk for a penny a pint, and sometimes 'kearning a bit.' He had had eight children, but they were all dead but two; one, a girl of seven, had died in a fortnight from the effects of a burn. The last who died was a young man of eight-and-twenty, who, it seems, had taken much to learning:

> I schuled him te fourteen, and he went on te mensuration and algebra. Ah, edication's a light harrow, ye may carry it any-where. I sent him down here te schule at Low Row, and paid sixpence a week. The price was tenpence, but the committee said, 'If ye charge him that much, maybe he'll be taken away, sin' his father's but a puir man.' There was Barker's son, he went te college, and was teacher at the free schule up here; he was his schulefellow; the tweeah went to schule together, and now they are both deead.

Consumption killed the son – a disease, I fear, common amongst these miners, since inhaling the noxious vapour and the lead-dust must make havoc with the lungs, and, moreover, the occupation is hereditary.

My friend paid £13 a year for his little cottage, and something besides for poors' rates and taxes. He had no vote, and seemed rather to deprecate the privilege than to desire it. 'If I'd a vote, they might summon me te York on a jury; besides, I know many a man who has a vote who daren't use it.' He hoped they would pass the bill for vote by ballot. He was a Wesleyan, but he thought 'we should never be asked what we'd been.' A man one instinc-tively took to, when the time came for parting it was with mutual regret.

An old tale was told me, setting forth the quaint simplicity of

these dalesmen. A miner, going into a little Roman Catholic church in the dale, was present at the Mass. He stared for a long time at each successive action in the ceremonial, until at last he saw the priest raise the chalice, hold it aloft, and drink from it himself without offering it to the other communicants. Then his patience fairly gave way, and he exclaimed, 'Eh, lad, I thought thee'd take it all theesel' in the end.'

The dialect of these dalesmen is not easy to understand, for they not only use a great many words a stranger has never heard of before, but they use common words in a strange sense. Thus a sick person is said to be 'silly'. Some old English words are used – to bray, is to bruise. They have their own way of naming things – thus red currants are 'wine berries'. In many words, however, it is only the pronunciation, as 'lili-uns' for children, that is, little ones; while the youngest is called the 'le-le-ist' . . .

When we left Reeth the clouds were dark and gloomy, and soon quite hid the distant fell. Suddenly the rain fell in torrents. At the approach of the second storm we took shelter in a cottage. Instead of the ancient hearthstone and open chimney and turf fire, such as one sees in the south, there was a modern grate, possessing every convenience, such as large ovens and boilers, while the pots and kettles were suspended by hooks of polished steel to a crane of the same material.

A huge pot as big as a bucket hung over the fire, filled with some savoury mess, which a young damsel was stirring. It is said there is little for the young women to do beyond housework and churning, which can be easily done by the mother and one of the daughters. The cheese and butter they make is collected by local men, who take it to Hawes, where it is bought by the dealers.

How miserable these little stone villages look in wet weather; no pretty little gardens, but stuck here and there without symmetry, black, grimy, and ruinous-looking. The whole of the vale, and far away up the sides of the hills, is divided into endless fields, each field surrounded by its dyke. In the corner of every field stands the 'cow-byre', a little stone building, the upper storey being used for hay, the lower to shield the cows in winter.

Wet and dripping I left Muker, but notwithstanding the rain I could perceive at every step the road was becoming grander. Now through the mist I saw the enormous fells rising on every hand. I heard the roar of the mountain torrents, swollen with the heavy rains; the brown, foaming waters dashing over slabs of limestone, now this side, now that. Soon I passed Thwaite, a little village picturesquely situated on a beck, whose dashing force covers its stony walls with spray. On I went, until I found that I was coming on the moor.

But where was Keld . . . to see which I had made this pilgrimage? Why, it turned out to be a little hamlet of stone cots, hid in a *cul-de-sac,* surrounded by illimitable moors. . . . And yet in this silent, remote spot hearts have been beating, brains working, and life going on as fresh and vigorous as any in the busy haunts of men. Here a noble-hearted Christian minister, who has been called 'the Oberlin of the dales', lived and laboured, and this it was which made the spot attractive, and drew me to it.

James Wilkinson was himself a dalesman. . . . Labouring day by day for the good of his people, thinking only how he might promote their mental and spiritual welfare; turning his thoughts into deeds; shut out from all external influence in this remote spot for twenty-eight years, James Wilkinson lived a poem, if he never wrote one. He used his great powers of organisation and untiring energy entirely for the good of others, his sole purpose in life being, as he himself puts it, 'to be spent in the ways of his great Lord and Master Jesus Christ.' In the quarter of a century during which he worked in Keld and its neighbourhood, hundreds – one might say thousands – of Yorkshiremen, with just such talents as his, rose easily to positions of wealth and influence far beyond the dreams of their forefathers. But such considerations never tempted James Wilkinson from his post. Ordained at Keld, he died pastor of Keld, having fairly worn himself out by his manifold labours. To form any idea of the intense earnestness of his spirit, one ought to see Keld, a miserable hamlet of about twenty cottages, containing not more than seventy inhabitants, hidden in an out-of-the-way corner of the moors, nearly ten miles

from direct communication with any of the main arteries of life in England.

Some idea may be formed of his energy by a short summary of the outward and material improvements which were effected during his ministry. Having succeeded in getting a new school-house erected, he turned his attention to the best means of arousing the mental energies of his people. Collecting a little company of twelve young men at his house, he formed a Mutual Improvement Society on the principle of self-reliance. In seven years the Society was able to think of building a Literary Institute, which was opened in 1862 at a cost of about £119. I visited this Institute in company with the librarian, who is also the postmaster of the village. It had two good rooms, in one of which was a large and well-selected library, comprising not only good books of reference but many of the best modern works of science, travel, and fiction. The books have been mainly selected by the members themselves. Whenever they have some money to spend they get a list from Mudie's Library, and each member is allowed to write down the name of the new book he wishes added. The list having been put up for a fortnight, each member votes for those in the list he likes best.

In the winter, evening classes are conducted by the librarian, who is evidently the chief man in the village. He dwells in a cottage built by his great-grandfather, and possesses a large and well-stocked garden and apiary. The interior of the cottage was the pink of neatness and comfort, and contained many curiosities. Up against the wall was a row of old china, which would have rejoiced the heart of a collector. He was a musician as well, and possessed both a dulcimer and a harmonium . . .

But to return to the pastor of Keld and its Literary Institute. The example thus set in the most remote corner of the dale spread, and now there is scarcely a village in Swaledale without its literary institute.

We may judge that all this outward fruit could not have ripened if there had not been earnest and constant endeavour in a more private way. Not only were there the regular Sunday min-istrations, with six or eight miles to traverse betwixt the two

chapels of Keld and Thwaite, but pastoral visits in winter-time, which were still more formidable undertakings. They were generally announced beforehand from the pulpit, and when the day arrived a little company would sally forth with their pastor, clad weather-proof, and, carrying lanterns and sticks, cross the trackless snow of the moor, leaping the frozen becks, to visit some lonely farm lying far away among the hills, and which but for such visits would be cut off from human sympathy for weeks together.

The people here at the head of the dale are mainly shepherd farmers, working themselves, assisted perhaps by a couple of men who live in the house, and eat and drink with them. If these men get married, they live out of the house, and receive about twelve or thirteen shillings a week. But they generally wait until they have saved a little money and can take a small farm and begin on their own account. This is not difficult to do, as every householder has a right of pasturage for his cattle and sheep on the moors from the 29th of May until winter. During winter the cattle are shut up in the cow-byres and fed upon hay, but the poor sheep have to do the best they can on the moor. This is a hard time for the shepherds, as the roads get snowed up, and the sheep in danger of being lost. However, they collect them in little places of refuge, resembling the Northumbrian 'stells'. Often the boys have to go out on the moor with great bundles of hay on their heads to feed the sheep.

During the summer-time, about six o'clock every afternoon, the cow-herds go out with great tin cases slung over their shoulder, uttering a shrill cry to call the cattle of the moors. Rarely have they any trouble, for the cows are so accustomed to the hour that they would return of themselves, even if there were no call.

The cottages are seldom on a level with the road, standing either above or below it. I was invited into one which lay considerably below the road-side, inhabited by a couple who had evidently married late in life. Spotlessly clean was their parlour, chairs, table, and floor, bright as hand polish and soap and water could make them. There was the tall mahogany clock-case, made at the

time of the wedding. There, too, was a shorter clock and a barometer. Dazzling was the burnished steel of the great fire range, notwithstanding the good fire which burnt in the grate, though it was only just August. From the ceiling hung suspended long planks of cedar wood, whereon they stowed away their oatmeal cakes and other commodities. Instead of pictures, the walls were ornamented with numerous mourning-cards, framed and glazed. They placed me in a great rocking-chair, and while the farmer sat opposite me in another, the good wife fetched a glass of milk and some oatcake. The farmer thought things wonderfully improved in the dale since his childhood; hardly any land was then enclosed, all was open moor. For even these quiet spots see great changes. The tide of humanity is ever ebbing and flowing. Thus, twelve hundred years ago, the Swale must have had a vast population on its banks if it be true that Paulinus baptized 10,000 converts in its waters. Now human beings are so scarce that a visitor is a curiosity. Immediately I entered the village the news was transmitted to the minister that 'a stranger in mannerly claes had come to Keld'; and in the evening a number of men and boys, who had assembled close by the house at which I was staying, were evidently discussing my apparition. Every now and then a figure passed by my window, casting a stealthy glance within, so that I thought it best for my own peace of mind and theirs to go out and make a clean breast of it . . .

FEN-LAND
AND FEN-MEN

(GOLDEN HOURS, 1873)

King George the Third and the author of the 'Political Register' have given the best descriptions of the Fen-land to be met with. The king's is the briefer and more comprehensive. 'What, what!' he exclaimed, 'Lincolnshire? All flats, fogs and fens – eh, eh?' but Cobbett's is the most graphic. 'Here', he writes:

> . . . I am in the heart of the Fens. The whole country is level as the table on which I am now writing; the horizon like the sea in a dead calm. You see the morning sun come up just as at sea, and see it go down over the rim in just the same way as at sea in a calm. The land covered with beautiful grass, with sheep lying about upon it as fat as hogs stretched out sleeping in a stye. Everything grows well here; earth without a stone as big as a pin's head, grass as thick as it can grow upon the ground, immense bowling-greens separated by ditches, and not a sign of a dock or thistle.

Nevertheless it lacks several features necessary to complete the picture. The cottages standing beneath the roadway, surrounded by water, and reached by bridges or planks across the ditches; the road itself a long straight causeway, locally called a rampire, running for miles by the side of a dyke, and on which you may trudge for an hour without a turn or change in the scene; the moist meadows below, intersected by numerous sluggish streams; and last of all, standing out against the gloomy sky, there are the

windmills, and the solitary trees, and the black poles of the sluices. Journey where you will, such are the scenes which meet the eye. . . . But the rich and prolific soil, dark in colour, and as fine in substance as flour, and when cut deep down into with a spade, like a piece of hard butter, compensates its owners for the entire absence of natural scenery . . .

At the meeting in connection with the agricultural labourers' movement, held in Exeter Hall towards the close of last year (1872), the Lincolnshire fen district was represented by a labourer, who, in an eloquent speech, described the sufferings of himself and his companions. He admitted that Lincolnshire Fen-men received a money wage higher than other parts of the country, and yet the burden of his speech seemed to be that semi-starvation and debt dogged their footsteps throughout life. 'I remember', he said, 'working as a boy for twopence a day, and for years going without stockings to my feet; I remember going hundreds of times to work with a bit of bread and a herring for dinner, having had bread and hot water for breakfast.'

During the autumn I was present at an open-air meeting which took place in the dark and in the rain at Croyland, where I believe that I heard the same speaker, together with a fellow-labourer from the Cambridgeshire fens. The latter, in a woe-begone strain, harped on a like string, relating the hardship and misery he and his people had at times endured from want of food, saying bitterly that it would be better if those who professed to feel so much for the labourer would leave off talking about good cottages, education, or sanitary reform, as the only thing needed, and, first of all, give them enough to eat.

Now, as this meeting was composed entirely of labouring people, with a few of the farmers and the tradesmen of the locality – men who knew by a life-long experience the true state of the case – it is evident this Cambridgeshire fen-man would not have made this want of the necessaries of life a leading point in his harangue if he had not been sure that it was here where the shoe pinched. For, though wages may be half as much again in Lincolnshire as they are in Dorset, what, after all, is 15s a week to support a family of

five or six persons? And this is the case of many a young married man. Deduct 1s 6d or 2s for rent, and you have about a couple of shillings for the weekly food and clothing of each individual – just one-sixth of the amount usually allowed a servant for board wages, and which may therefore be considered the sum judged necessary for one person's maintenance per week . . .

Certain it is that the question of mere existence must be uppermost in these fen-men's minds, or they could not possibly have forgotten some far worse evils of their social condition. I refer to the wretched slavery into which scientific improvement and material progress has brought their wives and children. For not a word did these representative fen-men say at either meeting concerning the infamous gang system.

It looks ominous, and, taken in connection with the singular reticence which I have found in getting information on the subject, I am inclined to think that a certain blindness has come upon the inhabitants of the district with regard to its wickedness.

The labouring men may dislike any interference with their supposed rights as fathers to sell their children into slavery; the farmers and the landowners may deprecate any interference with the labour market which would lessen their profits; but if England recognises its responsibilities to God as a nation, it must believe that He will not be satisfied with the plea of ignorance, or the plea of the exigencies of trade, or even with the plea of parental rights. The righteous Ruler of the universe will undoubtedly demand at its hands the blood of its young children destroyed body and soul by this agricultural gang system.

But before I proceed to unfold the evils which have followed in the wake of scientific improvement, let me record one benefit which has proceeded from it. It has vastly improved the health of the district. Malaria and other similar diseases which constantly lurked in the watery atmosphere have been banished, and the Fens, with one alarming exception, stand high in the Registrar-General's report. But the very cause which has brought about this one advantage, the bringing of so much land under tillage, has led to evils of such magnitude as far to counterbalance this solitary

good. These enormous tracts of land require constant labour to keep them well cultivated. The soil is so prolific that the weeds would soon choke everything else if they were not vigorously kept in check. The farms are generally very large, and run a long way into the fen. As a rule, there are no cottages upon them, and they therefore depend almost entirely for their labour on the native supply in the various villages, which lie on the highways, or rather, below them. The want of house-room naturally prevents any influx from other parts of the country, and the consequence is, that for about eight months in the year, every available woman and child is pressed into service.

As this kind of labour has been found to be more effectual under direction and in concert, and as, moreover, it is not always wanted to the same extent, a system has risen whereby a man, called a gang-master, contracts to supply labour when and where it was wanted. He is generally of the class called 'catch-work labourers', that is, a man who prefers jobbing to regular employment. He makes it his business to collect a number of women, young persons, and children, sometimes as many as forty, and form them into a gang, which he leads out day by day to those parts of the fen where he has engaged to work.

This system commenced in the Lincolnshire fens about forty years ago, the natural offspring of the great improvements science had made there. It went on for a whole generation demoralizing the people. At last, in 1865–66, a Commission was appointed, and the evils it revealed from the corruption which ensued in these mixed gangs of women, boys, and girls were of such a nature, that the very same year that the report was published Parliament passed an Act by which it was forbidden to employ any child under eight years of age in a public gang, or any female in the same gang with a male. It was also enacted that every gang-master shall take out a licence, and, in the case of a female gang, a woman was to act as gang-master as well as the man. The Act further gave the Justices power to limit the distance to which a child should walk, if they thought fit.

No doubt this Act has largely mitigated the evils of public

gangs, but private gangs are in no way affected by it. A large occupier near Spalding says: 'The result of legislation for public gangs will be great evasion of the Act under the form of private gangs, which will require dealing with just as much.'

A private gang is one formed and employed by a farmer on his own land; he therefore feels a personal responsibility in its character and proceedings. This is undoubtedly a great advantage, and if a farmer will really trouble himself about it, it may be made a very real one. But the enormous size and great length of the fen farms renders personal supervision in many cases a practical impossibility. How can a man who perhaps has farms miles apart, perhaps two or three hundred acres each in extent, and stretching in elongated fashion for miles into the fen, know much about the behaviour of his work-people? He must leave it to the master of his gang. If the latter is a strictly upright man, things may go on well; but if otherwise, a perfect sink of corruption may exist on the estate of the best-intentioned master in the world.

And even supposing that by strict and careful supervision the grosser forms of evil are kept down, the private gang system does not afford any alleviation in the labour-slavery which has been the lot of these poor fen women and children for two generations.

Let us picture to ourselves the life of one of these families, and we shall see more clearly how little benefit they have derived from the great wealth with which science has enriched their land; how, on the contrary, it has made their lives more miserable and more utterly hopeless than they otherwise would have been . . .

In one row of twelve houses at Langtoft (1864), a ganging village, the average to one bedroom was more than six persons. Up at earliest dawn, for they must start for work at half-past five or six, breakfast is scrambled through and the children hurry out into the street, to meet like a company of factory hands at a given rendezvous. Boys and girls, big and little, corrupt and innocent, they flock together; and there in the pure morning light the more depraved give the tone to the assemblage, by commencing some disgusting badinage . . .

The gang-master appears, and under his guidance they

'A Lincolnshire Gang' (engraving, Robert Walker Macbeth, 1876).

The Witt Library, Courtauld Inistitute of Art.

A Lincolnshire turnip-hoeing gang, *c.* 1914. The sun-bonnets were worn as a necessary protection against sunstroke.

Museum of Lincolnshire Life.

commence the toils of the day. Three, four, five, sometimes six miles they trudge into the fen, where in companies they begin their task, pulling weeds or potatoes, or topping beets, or peeling osiers, or whatever else may be the work of the season. And how do they work? Continually stooping to grub up weeds or potatoes, at other times kneeling on the damp earth, as in weeding carrots, and occasionally wet up to their middles, as, for instance, in weeding standing corn. 'It is dreadful,' says a large farmer at Spalding, 'to see the little things coming out wet and draggled. It is as bad for their health as their morals.'

If the ganger be a decent man, he will do his best to suppress such evil as he may chance to see and hear; but if, as not unfrequently happens, he is a man of no principle, he will permit the evil to have full sway, as the easiest means of preserving his power. Nay, it is on record that he himself is sometimes the leader and inciter of moral corruption. Anyhow, all are left to themselves during meal-times, and then untaught, hard-worked, overstrung humanity runs amuck; and innocent children witness scenes and hear words which corrupt their whole lives. Toil and sin – this seems the hard, the terrible lot of these poor fen-children . . .

A justice of the peace in the Isle of Ely says: 'I fail to see how the children thus usefully and profitably employed in the field are likely to have their morals less safely guarded than they would in a school-yard or in the village streets.' Happy man! he can never have known what it is to have the mind oppressed by a monotonous and disagreeable employment, or the nerves overstrung with protracted labour. If he had, he would have been aware how fearfully open such a condition of body and mind leaves even a man of strong principle to the most horrible temptations. And when the subjects of it are children of all ages, any one who has had the slightest experience of such a life will acknowledge that it is only too natural for them to run into all kinds of devilry.

Strong artisans, strong in the consciousness of their power, consider nine hours a day enough work for the father of a family, with all the responsibilities of life upon him, and they could quote the wisest of our kings in their favour; but here in Lincolnshire

children are made to work ten to twelve hours a day.

Ernest Hare, a *boy* of eleven, living at Deeping St. James's, told the commissioner that he was in a private gang. *He left home at 5 and got back at 7.* He was employed by a farmer who had two farms, the nearest of which was three miles from his home; the other at Deeping St. Nicholas, six miles away; and with reference to this latter, he adds, 'We'd have sometimes to go t'other end of it', which was three miles further.

Well might an inhabitant of this same village tell me that some people in Deeping never see daylight there all winter from Monday morning to Saturday night. They go off in the dark, and come home in the dark. Well might the police superintendent at Spalding say, 'They go too far, and work too long; *ten or twelve hours is too much for a young child.'*

And yet the landowners and farmers of Lincolnshire met in conference in their Chamber of Agriculture, and being interrogated by the Commissioner what they thought should be done, answered, first and foremost, that it did not appear to them that the present hours of work of women and children employed in agriculture are excessive, or injurious to the physical condition of either; and that, secondly, 'no restrictions should be placed on the distances to which it should be lawful for them to go to work.'

It is, as I have said, now forbidden to any *public* gang-master to have a mixed gang. But though this may prevent positive acts of immorality, it does not prevent that demoralizing influence which always ensues when a company of young people of all ages work unrestrained by the presence of their masters. This is especially the case with girls, since it is just the roughest and most depraved of the sex who are most constantly employed in this kind of labour, and who, by force of their audacity and superior skill, naturally assume the leadership of the gang. Their coarse and lewd conversation soon corrupts the whole gang, and so the moral evil spreads. This is the kind of training the future womanhood of the district has to go through, and it can easily be foreseen what sort of homes such young persons will form. Their slovenly and slatternly cottages, full of discomfort, alienate their husbands and

drive them to the beer-shop. Their ignorance of the arts of sewing and mending causes the children to go in tatters. As a farmer in Deeping Fen truly observes, 'No amount of wages will make the husband better off, for the wife does not know how to use the money.' In fact, a comfortable and happy home is an idea they have never been permitted to entertain, many being driven by the stress of their wretchedness to be themselves instrumental in destroying its very possibility.

Let anyone look into the Sixth Report of the medical officer of the Privy Council (1863), and he will there find a tale of horror as to some facts of social life amongst the labouring people of the fen districts. The account I refer to is Dr H. J. Hunter's report on the alarming mortality amongst infants in certain rural districts in England. And these districts are just the very ones of which I am writing, and others like them – that is, the reclaimed marsh lands lying near the mouths of the principal rivers which fall into the North Sea.

With wonderful accord this *mortality was traced* by seventy medical practitioners and other gentlemen well acquainted with the habits of the poor, who were consulted by Dr Hunter, the commissioner:

> . . . to the bringing of the land under tillage, *i.e., to the cause which had banished malaria,* and had substituted a fertile though unsightly garden for the winter marshes and summer pastures of fifty or a hundred years ago. It was generally thought that infants received no harm from malarious evils, but a much greater enemy had been brought against them when their mothers were forced into the fields.

By such authoritative testimony the cause is shown to be mainly due to the destruction of the maternal instinct in women whose lives are hardened and brutalized by unsuitable toil and continual contact with moral corruption, and by the neglect that must ensue when they are obliged to leave their babies to the care of others.

One-fourth of the infants lawfully born in these districts die

under one year of age, while of the remainder the average amounts to one-third. Whatever the immediate occasion of death, all the medical men agree in believing the real cause to be the mother's neglect, while 'the degree of criminality they attributed to the women varied from a sympathising excuse for their ignorance to a downright charge of wilful neglect with the hope of death – in fact, infanticide.'

The history of many an unfortunate infant is thus traced in the report: perhaps it is the immediate off spring of the gang system. Born into a household already burdened with too many mouths, its appearance in the world is unwelcome to every one. The young mother, called away to work, gives up her child to an old woman, who professes to keep a school for such babies. All the food the child gets from its mother is morning and evening. During the night she is too fatigued to attend to its wants; in fact, if she is to do her day's work, she cannot afford to lose her rest.

Both by day and night the child is either deprived of food, or fed, not with a bottle, but with a spoon. . . . Should the unhappy little creature struggle through this period of semi-starvation, its life is threatened by another domestic demon. 'There can be no doubt', says the report:

> . . . of the truth of the horrid statement made by almost every surgeon in the marshland, that there was not a labourer's house in which a bottle of opiate was not to be seen, and not a child but who got it in some form.

Each village has its own peculiar preparation, the favourite form for infants being Godfrey's Cordial, a mixture of opium, treacle and sassafras. Each mother buys the 'Godfrey' she favours most, so that, when she leaves her baby in the morning, she will leave her bottle with the nurse. Should the nurse substitute her own, and should it turn out more potent, as is sometimes the case, the children will sink into such a state that, in a fright, she sends off for the surgeon, who on his arrival finds half a dozen babies, some snoring, some squinting, all pallid and eye-sunken, lying about

A Lincolnshire waggoner and his team, *c.* 1914.

Museum of Lincolnshire Life.

the room. Happily, he is prepared for the emergency, applies the stomach-pump, and the poisoned infants come round.

Supposing they clear this danger and grow up, the habit thus induced often stays with them for life. It is well known that in no part of England is there such a quantity of this drug consumed as in the Fen-land. Wholesale druggists report that they send immense quantities into these districts, and retail druggists often dispense as much as 200lbs a year. It is sold in pills or penny sticks, and a thriving shop will serve 300 or 400 customers on a Saturday night, the largest consumers being the inhabitants of small hamlets or isolated cottages in the fens.

It is true that this is a report of a state of things which existed ten years ago in the fens; but it cannot be supposed a practice so widely spread should suddenly have ceased. In a late report, that of 1867, Mr Ellis, a surgeon at Crowle, in the Isle of Axholme, says:

> The mothers leave their children to go out to work; even children that are suckling are left a whole day – often thirty-five children in the charge of one old woman. Sometimes they give them Godfrey (opium) to keep them quiet while they are out. Twins and illegitimate children almost always die. I know of a case here where a woman has had five or six children, all of whom have died, having been given opium to keep them quiet.

And when the writer was in Spalding last autumn, he was told more opium was sold there than in any part of the kingdom.

Under such a system none but the strong live, and wretched as in a moral sense their companionship in daily labour too often is, it is probable, on the whole, that the open air and constant exercise prove the very best restorative these poor little ones can have, and cause many to grow up, in spite of such terrible odds, strong men and women. As soon, too, as they can work they get enough to eat. To this end they are sent to work as young as a master will employ them, and each generation repeats its parents' experience, beginning a little earlier, and growing more and more insubordinate than the last. As to the boys, they soon learn to master their mothers,

and will not go to school even when the winter months come on and there is not such a demand for their labour. The grossest ignorance accordingly prevails. Mr Leaper, the police superintendent at Spalding, reports that scores of farm labourers apply for admission into the Force who cannot even write their own names. The Vicar of Langtoft says, 'This year, out of twenty boys who came to me averaging sixteen years old, seven could not read at all, and ten could not write at all, while with others the power was too small to be of any practical use.' But it is contrary to the spirit of the god worshipped in these regions that the human machine should be too enlightened. As the Vicar of Burgh-le-Marsh says:

> The employers of labour do not wish the children to be wholly ignorant, but think that a very moderate share of scholarship is sufficient. Their view is that 'more than a little is by much too much'; they are afraid that the labourers will be spoilt for field work.

Parents bemoan the home misery, schoolmasters bewail their empty schools, and clergymen are in despair. It is impossible to cope with the evil. 'I despair', says one, 'of making the good overbalance the evil in this parish.' A few philanthropic farmers and landowners deplore the system, and individually fight against it, striving to repress its greater evils, or at least to keep their own lands free from them. But, notwithstanding its science, this enlightened age has its gods just as the most barbarous ages that have gone before it. And perhaps, of the whole Pantheon, none is adored more sincerely by Englishmen than that cruel Moloch, the Trade Spirit. At his altar the inhabitants of the fens are compelled to sacrifice their children. For if the facts I have stated be correct – and they mainly rest on the authority of the Government Commissions, which have never been, as far as I know, refuted – is it too much to say that these unhappy people are compelled to a sin not unlike that into which Israel fell in its most prosperous days – the sin of 'causing their sons and their daughters to pass through the fire' – a fire more terrible in reality than a material furnace – the fire of physical exhaustion and moral pollution?

161

A VILLAGE FAIR
IN SUFFOLK

(GOLDEN HOURS, 1871)

To dwell far from the great stream of life is ever the fate of the agricultural labourer, and this is why he naturally tends to barbarism. The early Christians had such a sense of his shortcomings in this respect that they used the term *pagani,* the country people, to express the state of mental and spiritual ignorance. But the Fair helped to send a few rays of knowledge into his poor benighted mind, and to keep alive those social qualities which in his case often seemed in danger of dying out. At the fair he discovered that there was a world beyond his village, and infinitely wonderful things in it. And even the sports, brutal as many seem to us now, brought out a spirit of emulation and kept up a sense of self-respect, which was a real good in men, whose souls were in danger of being crushed by daily drudgery and unintermitting toil.

But better than all was the opportunity it afforded for the reunion of families early broken by the exigencies of a dire poverty. The elder boys and girls cheered their labours all the year by the thought of seeing their parents and their brothers and sisters at the Wake . . .

Last autumn we stayed at a Suffolk village. . . . If you object to broken rest, do not take up your abode in a village on the night before the fair. It may be a place in which you could enjoy delicious slumbers every other night in the year, but on that particular morning you will infallibly wake long before daybreak conscious of much unpleasant bustle. . . . Heavy elephantine feet

have been passing and repassing ever since it was light, and when at last you rise and look out of the window, behold! the little triangular market-place is full of canvas and gipsy carts. Cheery-faced country people are busy setting out their wares, while dark, sallow-visaged, inscrutable-looking men stand idly about, probably speculating on the gains their round-abouts, their shows, and their pistol galleries will bring in. By degrees the visitors arrive – boys and girls with shining morning faces, bent upon a day's fun; the elders, too, in the best spirits, and loud in their mutual greetings.

Later on in the day we thread the line of little booths, and think how many generations of Hodges and Mollies, arrayed in new smocks and blazing ribbons, have found in them a source of delight, the mere anticipation of which was enough to sweeten the monotony of their existence from year's end to year's end. We look at those stores of dolls and whips and whistles, and think how in every age the children have looked forward to fair day as a day redolent with joyful surprises, when some good fairy seemed to load their little hands with all that heart could wish, or brightest fancy could ever conceive . . .

Shall we then despise the village fair, which showered blessings on the little ones, and provided them with many a happy illusion ere the hard realities of life had dulled their small imaginations? Nay, rather let us pause with delight before the gingerbread stall, and think how many little mouths have watered as they surveyed those wonderful figures in gingerbread, those piles of hardbake, those bottles of bull's-eyes, those sticks of sugar-candy . . .

And now as evening advances the flaring little lights bring out all the latent beauties of the cheap toys and the still cheaper crockery. You see piles of hideous-looking ornaments, and wonder at the bad taste that can buy such rubbish and call it pretty. From the village inn comes the sound of music, and, passing the door, all may see a rustic Adonis dancing a jig on the sanded floor to the squeaky notes of the village fiddler. Later on the merriment increases, but it is time for all right-minded people to go home . . .

IN
OXFORDSHIRE

(GOLDEN HOURS, 1872)

(In Oxfordshire lies) the district which has Blenheim Park for its centre, and the Marlborough estates for its circumference. A park fourteen miles round, enclosing an area of 3000 acres, worthy, from its antiquity and beauty, to be compared with Windsor. A regal palace, rather than an old grey hall, standing in a fairyland of gardens and streams and fountains and islands, with picture galleries, whose wealth of Rubens and Titians moved a great German art critic to declare Blenheim alone worthy a journey to England. The possession of such an estate is enough to elevate its owner to the very top of the social column, even if he owed it to modern commerce or to ancient rapine. But Blenheim, as everyone knows, is held by the better title of service done in the cause of European liberty. Still more, its present owner, as a Christian man, and as one who has been a minister of the Queen, must be supposed to take a higher view of his duties than that which ordinarily obtains in rural districts. At Blenheim, therefore, if anywhere, we ought to find the rural system of England producing good fruits.

In passing rapidly through the villages which lie under the Blenheim aegis, one's sense of the orderly and the beautiful is certainly gratified. The white cottages and pretty porches overgrown with jasmine and honeysuckle, the small gardens just now blazing with gorgeous hollyhocks, and often well-stocked with fruit-trees, seem at first sight to leave little to be desired.

But look deeper. Talk with the peasantry, and you will find

discontent everywhere. Not a grumbling, unreasonable discontent, but a deep sense that things are very far from what they should be.

In his now famous manifesto to his tenantry, the Duke (of Marlborough) recognises this state of things, and attributes it to agitators and declaimers. No doubt the Union propaganda has done a good deal to produce the present outspoken expression of feeling, but would it have had the amount of influence it has had if it had not found the soil prepared, the seed sown, and the crop itself ready to be gathered in? What the Union chiefly has done has been to help the general discontent to express itself, and to bring about such a mutual understanding as should enable it to do so with some hope of removing the causes.

No one could read Mr George Culley's most favourable report of the condition of Oxfordshire labourers, given in the 'Agricultural Commissioner's Blue-book of 1869', and suppose for one instant that the labourers themselves could be contented with it, or that they would not be more and more discontented as they became thoroughly alive to its evils.

What were the labourer's wages in the Woodstock district lately – that is, before the Union movement commenced? Ten shillings a week! At harvest time, with the help of his wife and children, he could make four or five times as much, but it only lasted two or three weeks, and he had to work from early dawn to sunset.

Mr Culley, in his report, gives the following statement, as made to him by a labourer's wife at Combe, a pretty village close by Blenheim, and where some of the Duke's labourers live:

My husband is a farm labourer; he has ten shillings a week if they make all time; sometimes he loses a day or two from wet, and they take it off. I can't say what my husband gets in piece work; in harvest, if I help him with a little boy, we can cut and tie an acre a day, and we got nine shillings an acre last harvest; the crops was light, the rabbits had eat so much, you see, sir, or we would have got ten shillings. We had a fortnight at this.

Ox-ploughing team, *c.* 1900.

Oxfordshire County Libraries.
(Copyright George Bushell and Sons)

This appears an average case. Whatever way we look at it, an Oxfordshire labourer's wages, all things considered, can hardly amount to much above twelve shillings a week. These people had only two children, but most labourers, as we know, have many more. Could such a pittance keep more than bare life in their bodies?

In my late perambulation through this district, in one day I came across several cases, showing what is the result of this semi-starvation on the constitution of the people.

Early in the day at Bladon I met with a poor distorted creature, who had had erysipelas in his legs for the last thirteen or fourteen years, brought on by overstraining himself at his work. He had commenced labour at nine years of age, and his was doubtless an extreme form of a common evil, noted by Dr Batt, of Witney, in his evidence given in the Government Report: 'Children are employed too young in heavy ploughed land, it tells on them later in life; when they get about fifty they go at the knees, and are very much bent.' But that it became more than mere distortion with this poor man was certainly due, as Dr White of the Woodstock Union says, in referring to the fact that farm labourers are not so healthy as they should be, 'to the low wages, which will not allow men with families to procure food in quantity or quality sufficient to keep up the standard of health, and they are therefore more easily affected by outside influences inimical to health.'

At the next village, Long Handborough, I came up with a man who had a most wretched look. He had caught a severe cold a year or two before, mowing, and ever since his eyes had been so bad that he could not do any regular work, but was obliged to live by such jobs of porterage as he could pick up at the railway station. And late in the same day I met with another.

No one can walk far along a country road or enter a village without meeting those who in its heaviest form have borne the primeval curse. Poor, rheumatic creatures, dragging their unwilling limbs over the stones, deaf, dark, and dull. Or you enter a cottage, and as the woman talks with you she holds her hand to her side. She has a heart complaint. And yet she has been regularly

in the fields, bringing up a family at the same time, working sometimes as many as fourteen hours on a stretch. But all she says is, 'that she must if they would get bread'; nevertheless she adds, 'this fieldwork ruins many a woman's constitution'. You ask her about the children. It is a common tale, the natural result – she has lost four out of seven.

And thus the lives of men, women, and children are as really sacrificed now as ever they were in old heathen times, not certainly to appease some cruel deity, but in order that England may produce a highly-bred race of men and women, living a life so perfect in all its conditions of happiness as to excite the envy and the admiration of the world.

Much may doubtless be said on the question of cottages being built as farm buildings, to be used by the tenant's own labourers, and his alone; but in the Duke's manifesto, the reason avowed for putting both cottages and allotment-grounds into the hands of the farmers is the attitude of the labourers in forming a Union. Moreover, these cottages are mainly in villages, so that the result is to place one class of the community directly under the control of another. This is still more shown in the determination to take away the allotment-grounds, since it proves that it is considered unwise to allow the labourer to feel, even in the smallest degree, independent of his employer. As there are 914 allotments, the greater proportion of which are forty poles each in extent, and 360 cottages on the Duke's estates in Oxfordshire, it will be seen how numerous are the persons likely to be affected by the manifesto.

And this brings me to speak of the cottages themselves as the second item in the grounds of discontent which an intelligent and religious labourer may righteously feel as he contemplates his condition.

Not that I mean to say that the cottages in this district are worse than elsewhere, or perhaps so bad as I have seen them in some parts, nevertheless such is the condition of numbers in the Woodstock Union, that the Medical Officer of Health ascribes the unhealthiness of the people to the two causes of low wages and the unwholesomeness of many of the cottages.

As illustrations of the sort of places the Oxfordshire labourer inhabits, I will describe two cottage interiors I sketched. The first, at Long Handborough, was clean and tidy enough for the most scrupulous persons, but there was no floor but rough stone flags. The draught was kept out by a thin screen of calico, but it must be very cold in winter. The fire-place was a most primitive arrangement; a couple of bricks, with a rest placed transversely to support the saucepan, a few sticks and a little coal.

The other was at Wootten, and was a cottage in which the good dame had dwelt since her birth. She allowed me to go up into the sleeping-room to sketch. As far as I can remember, it would have accorded with the average size of rooms in Wootten, and would probably be nine or ten feet square. The great four-post bedstead, finding as it does its last refuge with the rural poor, after it has been discarded everywhere else, touched the unceiled roof. Many gaudy little pictures adorned the walls, and a quantity of crockery from the pedlar's basket loaded the narrow shelves. Flower-pots filled up the long window-sill; the window itself only opening in one compartment. Nevertheless it afforded a pleasant view of the mediaeval-looking village of Wootten, with its precipitous winding streets, crowned by the old church, and the river Glyme running at its base, spanned by a many-arched bridge.

She seemed much depressed at the struggle going on in Wootten between the farmers and the labourers, as in no place have the former shown themselves more determined to crush the attempt on the part of the men to form a Union.

It appears that the labourers at Wootten, on the 29th of May last, formed themselves into a Union. They began with only sixteen members, and their first requests coming when the excitement about the Warwickshire strike was at its height met with success. Their employers agreed to advance them first to eleven shillings, and then to twelve shillings. After a time, the labourers, finding their numbers increase, and the principles of the Union more thoroughly understood and accepted, thought themselves justified in asking still better terms: sixteen shillings a week, nine hours work per day, and fourpence an hour overtime. This

request the farmers determined to resist. They accordingly commenced a lock-out, and discharged every man belonging to the Union. The consequence was 120 hands were immediately thrown out of work.

The husband of the woman whose cottage I have here described was one who thus lost his situation. With the exception of eighteen years, he had worked for the same family since he was a boy, and his wife had served them also.

As I stood talking, two soldiers crossed the bridge. 'A'n't that a sight to aggravate one?' she exclaimed; and truly it was a shame to think that the Queen's troops should be sent to take the bread literally out of the mouths of the poor.

Not a greater mistake has been committed during the whole of this struggle than this obtaining soldiers to gather in the harvest. It is a mistake which the people will not forget, and which has envenomed a dispute hitherto carried on by the men without the least desire or sign of violence.

Whether it is to be attributed to the Farmers' Protection Society, or to some individual farmer at Wootten, or to more potent influence, does not appear certain; however it was, some one had sufficient interest to induce a commanding officer at Aldershot to send down ten men of the 46th Foot to Wootten. Accordingly the day after Parliament rose, to the chagrin of the people, the red-coats marched into the fields.

The whole thing was done without the knowledge of the War Office, and in direct violation of Article 180 of the Queen's Regulations for the Army, which says that soldiers may be allowed to assist in gathering in the harvest, when application is made for that purpose, 'provided that the employment of the population is not interfered with'.

As there were more than sixty or seventy able-bodied men ready to work, no plea could be advanced as to the scarcity of labour; on the contrary, it is manifest that the introduction of these soldiers, who thus laid aside the sword for the sickle, took the labourers' harvest away; robbing them of the only opportunity they have in the year to make a little money to pay their

debts. Moreover, it was a most unfair interference in the struggle between the employer and the employed, destroying the only chance the latter had of making better terms with his master; and in view of the long winter, with its scarcity of work, and cold, pinching poverty, it would certainly have compelled the labourer, if it had not been for the National Union, to cast himself entirely on his master's mercy . . .

It is a happy thing that the new movement for union among the labourers is under the leadership of Christian men, who in their own religious communities have had some practice in fellowship; for the labourers, feeling their ignorance and inexperience, follow their leaders unreservedly. A little while ago the men of Wootten and the neighbourhood marched into Woodstock to the number of 200 or 300 men. One who witnessed the sight, said that he never saw a more orderly procession in his life, and when it was over their leader dismissed them all, saying, 'Now go home, lads, and don't let anyone have a word to say against you.'

For the mass of the labourers are like men feeling their way in the dark; they crave for guidance. As my informant, a young labourer, whose health had been ruined by the abject slavery of his great employers to bad customs of modern society, very touchingly put it, 'They want some one to tell them whether their thoughts are right or not.' They have no helps; they are too poor to buy books or to take in magazines. An occasional *Cottager* or *British Workman* or *Police News* finds its way amongst them, and is preserved and pasted on the cottage walls for the sake of its pictures.

But it is evident that Methodism has been quietly doing a good work amongst them. The Primitive Methodist United Free Church has a circuit in this neighbourhood with eighteen chapels, each managed by its own congregation, and ministered to by local preachers. Two regular ministers superintend the whole circuit. Under this system Oxfordshire labourers have learnt something of the art of self-government, and how to submit loyally to the men of their own choice. It has taught the leaders how to organize and how to sustain the burden of a great undertaking. Thus they

have learnt to have faith in the ultimate triumph of a principle; thus they have obtained power to endure in hours of weakness and apparent defeat; and thus they have learnt how to retain calmness in hours of prosperity . . .

IN SOUTH WARWICKSHIRE

(GOLDEN HOURS, 1872)

. . . from the heart of old England has come the impulse which bids fair to revolutionise the condition of our agricultural labourers. I lately made a pilgrimage to the spring-head of this movement – to Barford, where dwells its leader, Joseph Arch; to Wellesbourne, beneath whose now historic chestnut the leaders of the movement have found a rural forum . . .

Ere long I came upon Barford, a neat village mainly built of red brick, the cottages fronting the street. I saw some very large buildings, evidently old homesteads, one of which was going to decay. At the end of the village I found Mr Arch's dwelling-place, an unpretending modern cottage. It is his own, however, and so is the piece of land upon which it is built. Unfortunately, he had just set out on a tour, in order that he might meet night after night great gatherings of his fellow-labourers and urge them to union. From Mrs Arch, however, I learnt much that was interesting concerning the origin and spirit of the movement. She was evidently the wife for a public man; self-reliant, and heartily believing in her husband's call to work.

During the early years of Joseph Arch's married life, he was a labourer on nine shillings a week. But when his family increased he threw up his situation, and soon made more by jobbing for the farmers round. As he could not remove his home, he was obliged to be away for a long time together, and often endured great hardships, seeking to save every farthing he could, sometimes sleeping in barns or outhouses, or beneath hay-ricks, and even on

wood-stacks. Thus he received a physical education inuring him to the arduous work he has now undertaken, the Bible and the weekly newspaper being his only means of mental training. Little schooling, indeed, was possible for a lad who commenced to toil on the land at nine years of age.

Mrs Arch said that they had often talked of the condition of their class, but could not see their way to do anything. They were Methodists, and Arch being a man of deep religious convictions, and gifted with natural eloquence, became a local preacher.

One day Arch, when he was engaged making a box for his son, who had gone into the army, two men from Wellesbourne came to see him. At first his wife refused to call him, and would only consent on their telling her what they wanted.

'We want,' said they, 'to talk to Joe about forming a union; other trades have a Union, and we don't see why we shouldn't have one.'

'You form a Union!' she replied; 'why, you ain't got spirit enough to do it.'

'Yes, we have; only Arch must lead us.'

'Very well,' she answered, 'you must tell him so yourselves, and he will do it.'

The man they sought entered heart and soul into their wishes, and the following Wednesday he went over to the village; and then and there, on the 14th day of February 1872, was held the first of those now famous Wellesbourne meetings.

From farm to farm the tidings had been carried. The men of Wellesbourne, a village, or rather two villages, numbering 1,500 inhabitants, was there almost to a man. From the neighbouring hamlets the labouring men came in such numbers that a thousand and more had soon congregated in the little triangular green where stands the great chestnut. Arch urged upon them in his own earnest, sledge-hammer way the necessity of combination, and proposed a Union. The tinder was ready, and the spark was struck; the men came forward so fast to give their names, that they could not write them down rapidly enough. A week after there was another meeting, more names were given in, a committee

was formed, a secretary appointed, and an organization instituted. Notices were sent to the farmers, asking that wages should be advanced from twelve shillings to sixteen shillings a week. The farmers made no reply, and so on the following Saturday the men struck. There were more than a hundred who thus 'came out' in Wellesbourne alone, while from the neighbourhood around nearly a hundred more joined them.

Of course the masters were somewhat surprised and much annoyed at this sudden outburst of their labourers. So war was proclaimed in the disturbed district, and the first action taken was to serve the men who joined the Union with notices to quit their cottages. Just as I entered Wellesbourne I saw several very nice large cottages, let, no doubt, much beneath their value. Sir Charles Mordaunt, the landlord, had given them all notice to quit because they joined the Union. A placard was issued, and posted up about the county, in which the Wellesbourne farmers declared their resolution to employ none who thus acted, and to eject them from their cottages.

Nevertheless the cause prospered. The 200 men who first joined the Union almost all found work, so that when I was there only 29 remained unemployed. Some had been engaged in a soap factory in Liverpool, some in the dockyards at Gateshead, others had emigrated to the Colonies. Very painful, however, to all concerned are the immediate effects of this revolution, uprooting old ties, and introducing much bitterness into the social life of the district. Hard must it be for the men to see the home, tended and loved for many a year, in the hands of strangers; while the masters will feel the want of their old, trusty labourers when harvest comes, and already complain bitterly of the ingratitude of those for whom they have sometimes found work at a loss to themselves. However, it is a law of the universe that wrong done must be avenged. . . . So now the present race of farmers, the present race of landlords, nay, the nation at large, will have to suffer for the accumulated wrongs endured by the agricultural poor of this land for generations . . .

(In) the neighbourhood of Stratford, in the hamlet of Shottery, I

saw enough to give colour to a statement made the other day in the Chamber of Agriculture at Warwick, by an eminent Warwickshire farmer, that it was his opinion that the cottages lay at the root of the present difficulty.

One of the villagers, accompanied by her little son, was crossing the meadow. About Stratford, she said, the labourers had only 11s a week up till lately; now they were to have 12s. They were not allowed to keep pigs, and had no allotments. She had a cottage with two rooms up-stairs and a pantry below, for which she paid 1s 9d a week. Her little boy went to school; but their betters need not be afraid that these young rustics are taught any superfluous lore, since this Shottery boy, living probably within a stone's throw of Anne Hathaway's cottage, had never heard of the name of William Shakespeare. Nor was he a singular exception, for I asked a baker's boy, who gave me a ride in his cart, and who lived at Hampton Lucy, close to Charlcote Park, the same question and he too had never heard of such a man as Shakespeare.

Passing through the village I saw four old cots standing in a row together. I had no means of measuring, but I should hardly think each house could have been more than 8ft wide and about 15ft deep. There were but two rooms. In one I found a woman with four children, and she was on the eve of adding to the number; they all slept, six of them, in one small room.

Next door things look much more comfortable, as it was the home of an old couple, who lived there alone. The little room was very clean, and was furnished with a tall clock, which nearly touched the ceiling. There was a rack, too, with a number of plates of the willow pattern, and some small religious pictures. The old woman had herself worked in the fields until lately, when she hurt one of her eyes. Women are not continuously employed in Warwickshire; but at certain seasons it would appear that many do labour out of doors. In springtime they are out couching and weeding the crops, in haymaking and harvest they bind up and rake, and at other seasons they pick potatoes and clean turnips. It is not at all economical for married women thus to engage themselves, as they only get 1s a day in winter and 10d in summer,

working from eight in the morning to five in the afternoon, with intervals for meals. All this time they are wearing out their clothes, and leaving their homes and babies to the care of some little daughter. Every now and then sad accidents happen. A medical doctor of the union of Warwick says: 'I have known at least eight cases in which children left at home have either been burnt or scalded to death. I have occasionally known an opiate in the shape of Godfrey's cordial or Daffy's elixir given by the mother to the children to keep them quiet.' The women who thus work rather like it, and it no doubt suits certain temperaments better than the more quiet employment of domestic life. Probably they worked as girls, and of such it is said that they are just the ones who dislike the control of domestic service.

Leaving Shottery, so pretty and yet so miserable, I made my way across the meadows into the Alcester Road . . .

Alcester is a sleepy town lying on the banks of the Alne, just at its junction with the Arrow. There is a considerable manufacture of needles carried on in the place; but the neighbourhood is purely agricultural, and contains some pretty hamlets, where the cottages are mostly surrounded by good-sized gardens, well stocked with fruit trees.

In one village, however, which I visited, about two miles from Alcester, I saw no such gardens, and the cots were extremely old. But if those of its inhabitants with whom I talked were not singular exceptions, it was a garden in a higher sense.

Sitting down by the roadside to sketch, I saw a comely, sweet-faced old dame come trudging up the lane. She had a warm kerchief over her shoulders, and looked as clean as a new pin. She was, indeed, a picture of health and happiness, and never spoke but a merry smile played over her lips. And yet she had only two shillings a week and a loaf to live upon, eked out by the proceeds of her little garden. Doubtless she got some help from her children and neighbours; but this was all she had to rely on, and out of this she had to pay her rent. How she managed to live, and withal to look so blooming and happy and clean, was rather marvellous. But she evidently had a secret source of joy which the world could

neither give nor take away. The Lord, she gave me to understand, was always with her, making her happy. Some of the healthiest little ones I ever saw came running up to her; she said they were her grandchildren. With warm affection she dwelt on the memory of her husband, who had been her guide and companion in every sense . . .

Entering a cottage, a poor wretched place, full of fierce draughts, I found an old man sitting over a little coal fire made between some bricks on the hearth. He had lost all his teeth, and a bad asthma made him pant sadly for breath; but he too was content with his lot. . . . He had had several children, but did not appear to regret it, or to think that that fact had increased his misery. A sick wife had been his life-long affliction; the poor old body lay above sixteen months bedridden. Withal he was no grumbler, but disposed to think he had all that he was entitled to. 'Yes,' said he, 'I liked to go to church as long as I could; I was bred up to church. Our parson be very kind; he comes to see me often, and does good to body as well as soul.' Referring to the Labourers' Union he said:

> I don't think much o' this 'ere Union, and I'll tell yer why, sir. Here have I served one man or his father this forty year, and never had a misword. All the work I have done he's paid me for. How do you think, sir, such a maayster 'ud like it if I was to fly in his face and ask him for more wages? We must all do our duty, sir. The maaysters must do their duty to the men, and the men must do their duty to their maaysters . . .

The old labourer's views of life were especially fitting for a man on the brink of the grave. It was well for him to depart in love and charity, and with a good word for all. But his miserable circumstances cried out against the system under which he had lived. He may have had a master who neither defrauded or abused him, but his life had been little better than the endurance of a sentence of perpetual imprisonment with hard labour . . .

Christianity teaches contentment founded on trust in God, but

nowhere contentment founded on the love of ease and the fear of man. But it teaches everywhere to its followers a burning indignation against all wrong and injustice. This 'capacity for indignation' is the root of all virtue. Therefore I believe the Christianity of the leaders of the Warwickshire Labourers' Union to be a far nobler type than that of this good old labourer.

How much the world gains when its inevitable changes are brought about by men who believe in their responsibility to God, may be seen in the unusual moderation and good sense which has marked this movement. And surely its wonderful success may be accepted as a proof that it was the right act at the right time, and therefore of its being strictly within the divine order of things. When 1872 opened, the men of South Warwickshire had scarcely dreamt of agitating. When in February they first sent in their demands, we have seen how little the masters comprehended the situation; so that they quite ignored the notice, believing it was got up by a few discontented spirits, and that the great mass of the labourers would sink again into their old subserviency directly these persons had withdrawn. But they soon found out their mistake. Village after village took up the cry. . . . A great mass meeting was held at Leamington on Good Friday. The Warwickshire Agricultural Labourers' Union was there and then formally inaugurated, rules framed, and officers appointed. It was evident the men meant what they were about, and accordingly the masters began to understand that they must change their attitude.

At a meeting of the County Chamber of Agriculture, held at the Shire Hall, Warwick, April 13, it was admitted that the labourers had a right to form a union, and one of the speakers strongly deprecated the attempt to prevent it by refusing to employ any man who became a member. It was urged that they should meet the labourers in a friendly spirit, and that the Council should try to bring about a conference between the landowners, the farmers, and the labourers. They also unanimously adopted a resolution in favour of piecework where practicable, and against the payment of wages in kind.

The meeting of the Chamber in May was still more conciliatory.

One resolution was passed in favour of stringent regulations for the education of labourers' children; while others were agreed to urging all farmers to pay their men the day before the local market, and against the practice of supplying men with beer at the hay and corn harvests.

Wages have risen from 12s to 14s and 15s, so that the labourers of South Warwickshire may fairly congratulate themselves upon having already gained a great moral victory.

And thus a great agricultural revolution has commenced, the end whereof no sensible man would dare to prophesy. From Northumberland to Cornwall, from Norfolk to Hereford, one hears everywhere the tidings of rising life. The central wave is spreading, and the adjacent counties are forming Unions; and now they talk of a congress of representatives, that they may form a National Union. The heart of old England has heaved, and every member of the agricultural community throughout the country begins to feel the glow of a new life.

THE RURAL
REVOLUTION

(CONTEMPORARY REVIEW, 1895)

Although a complete analysis of the results of the Parish Elections on December 4 and 22 (1894) is only possible to the Local Government Board, we have enough material in the reports published by the provincial newspapers to enable us to form a fairly correct idea of the direction such an analysis would take . . .

In treating, first of all, the results from East Anglia, we have a standard by which to test the rest of England and Wales, for there the tide of popular enthusiasm has reached its highest level, and it is there, in consequence, the local newspapers have seen the meaning of the national movement, and have taken more pains than, with some notable exceptions, has been done elsewhere to supply the necesary data to the fullest possible degree . . .

(In) the three East Anglian counties, the Councillors representative of labour would number something like 2507, distributed as follows:

	Norfolk	Suffolk	Essex
Agricultural labour. . .	724	617	205
Other forms of labour. .	378	386	197
Total labour Councillors	1102	1003	402

(In) a great many places in Norfolk and Suffolk the government of the parish will for the ensuing year be in the hands of the representatives of labour: this is a very great thing, and for more than three centuries a quite unprecedented fact.

It is remarkable that where labour has obtained a victory it has been overwhelming. Thus, while in some parishes not a single labourer and few working men obtain a seat, in others they have nearly taken possession of the entire Council. Elmslett, for example, returns five labourers, a farmer, and a carrier; Whatfield, five labourers, a farmer, and a shoemaker; Reydon, five labourers, a farmer and the clergyman; Great Wratting, four labourers, two shepherds, and a farmer; Westleton, six labourers, three farmers, a shoemaker and a carpenter. At Whepstead the Council is composed entirely of working men, but how many are rural labourers is not said. The *Westminister Gazette* of December 11 mentions that at Brisley the council is composed of eight labourers and a farmer; at Carleton Rode of seven labourers and a farmer; at West Rainham of seven labourers.

Swanton Morley is a parish which has long been in the van of the rural struggle. At the parish meeting nearly every man was present. The indomitable Norfolk labour leader, George Rix, C.C., was voted to the chair, and the battle began. The labourers' nominations comprised four agricultural labourers, two small farmers, a few years since labourers, one working farmer, and finally the chairman, himself a former day labourer at 1s 2d a day (1849), but now a grocer and farmer. The show of hands was two to one; a poll was demanded, with the result that the seven representatives were all returned by a good majority.

At Coombs in Suffolk an even more signal victory was achieved on behalf of labour. The number to be elected was thirteen and labour asked for nine seats. Seven were offered, with power to choose a chairman outside the Council: apparently, however, no agreement was come to, for at the nomination the non-labour party put up nine candidates, to which the labour party replied by nominating thirteen. Desirous, however, to save the parish the expense of an election, six of the latter offered to retire, but finding their opponents not content with this, but wishful to have the appointment of the chairman, the whole thirteen went to the poll and were elected.

Of 927 Councillors chosen in 111 parishes in Suffolk only

thirty-eight bore the title of nobleman or gentleman, and out of 1011 in Norfolk only twenty-nine. At this rate, if we had the whole of the figures for the two counties, we should probably find that the Suffolk gentry only appear in the Councils to the extent of rather more than 8 per cent, and the Norfolk gentry between 5 and 6 per cent. The clergy are in a still worse position. In Suffolk, out of 927 Councillors, only twenty-nine clergymen are returned; and in Norfolk out of 1011 Councillors only twenty-four; that is, in Suffolk the clergy appear to a little more than 3 per cent on the Parish Councils, while in Norfolk not more than 2½ per cent. This position of affairs has been occasionally aggravated by the resentment displayed by those who have for so long exercised the supremacy. At Ingham, in Norfolk, where two labourers, a groom, and a marsh labourer were elected, three persons of the hitherto governing class refused to serve. However, this policy has not been generally imitated, and some of the East Anglian gentry, displaying the usual courage of the race, have entered the Councils to fight, as one hopes, not merely for their own interests, but against that personal selfishness and corruption which undoubtedly will spring up under the new conditions as under the old. As things are and men feel and think, a parish meeting presided over by an admiral, and electing two farmers, three labourers, a groom, and a baronet, seems likely to promise more progress in a material and practical sense than an election which puts the parish entirely into the hands of one class. But then, on the other hand, there is the moral education the people get when they feel responsibility, and are left to learn by their own experience. Perhaps the danger in some places just now is that the pendulum may swing too far. For good or evil, the judgement of the people of Norfolk and Suffolk has gone forth unmistakably.

By what sentiments the leaders of the incoming hosts are animated may be gathered from the following passage in a letter received from one who has great influence among them:

I am more than satisfied with the manly and independent action of the agricultural labourers, etc, in the county of Norfolk. I have reason to believe that in scores of villages in Norfolk,

Norfolk unionists, *c.* 1876. The bearded man at the centre of the front row is probably George Rix, the Swanton Morley labour leader mentioned on p. 183.
Norfolk Museums Service (N.R.L.M., Gressenhall, C. Jolly).

The interior of Blo' Norton Primitive Methodist Chapel, *c.* 1900. Methodism was a powerful influence on the agricultural labourers' union movement and on rural politics.
Norfolk Museums Service (N.R.L.M., Gressenhall).

John Brinkworth, a hedger and ditcher of King's Stanley, Gloucestershire. The photograph dates from the late nineteenth century and was taken when he was 81 years old. Retirement was impossible for many farm workers – pensions were non-existent and work or the workhouse were often the only choices open to the elderly.

Museum of English Rural Life.

where Methodism has a good hold, the Parish and District Councillors will be composed of their best and most active laymen. I feel very keenly the responsibility that rests upon me to guide these, my life-long friends and supporters, into the paths of steady, thoughtful and seasonable action. The future is pregnant with benefits to the toiling masses of our countrymen. . . . I think, if we, as life-long reformers, are true to our principles, and keep pegging away at the work, we have nothing to fear from mongrel Liberals and stupid Tories, but shall, as time goes by, be led from victory to victory, and ground our arms at the feet of Justice, Mercy, and Truth.

If we go from the extreme east of the country to the extreme west, from East Anglia to South Wales, we shall find there the same movement among the people. As the *Cardiff Times* said a few days after the nomination meetings and first elections:

From North Pembrokeshire and South Cardiganshire, from the Lleyn promontory in Carnarvonshire, and from Anglesey, the 'mother of Wales', from the busy haunts of men in the Rhondda Valley and Merthyr Tydvil, the same tale is being carried. The working man is abroad! He has recognised the magnitude of his opportunity, and he has determined to make good use of it.

The *Tyst* is evidently alarmed at this, and preaches moderation to the working man:

There is a great danger that the working men of our country, should by being selfish, carry things to such extremes as to turn the stream of everybody else's sympathy and encouragement to another direction, and then it is only a question of time for them to enter into a worse bondage than before. 'This is an Act for us,' say some of them, 'and let us keep all others out.' Never was there greater need than now for safe leaders for our working men. What is somewhat dispiriting is to see them somewhat unwilling to follow their tried leaders, and their reckless readiness to follow false leaders.

Good old mother hen is desperately anxious, and cackles loudly when her runaway ducklings make for the water, but an unerring force is leading them to their natural element, and they will soon be displaying powers she little dreams they possess. There is little doubt that the new Act has created a very great stir in rural South Wales. The Welsh country-people have all become alive to their responsibilities as citizens, and every one who feels within himself or herself the least ability for public life is anxious to take a share in the regeneration of their parish. The nominations were, in consequence, so numerous that the returning officers could not, even with the help of additional clerks, examine the whole of the documents sent in, and the Local Government Board had to extend the time allowed for making the returns by two or three days. A brilliant morning star rose in the dawn over the hills of Carmarthenshire. The young daughter of a local farmer was chosen a member of the first Parish Council elected in that lonely and remote district.

In testing the returns from South Wales by the East Anglian standard we must not forget the very different proportion in which farmers and labourers are found in the two districts. In Norfolk, for example, the labourers are five times, and in Suffolk six times as numerous as the farmers in those counties; whereas in South Wales the farming class are a good deal more numerous than the rural labourers. This at once suggests a closer comradeship and a more frequent interchange of positions than is the case in East Anglia. Moreover, the farmer and the labourer are in sympathy religiously, which is not the case to anything like the same extent in Norfolk or Suffolk. In South Wales, the great majority of the farmers being Liberals and Nonconformists, many labourers find in them representatives whom they trust, and who they know have more time to devote to public affairs than they have themselves. The thousand-and-one little chapels have been normal schools where the people have learnt the art of self-government and whom to trust. That the question in rural South Wales has pre-eminently been one between the democracy and the old governing classes appears from the fact that the clergy, gentry,

and professional classes together form about a ninth part of the councillors from 78 parishes in South Wales. . . . 'Looked at from any point of view,' says a Welsh newspaper (the *Cardiff Times,* December 8 1894), in full sympathy with the village awakening, the results are full of encouragement for the friends of the democracy, and especially for those who have foretold the immense possibilities that lie dormant in the Welsh people . . .

The enthusiasm in Wales may be somewhat due to its Celtic blood, for the same thoroughness in democratic action distinguishes both Cumberland and Cornwall. In 12 Cumberland parishes the democratic character of the returns is manifest . . . The Cornish working men, rural as well as others, appear to have been very much in earnest about the elections. In one parish, it is said, politics were little thought of, every one considering it a fight between the farmer and the labourer. In another parish, Linkinhorne, the working men obtained five seats out of thirteen; at South Petherwin two labourers were at the head of the poll, and in another parish in Cornwall the new Council did a democratic act in electing a Bible Christian minister as their chairman. That the successes of the working men in Cornwall were not still more numerous and thorough is attributed to lack of organisation.

In the south-western counties there is reason to believe that the people of the villages have received and carried out the new law with an energy and an enthusiasm never witnessed in rural England for many generations. The parish meetings seem to have been well attended; the labourers, and in fact all classes, were properly represented. If the labourers do not at once make a show in the results in accordance with their numbers, we must remember it is only yesterday, as it were, that the labourer was supposed to be competent to take part in the government of his village, and that even to-day thousands will look askance at his arrival in the seat of power . . .

(In Devonshire) there must be some 447 labourers and some 338 working men in the Parish Councils of that county. And if this is seen to have been more or less the case all over the country, the moral effect of this great change in rural affairs can hardly be

over-estimated. Such, indeed, is the view of a Somerset news-paper (the *Weston-super-Mare Gazette*), which, in reporting the results of the first parish meetings and nominations in the county, says:

> It is not, perhaps, an exaggeration to affirm that never were the villages of the land so stirred as to-day. People of all degrees – squire and labourer, farmer and shopkeeper, vicar and local preacher – are showing great eagerness to serve on the new councils; and there is abundant evidence to show that great changes and developments in village life and its amenities are likely to flow from the infusion of new blood and new interests into the administration of the affairs of rural England.

From the evident enthusiasm of the Somerset people, we may at least hope labour succeeded there as well as in Devonshire. . . . Wiltshire must apparently be a county in which labour has been peculiarly successful. The Gloucestershire returns that we have been able to utilise present very similar results . . .

Proceeding along the southern counties, we find the rural mind waking up everywhere, and with more or less resoluteness, determined to leap on the horse Opportunity. Thus we are not surprised to hear that even the sweetest and gentlest of our rural labourers, the people of Dorsetshire, have displayed great activity in the elections, defeating in several places their employers at the polls . . .

(In) North Kent, in the Rochester and Chatham districts, the labourers have done well. . . . In the village of Stoke, near Chatham, the entire Council is reported to be composed of men of the labour party, the vicar and farmers being completely defeated. Ninety-nine per cent it is said of the electors voted . . .

In a portion of Surrey, into which the most select form of villadom has made, and is continually making, large advances, but otherwise a purely agricultural country, we find the Councils in twelve parishes to consist of thirty-three traders, twenty-two gentlemen, thirteen professional men, fifteen working men, and

five clergymen; while the strictly rural population has only thirteen representatives of the farming class and eight of the labouring . . .

As we quit the metropolitan counties and go north, popular feeling seems better able to assert itself. At Welwyn, in Herts, there were eleven candidates for four seats in the Rural District Council, and three of them were won by labour men, a clergyman, who stood in the Conservative interest, being behind them all, with less than half the votes given for the first labour candidate elected. An analysis of the votes given came out thus:

Labour 438
Conservative 156
Liberal 101

And in the same place the labour party won five seats out of ten on the Parish Council.

In Bedfordshire, three Parish Council elections give the following results: five farmers and market-gardeners, six labourers, six working men, six tradesmen, and two clergymen. . . . In Huntingdonshire, a lively interest was taken in the elections, and at Warboys three labourers were returned. At Kirtlington, in Oxfordshire, the working men succeeded in forming a Parish Council entirely composed of their own nominees. This thoroughly agricultural county seems, judging from the results which have been published in detail, to be much nearer than most others to the Norfolk and Suffolk standard. . . . (The) agricultural labourers in Oxfordshire did more than twice as well as the labourers in Berkshire, taking into account the relative proportion in each county of labourers to farmers.

In the heart of England, in Warwickshire and Leicestershire, to judge from the newspapers, the labourers have not done great things. In the former county, although there are many ardent souls among the labourers, several causes have concurred to disorganise and destroy the great agricultural labour movement commenced there so hopefully more than twenty years ago. Too much of the old leaven of individualism killed this promising

movement, and this, I believe, is the secret why Warwickshire appears at this crisis to experience but little of the joyous thrills of the new birth. The Leicestershire labourers, I hope and believe, have done well, but (the) Leicestershire newspapers that I have seen are too much affected by the political bearings of things to bring out the real point in the late elections . . .

As we turn again to the east the sun appears to be rising, and we feel distinctly warmer. Lincolnshire evidently feels something of the glow of Norfolk. . . . (And here) we meet the same phenomenon which we have had almost everywhere else – the rejection of the clergy. . . . The neighbouring county of Notts exhibited in some places similar democratic tendencies . . .

The more we go north, the more we may be sure the people knew how to secure their due representation in both Parish and District Councils. In Durham the most striking feature of the elections was the great number of miners returned. Their representatives are hewers, engineers, overmen, check-weighmen etc. At Altofts, near Normanton, in Yorkshire, a miner was at the head of the polling for the Urban District Council, and at Methley, near Leeds, the working men won nine seats out of twelve on the Urban District Council. At Hutton Cranswick, near Driffield, a shoemaker headed the poll for both the Parish and District Council elections.

The people have not, perhaps, everywhere fully realised the superior importance of the District to the Parish Council, and they do not seem to have displayed the same energy with regard to it. Of course, there are many instances all over the country of working men obtaining seats on the Urban District Councils; but it is comparatively rare that they have sought and obtained a position in the Rural District Councils. It is difficult to tell whether men who are described as cabinet-makers and carpenters are *bona fide* working men; but when the District Councillor elected at Helions Bumpstead, in Essex, is described as 'a factory hand' one can have no doubt. At West Dereham, in Norfolk, a labourer was elected as the District Councillor; at East Rudham, a tailor and carpenter; at Edgefield, another carpenter; at Binham,

an ex-policeman – all in the same county. From Suffolk we hear of a farm horseman at Baddington, a stone mason at Wickham Market, another at Saxmundham, being returned as District Councillors. On the District Council, which takes in all the parishes about Stowmarket, the labour party have a majority, and expect to see the chairman they select, a magistrate. At Caistor, in Lincolnshire, a blacksmith and a lady were returned as District Councillors; and at Toynton All Saints, in the same county, a cottager was elected. In some very unexpected parts, the labourers and working men made their way to the District Councils. At Tredington, in Worcestershire, a labourer defeated a captain of reserves in the election for the District Council. At Bidford, in Warwickshire, the working men's candidates were returned to the District Council; and at Stow-on-the-Wold, in the same county, a labourer was returned. A working man was chosen vice-chairman of a District Council in Sussex, of which Mr Stansfeld is chairman. Several working men occupy seats in various Sussex Urban District Councils; and at Ringmer a sweep gallantly attempted to take the seat for that parish in the Rural District Council. But perhaps the most striking of all the democratic victories in the recent elections was the return of Mrs Dickenson, a miner's wife, as Guardian in the Hunslet Union, Yorkshire.

It has been said the number of women returned in the late elections is a negligible quantity. But even in the partial returns I have come across the number amounts to between eighty and ninety. It is true the greater number have been elected as Guardians or on the District Councils. But in many of the counties women were returned as Parish Councillors. In Devonshire, Herefordshire, and Worcestershire they are just represented. In South Wales the few returns I have collected give eight women Parish Councillors. In Bucks two women have been elected; at Girton, Oxford, a woman student has been elected, and at Guilder Morden, Cambridgeshire, the daughter of the secretary of the Local Government Board is a member of the Parish Council; in Norfolk, nine women have been elected on the Parish Councils; in Suffolk, one; in Essex, one; at Killingworth, another; and at

Hawarden, in Cheshire, the election of a woman as Parish Councillor is reported. And these, probably, are representative of many others which have not appeared, or which I have not observed. The elections of women as Rural District Councillors and as Guardians have been numerous, and they have generally been at the head of the poll, their heavy majorities showing with what enthusiasm their elections have been carried. In South Wales, at least twenty-seven women's names appear as Guardians; nine were among the elected at Cardiff, where, with one exception, all the women candidates headed the polls in their respective wards. In Gloucestershire it is reported that there are about twenty women on the various Boards of Guardians. At Bristol two have been elected, and one at Newnham; in Wilts, at Swindon, three; and at Chiseldon, another headed the poll for the Rural District Council. In Warwick-shire, at Alcester, a surgeon's wife was elected on the District Council; and in the same county we have the now famous example of the Countess of Warwick. In Lincolnshire, at a place described as Greetwell Wilton, a woman was unanimously elected to the Rural District Council, and on the Biston Union two women have seats. In Yorkshire, at Wakefield, two women were elected; and at Batley, one to the Rural District Councils. In Sussex and in Surrey we have two striking instances of the welcome women have generally received from the working men. At Battle a woman headed the poll with more than double the votes of the two other successful candidates; and at Dorking a woman headed the poll by an immense majority over the next successful candidate – 639 votes to 359.

This unity of women and labour is one of the auguries of the time. The two enslaved classes signal their emancipation together, and this is all the more striking as the representatives from each have a history and an experience the most totally opposed it is possible to conceive. But as the entrance into some sort of liberty, equality, and fraternity of the masses in the Middle Ages was heralded by the mutual sympathy of the high-born dame and the lowly minstrel, incarnation of the genius of 'the common man', so the apparition of the same fact to-day is the augury of another great emancipation in human history.

But the most striking fact, because it has been so universal, is the reprobation of the clerical power which the rural people of England have deliberately, and with the most surprising unanimity pronounced. . . . Who can say it is not a just judgement when one reflects in what a curiously un-Christian manner Christianity has been presented in most rural parishes? The care of souls undertaken, not because a man feels he has a special call to be the pastor of a particular parish, but either because he has interest with the patron, or because he is considered deserving of reward for work done elsewhere. Then, again, the ghastly contrast between the dwelling-place of the shepherd and those of most of his flock. While the shepherd has often had rooms enough and to spare, his poor sheep have been driven to herd together in their old age as so many criminals, separated from their wives and children, doomed to a pauper's death and a pauper's grave. How can the people forget these things? They may grumble about the charities, but the way in which they have been administered is only part of the scandal of the whole position, the impossibility of simple men believing in Christian ministers who live in palaces and closes, rectories and vicarages, while so many thousands of their brothers and sisters live out their lives in such terrible discomfort.

Are we to suppose that 'the Medes and Persians' among whom the old clerical kingdom is to be divided are the various dissenting ministers to whom the rural people will now turn? The universal answer is distinctly negative. Nothing is more striking; the clergy are not rejected in order that the ministers may be welcomed. Both alike have received their *congé*. If we ask what the dissenting ministers have done to deserve this censure, the answer will be that they have done nothing but follow in the wake of the clergy: as the clergy have lived as part of the gentry, so they have lived as part of the middle class; neither of them being in consequence truly in sympathy with the 'common man'. Of course there are many exceptions to this, both among the clergy and the dissenting ministers – many who have suffered life-long poverty, and that often in its most cruel forms; but this, had they been willing to glory in it, was the best sermon they could preach to a

195

Christendom lost in wealth and comfortableness. What will the gentry do? They have the history of Europe for a whole century to teach them, and from it they may plainly learn the folly of struggling against the inevitable. Let them accept the revolution and lead it. But will they have the grace to do it? Yes, it is possible, for the English aristocracy have shown a *savoir faire* unknown in other lands. But will they understand how much is needed, how complete a conversion is required? Will they be able to do for themselves what their spiritual guides should have helped them to do long ago – that is, understand the intrinsic injustice and iniquity of their position, and the duty it entails upon them of living entirely and wholly for the common weal. Let them not ask the confidence of the people as a right, but earn it as men earn their bread, and they will find it tastes sweeter than all the gingerbread of stars and garters and ribbons and titles. Let them enter the homes of the poor and live in them and with them, at least some time in their lives, and so will they understand the stuff life is made of, and learn how to be true princes and leaders of the people. Let them have done with the foolish notion that they can stop a current which has been flowing down the Christian ages, and which, having overcome endless obstacles, has been for a century past ever widening. They may refuse, but the course of time will not wait until they are ready, still less will it consent to their turning it back. Prometheus, having stolen the divine fire, is now giving it to us Englishmen, and especially to those whom aforetime in the pride of our hearts we called clodhoppers; and to-day the turn of the clodhopper has come, and it is they who will have the making of the new England.

Made in the USA
Charleston, SC
18 March 2012